D0332685

Staging the real

MANCHESTER
UNIVERSITY PRESS

Staging the real

Factual TV programming
in the age of *Big Brother*

Richard Kilborn

Manchester University Press

Manchester and New York

distributed exclusively in the USA by Palgrave

Published by Manchester University Press
Oxford Road, Manchester M13 9NR, UK
and Room 400, 175 Fifth Avenue, New York, NY 10010, USA
www.manchesteruniversitypress.co.uk

Distributed exclusively in the USA by
Palgrave, 175 Fifth Avenue, New York,
NY 10010, USA

Distributed exclusively in Canada by
UBC Press, University of British Columbia, 2029 West Mall,
Vancouver, BC, Canada V6T 1Z2

British Library Cataloguing-in-Publication Data
A catalogue record for this book is available from the British Library

Library of Congress Cataloging-in-Publication Data applied for

ISBN   0 7190 5681 0 *hardback*
          0 7190 5682 9 *paperback*

First published 2003
11 10 09 08 07 06 05 04 03   10 9 8 7 6 5 4 3 2 1

Typeset by Freelance Publishing Services, Brinscall, Lancs
www.freelancepublishingservices.co.uk
Printed in Great Britain
by Bell and Bain Ltd, Glasgow

Contents

Acknowledgements

I would like to thank all those who have had a part in the production of this book. In the current broadcasting environment there are enormous pressures on programme makers, so I am especially grateful to those who took time out from busy production schedules to answer my questions and to correct any mistaken impression I might have had about their working methods. My particular thanks go to John Willis, Roger Graef and to Jeremy Mills, Andrew Bethell and Chris Terrill.

I have also benefited from many discussions with friends and colleagues who themselves are involved in reflecting critically on documentary and factual programming in all its many guises. John Corner, Annette Hill, Derek Paget, Jane Roscoe and Brian Winston have all helped to shape my own thinking on documentary matters. I should also mention in this respect the stimulus provided by the *Visible Evidence* conferences where academics from all over the world gather to discuss documentary.

As always, I am grateful to my colleagues in the Department of Film and Media Studies at the University of Stirling for all their encouragement – and also to several generations of students who have been prepared to debate Flaherty's *Nanook of the North* with almost as much enthusiasm as the latest series of *Big Brother*.

My thanks to Manchester University Press for all their support and in particular to Matthew Frost for his splendid nurturing ability. I would also like to give special thanks to my colleague John Izod who provided valuable comments on the original manuscript and who suggested one or two additional lines of inquiry.

Finally I would like to thank Eva for all her help in seeing this project through.

Introduction

The aim of this book is to examine developments in TV factual/documentary programming since the early 1990s. *Staging the Real* is an addition to a growing number of books which engage with issues relating to documentary film and TV factual programming (Bruzzi, 2000; Corner, 1996; Dovey, 2000; Kilborn & Izod, 1997; Paget, 1998; Roscoe & Hight, 2001; Winston, 1995 and 2000), but this volume distinguishes itself from work already published in that it focuses almost exclusively on the medium of television. For better or for worse, television has been the major shaping force in determining the course of documentary in recent decades. Unlike the United States where the existence of an independent documentary film tradition still provides at least some opportunities for the production of innovative and occasionally subversive documentary work, in Europe it is television to which (would-be) documentarists have become increasingly beholden, both for the funding they receive and for the possibilities to get their work aired (Corner, 2000: 682).

Staging the Real sets out to examine some of the new factual formats which have come to the fore in this period, but will at the same time be considering how these developments have been shaped by changes in broadcasting institutions and in the wider media environment. The main focus will be on the situation in the UK, but, given the extent to which television now operates on an increasingly global scale, references to developments in other parts of Europe will occasionally be included.

In the eyes of some, much of what has occurred in the domain of factual television is indicative of a more general cultural malaise. Programming that allegedly makes few demands on its audience is now seen to dominate the schedules of mainstream broadcasters, while programmes that stimulate debate or provide some form of cultural enlightenment are, it is claimed, a much less visible presence. In particular the proliferation of the various forms of 'reality television' is seen as a development which panders to lowest common denominator tastes. Docu-soaps (see Chapter 4) when they sprang to the fore in the second half of the 1990s, were widely regarded as a trivialising if not contaminating force, while the increasing emphasis on contributors' performance ability and the strong entertainment orientation of other factual formats (most notably of game-docs such as *Big Brother* or *Survivor)* were regarded as having lowered the esteem in which documentary had once been held.

The proliferation of popular factual forms and the widespread popularity these have enjoyed with the television audience have, not surprisingly, been seen as part of a more general 'dumbing down' whereby – faced with the multiple uncertainties and pressures of contemporary living – people seek refuge in the many forms of bland trivialising entertainment that the mass media provide.[1] While not wanting to dispute that many of the new factual formats are primarily vehicles for the provision of light, undemanding entertainment, this study does not take the unduly pessimistic view that they pose a major cultural threat as some critics would have us believe (Mosley, 2000), and that what we have been witnessing since the early 1990s necessarily represents a lamentable decline following the achievements of a Golden Age. When one examines the record of television in the field of documentary in earlier decades, one is certainly not overwhelmed by the number of cutting edge, thought-provoking or culturally enlightening programmes produced and aired on a regular basis.

Any attempt to throw light on TV factual/documentary programming is also going to involve a study of what has been happening in the wider field of television during the period under review. Unlike documentary work that has been primarily conceived for the larger screen, factual/ documentary programming has always been subject to the constraints and pressures that the medium imposes. This point is given such heavy emphasis because the changes which television has gone through since the early 1990s have had a significant impact on the type and volume of factual/ documentary work that has found its way onto our screens. The 1990s were a time during which all broadcasters became accustomed to operating in a far more commercial environment than hitherto. First and foremost, there was an exponential growth in the number of channels, meaning that television became an increasingly crowded marketplace. Slowly but surely audiences began to fragment as new providers jostled for the viewer's attention. Some of the new channels concentrated on various types of factual and documentary programming (e.g. Discovery Channel, Animal Planet, National Geographic). Most of the new services were initially delivered via cable and satellite, but as the decade wore on, the new digital technologies began to have an ever greater impact on the range of programmes available for viewer consumption. Now in the first decade of the new century viewers are confronted with a bewildering array of factually oriented programming, much of it targeting 'special interest' audiences. While those with the wherewithal to pay for these largely subscription based services now have access to what seems to be a vastly enhanced range of factual/documentary material, questions continue to be raised about programme quality. In today's harshly competitive broadcasting world the costs of acquiring and/or producing this material have been ruthlessly driven down – and this has not always been achieved without a concomitant sacrifice of quality. The economically driven need to extend the shelf life of certain products has also resulted in a marked tendency to indulge in excessive recycling of material.

The radical transformations that have taken place within the wider broadcasting environment – the proliferation of channels, the fragmentation of the television audience and the growing commercialization of the whole televisual sector – have, of course, intensified debate about the future of public service broadcasting. The role of public service channels in the (re)shaping of factual/documentary programming will be considered in more detail in Chapter 2, but the following point is offered in passing. Public service channels have been traditionally committed to providing a range of programmes that will inform, educate and entertain their respective publics. As such, the production and airing of serious factual/documentary programming has always been a part of their remit, though it has been the subject of debate as to how far programme makers could go in their treatment of politically sensitive issues. The challenge in recent times for public service channels has, however, been of a very different order. It has been how to adjust to the demands of the new television age without reneging on those core public service values. An institution such as the BBC has therefore been subject to ever closer scrutiny regarding its sociocultural role, but at the same time has had to demonstrate that it was offering value for money in terms of the range and quality of the services it was providing. Accordingly some of the liveliest debates in the last few years have related to the attempts by the BBC to introduce onto its 'mainstream' channel (BBC 1) various types of popular factual programming. For those wedded to the Reithian notion that the Corporation's principal mission should be one of raising levels of public awareness about a range of socio-political issues, BBC 1's apparent growing dependence on lightweight factual material such as reality shows and docu-soaps was tantamount to a derogation of public duty (Dunkley, 2000: 20). For others it simply represented the necessary adjustment that had to be made if the BBC were to have any chance of surviving in the far more competitive broadcasting environment.[2] It was the price you had to pay if you were going to retain slots elsewhere in the schedules (primarily on BBC 2) for the type of serious and sometimes challenging documentary work that audiences have come to expect.

The account provided in the following chapters is one that constantly reflects the need of broadcasters to develop forms of factual/documentary programming that extend the range of what would traditionally have been regarded as documentary. Many of the programmes that have captured the public imagination in recent years are the result of programme makers amalgamating diverse elements from established television genres. This hybridizing tendency is one of the most notable features of the more popular factual formats. It is a topic which will be returned to in Chapters 3 and 4 when among other things the emergence of formal hybrids such as the docu-soap and the game-doc will be discussed.

The discovery by broadcasters that factual formats could be so popular with viewers also had consequences for those working in the TV industry specializing in factual/documentary production. For a time during the 1980s it had seemed that documentary was a distinctly endangered species, but the emergence of these new and engaging formats gave a much needed fillip to those working in the broad factual/documentary production sector. Chapters 1 and 2 have more to say about what forms this 'renaissance' of factual/documentary TV genres took, but for the time being the point is simply made that, while for some observers it was seen as cause for celebration, for others it brought gloomy confirmation that television was fast becoming just one huge entertainment machine (Willis, 2000: 100–1).

Factual and/or documentary?

The fact that television throughout its history has always been a rich repository of different genres has always created certain methodological and definitional problems for those wishing to write about TV documentary.

Where do you draw the boundary between documentary and current affairs programming? Can you legitimately designate a programme 'documentary' which makes only intermittent use of documentary techniques? Should one rely more on broadcasters' and programme makers' claims about the documentary status of their work or on the audience's readiness to define it as such? To avoid getting drawn into a lengthy debate on some of these definitional issues (see Kilborn & Izod, 1997; Nichols, 1991) this book will persist in employing the portmanteau term 'factual/documentary' to refer to the corpus of work examined here. This is partly to examine a relatively broad spectrum of programmes ranging from the softer reality formats to the more serious heavyweight documentary, and partly out of a recognition that much of the programming in question displays distinctly hybrid traits. A further justification, if one were needed, is that broadcasters themselves regularly employ both terms ('factual' and 'documentary') in their various attempts to advertise and otherwise promote these products. As far as broadcasters are concerned, the term 'factual' can encompass a wide range of programmes, including documentaries, though in recent times it has been used increasingly to refer to the relatively lightweight entertainment-oriented formats such as the docu-soap. 'Documentary' on the other hand carries with it a different set of connotations. Its use by programme promoters suggests that the work in question is going to make greater demands on the viewer's attention. The question which needs to be raised, therefore, is with what legitimacy the new hybrid forms of the factual (which clearly have many generic affinities with the talk-show and the game-show) can claim to be documentary, when they are so manifestly not concerned with engaging with important issues relating to the socio-political world.

Mindful of the far-reaching changes that have occurred in television since the early 1990s, some would argue that the radical transformation of the factual landscape could probably have been predicted and that all forms of programming were bound to become more entertainment-oriented than hitherto. This raises the further question as to the future of factual/documentary programming in the longer term. Commercial pressures on broadcasters are hardly going to get less intense. Also, as interactive technology continues to advance, consumers will be offered a further range of options for relating to audio-visual material delivered via either television or computer screen. All these developments are bound to have an impact on the range and type of work to which consumers will have access. As they peer into their crystal balls, it has seemed to some observers that the far-reaching nature of these changes could well signify the move into a post-documentary age. John Corner, for instance, in the concluding paragraph of his seminal article 'What can we say about "documentary"?' makes the following observations:

> However barbaric it might seem to use the 'post' prefix, *there is a very real sense in which we are moving into the 'post-documentary' era*. We are doing this not as a result of documentary's collapse under the pressure of postmodern doubt or of digital image technology but, by contrast, as a result of the widespread dispersal (and, in part, perhaps dissipation) of documentarist energies and appeals across a much larger area of audio-visual culture. (Corner, 2000: 687–8, my emphasis)

While I agree that there is some evidence to suggest that – given the economic conditions under which film and programme makers now have to operate – energies *are* being dispersed, I do not wholly share Corner's view that we are on the threshold of a 'post-documentary era'. For all the attempts of broadcasters to make life difficult for those programme makers committed to producing serious and thought-provoking work – by not providing adequate enough budgets for them to undertake well-researched investigations and by scheduling the work they do commission in late-night 'graveyard' slots – the traditional documentary shows an astonishing capacity for survival. In the words of Peter Moore, a former commissioning editor for documentaries at Channel 4:

> The intelligence and inquisitiveness of documentarists keeps the genre alive. They're difficult blighters to keep down. They're like moles who keep coming up on the televisual lawn, however often the heavy mower is used. (Izod & Kilborn (eds), 2000: 102)

Notes

1   The situation has, interestingly enough, not changed significantly since the events of 11 September 2001. Initially it was felt that viewers, especially in the United States, would lose their appetite for the more cynical reality shows. A year after the terrorist attacks, however, reality programming still bulks as large as ever in the schedules of US broadcasters.

2   The period during which John Birt was Director-General of the BBC saw the progressive dissaggregation of departments and the introduction of a 'publisher' model of broadcasting (see also Chapter 2).

1 New forms of the factual

The final decade of the twentieth century was a period of significant change for broadcasting. The proliferation of channels, growing commercialization, the gradual erosion of public service broadcasting, the introduction of digital services, the fragmentation of audiences, the rise of the niche broadcaster: all played their part in transforming the media landscape we once knew. A new era was ushered in where broadcasters were forced to operate under a changed set of imperatives and where audiences developed different tastes and preferences.

This chapter considers what impact these developments had on the provision of factual/documentary programming. For better or for worse, during this period factual programming, in all its many guises, assumed an importance within overall programme provision which many would not have considered credible even a decade before. For some critics the arrival of reality shows such as *Big Brother* (Endemol, 1999) represented a major step forward in that they considered them to enable a new form of engagement with television (Bazalgette, 2001: 10–11). For others the explosion of popular factual programming represented an unmitigated disaster. Any residual commitment to the public service values of educational or cultural enlightenment was allegedly abandoned in the headlong rush to create a saleable product:

> The change in factual programming over the past 15 years has been disastrous … Serious current affairs programmes have either disappeared altogether or been drastically reduced, pushed to the margins of the schedules, or on to networks which are virtually unwatched. (Dunkley, 2000: 20)

Chapters 1 and 2 consider these developments from a number of different perspectives: economic, political, cultural, institutional and technological, in order to provide a better understanding of the multiple forces which have wrought such significant changes.

The rise of the pop-doc

All those who operate in today's broadcasting world have been forced to recognize the growing importance of the commercial imperative. In an increasingly competitive media environment the battle for ratings is more intense than at any point in television history. One of the most tangible consequences of the growing commercialization of the whole broadcasting sector is that all established TV genres have, to a greater or lesser extent, become commodified. In practical terms this has meant that programmes within the larger domain of the factual/documentary are required, in the language of broadcasting executives, to 'earn the right to be there'. Factual/documentary programming is now seen as having to fight for its place in the schedule alongside other genres. No longer is there any sense of it occupying privileged or protected space. It has, for better or for worse, to coexist with the vast swathes of other material devised to capture and hold audience attention.

The commodification of broadcasting has introduced new criteria for all those who seek to get work commissioned by broadcasters. Those engaged in producing factual/documentary work have been forced to adapt to television's more market-oriented requirements. For those producers wedded to the belief that documentary should be primarily defined by its enlightening and thought provoking qualities the changed priorities of contemporary broadcasting have been difficult to accept. They see these developments as a more or less systematic attempt to replace the more serious and challenging forms of documentary with so much lightweight, undemanding pap (Watson, 2000: 10). Though these commercial imperatives have certainly resulted in a major reappraisal of the function of factual programming, it would be unwise to conclude that serious documentary is about to disappear. A wide range of material continues to get made and aired. The one difference that can be discerned, however, is that – compared with earlier generations – today's producers of factual/documentary programming are subject to much more stringent requirements relating to programme accessibility. This is not simply a question of giving an audience what it wants to see and hear. It extends to matters such as style, register and mode of address. Whether the programme in question belongs to the 'softer' or to the more challenging categories of documentary work, today's programme makers arguably lay more emphasis than their forebears on producing material that takes more into account

The discovery by schedulers that audiences clearly had an appetite for this kind of 'real-life' material served up in easily digestible form led to a sustained attempt, which continued through the 1990s, to develop further styles and formats of programming that capitalized on the audience's growing demand for undemanding reality material. Chapters 3 and 4 examine in more detail these styles and formats, but by way of introduction some general points can be made:

1   The rise of the pop-doc since the late 1980s is primarily the result of a broadcaster-driven need for a relatively inexpensive form of material to supplement and complement existing formats. Just how pressing this need was is demonstrated by the speed with which pop-docs colonized designated areas of the prime-time schedule of the major networks and the zeal with which programme makers cloned material and ideas from formats which proved successful.

2   The primary concern of programme makers attracted to work in this area of TV production is the creation of lightweight entertainment vehicles. The design requirement is for forms of programming which, in both style and approach, will not make undue demands on viewers' powers of concentration. Engagement with real-life subjects is kept at a quite superficial level. The aim is that of diversion rather than enlightenment. As such, the growth of the pop-doc might be regarded as part of a more general tabloid tendency within broadcasting whereby all programming categories, including the factual/ documentary domain, become in effect an extended arm of the TV entertainment machine. Thus, though broadcasters – by various promotional sleights of hand – may seek to persuade viewers that these programmes are giving us 'important insights into the ways we run our lives' or are designed to 'take the lid off taboos that have been a barrier to social progress', they cannot really disguise the basic commodifying intentions which underlie such infotainment formats.[1]

3   With the whole emphasis being on extracting maximum entertainment potential from factually-based material, television has begun more and more to fashion this same material according to its own requirements and specifications. To an increasing extent real-life situations are contrived or fabricated to enhance their dramatic appeal (see Chapter 6). By the same token those individuals who were

selected to play a role in these real-life entertainments were required, more and more in the later 1990s, to produce the appropriate level of performance which the particular reality format demanded. John Grierson in an earlier phase of documentary's history may have referred to his subjects as 'social actors', and documentary film makers may have regularly auditioned people to assess their suitability for a role in their project, but in the last decade of the twentieth century those who participated in TV factual programming regularly acquired the status of semi-professionalised performers, acutely aware of the roles they had been allocated. Small wonder therefore that one of the traits that has come to be regarded as a defining feature of factual programming produced in the 1980s and 1990s is the progressive blurring of the boundaries between factual and fictional discourse.

4   As competition amongst broadcasters has increased, so programme makers have been encouraged – or driven – to find new ways of speaking to their audiences.[2] Though TV producers sometimes make the claim that the formats developed for this purpose broke new ground and were stylistically innovative, they can be seen, more often than not, to combine elements from established TV formats. This process of hybridization can take several forms, though one can make a broad distinction between the 'additive' and 'integrated' modes. The first occurs in magazine-type programmes where one can identify different generic influences, but where the specific generic features are still discernible within the overall mix. The 'integrated' mode is exemplified by those formats where a more thoroughgoing amalgamation of styles and approaches has taken place. Programmes such as *Crimewatch* (BBC 1, 1984–) and *999* (BBC 1, 1992–) would be instances of the former, while more recently developed factual formats such as the docu-soap and the game-doc belong to the second category. Docu-soaps, as the term suggests, combine structuring features derived from soap-opera narrative with elements of the observational documentary and from the ubiquitous talk-show, while a programme such as *Big Brother* (Channel 4, 1999) amalgamates game-show, talk-show and peep-show elements while retaining vestiges of the observational documentary.

While some observers have regarded the hybridizing impulse as part of the questionable tendency of contemporary broadcasters to popularize their factual programming output, others have interpreted it as evidence of a desire to move the genre on. The claim is that all genres have to be involved in a dynamic process of renewal in order to stop them from atrophying. The borrowing of stylistic and structural elements from other modes of programming is one way of re-animating 'tired' genres, even though what has been happening in the domain of TV factual programing might be regarded not so much as generic transmutation as the creation of a totally new species.

5 Virtually all the popular factual formats that have emerged in the last few years have put very high premium on the notion of performance. Producing a performance for the diversion or edification of an audience is, of course, deeply rooted in almost all forms of fictional dramatic entertainment, through whatever medium they are delivered. The ability to produce a convincing performance on the basis of a given script is likewise a fundamental skill that all actors have to acquire. In the new reality formats that have come on stream in the 1990s, however, performance ability has equally become a major criterion for the selection and involvement of those chosen to participate. This notion of 'performativity' will be discussed further in Chapters 4 and 6, but for the time being two points can be made.

First, in their choice and deployment of real-life performers, programme makers are well aware that they are looking for a special kind of performance ability. What they are seeking is an ability to project an aura of real-life ordinariness coupled with an ability to accomplish a series of tasks with some measure of aplomb (e.g. being able to sustain a convincing performance in dramatic situations set up by the show's producers, or being able to slip effortlessly into confessional mode in those intimate straight-to-camera diary room sequences which are a regular feature of many of the factual formats). For the viewer, part of the appeal of the reality formats is checking out how well subjects are able to maintain this level of performance in accordance with the rules of the game that the TV imposes. At another level, however, there is also a recognition that watching how others stage their real-life performances for the purposes of televisual entertainment does, in quite significant ways, mirror the manner in which all of us, in our everyday lives, are called on to produce a not dissimilar kind of performance. What is suggested here is that the success of these reality formats may be attributable – more than one might have imagined – to the pleasure that audiences take in measuring the subjects' ability to generate an appropriate performance as a reflection of that real-life role-playing in which all of us are required to indulge on a daily basis.[3]

Second, it is possible, of course, to view this intense, media-fuelled fascination with real-life performance in a more negative light, namely as reflecting the values of a consumer-oriented culture which places higher value on an individual's capacity to maintain a crowd pleasing performance than on their ability to stir the imagination or to be genuinely thought-provoking in what they say. The dependence of the new factual formats on the contributions of 'real life' performers (people like you and me) may give the impression that new democratizing forces are being unleashed. The reality, however, may be that this participation is, in the vast majority of cases, a highly constrained affair. As Rory Bremner, himself a keen observer of how audiences respond to TV performers, has remarked:

In the countless people shows that fill our daytime television schedules, the audience has become the star. The public are the turns, the presenter merely the ringmaster. The trouble with this 'inclusive' culture is that it knows no bounds. The public make programmes, the public participate in programmes, the public become performers. Anybody can get up and do it! It seems to me that all this 'inclusion' and democratization fosters a culture which values participation over ability and popularity over excellence: the karaoke culture. (Bremner, 1998: 24)

The point that Bremner is making is that the deployment of people performers is very far from affording a voice to the people. The terms on which these 'ordinary members of the public' are allowed to perform are determined almost wholly by the broadcasters. Moreover the mere fact that the shows are popular is in itself no criterion for judging their value. As Bremner concludes: 'the identification of popularity with quality is dangerously fallacious' (*ibid.*)

Consuming reality

Pushing ordinary people onto the television stage and encouraging them to deliver suitably tailored performances which are lapped up by multi-million audiences as if everything had life-or-death significance has, naturally enough, raised questions about the wider cultural significance of the new reality formats. What does the fact that more British people get involved in voting for contestants in the *Big Brother* show than in casting their vote at the election for the European Parliament have to tell us about the cultural life of the nation? To what extent do we share Germaine Greer's view that 'Reality television is not the end of civilization as know it; it *is* civilization as we know it. It is popular culture at its most popular, soap opera come to life'? (Greer, 2001: 1). An audience's obvious enjoyment of these shows and their readiness to engage in various interactive forms of involvement is not, however, directly symptomatic of disastrous cultural decline. It is merely a sign that audiences are using television as an instrument to which they can turn when seeking respite from the more pressing realities of life. What the huge success of *Big Brother* (and of other programmes in the same mould) does demonstrate, however, is that significant changes are occurring in the way that audiences are consuming entertainment products in an increasingly interactive media environment.

The question of the cultural significance of the audience's response to these popular reality formats will be returned to in Chapter 3, but it is important to distinguish between actual and presumed audience responses. On the relatively few occasions when searching inquiries have been made as to how members of the audience actually respond to the types of TV programming we are considering here, the picture that emerges is one that suggests that viewers are far more critically aware than they are often given credit for, thus belying some of the more gloomy prognostications of the cultural pessimists. As the authors of one such investigation conclude:

> People's critical judgements draw on social knowledge: they depend on shared discourse of production/genre knowledge, a shared representation of expertise and ordinariness, and a shared set of values about the public sphere and public interest and about the place of commercial interests and private experiences. (Livingstone and Lunt, 1994: 90)

These findings were reinforced by the findings of a later research project which investigated, among other things, the public's perception of the use of 'real-life performers' in a cross-section of contemporary factual formats. The view emerging from the focus groups revealed a clear-sighted awareness of how events were being specially contrived for the purposes of televisual entertainment and how, to an increasing extent, the contributors themselves were being manipulated to ensure they delivered a suitably tailored performance (see Hibberd et al., 2000: 27–34).

The recognition by those working in the media industry that audiences are becoming increasingly knowledgeable (and probably cynical) about the strategies employed in the construction and delivery of various forms of factual entertainment is reflected in a growing body of work which satirizes the strenuous efforts of programme makers to extract yet more mileage out of reality formats. The proliferation of the 'mockumentary' (aka spoof or 'faux' documentary) might even be seen as a tacit acknowledgement by film and programme makers that they admit to having overtaxed the audience's patience in their playing of the reality card. Films such as *The Truman Show* (1998), *The Blair Witch Project* (1999), *EDtv* (1999), *Best in Show* (2000) and *Series 7: The Contenders* (2001) have all, in various ways, tapped into audiences' knowledge of how film and programme makers operate and of the techniques deployed to persuade the public that what they are witnessing is vibrantly real. Some of this work such as Michael Moore's highly successful *Roger and Me* (1989) attempts to prick the bubble of pretentiousness that has characterized certain types of documentary production. Other work, such as *Series 7: The Contenders* (2001) parodies the rapidly proliferating 'survivor' formats by offering a fictional scenario in which 'real life' performers engage in a fight to the death. All these mockumentaries trade on viewer familiarity with the targeted programming and derive many of their humorous effects by deliberately subverting the styles and conventions associated with the reality formats. Much of this work also attempts to deconstruct the familiar styles and conventions of traditional documentary and as such might be considered a contribution to the re-animation of the documentary form (see Roscoe & Hight, 2001). The mockumentary phenomenon is examined further in Chapter 6, but it is worth commenting here that the proliferation of such work in itself provides recognition of the pleasure that an audience can derive from participating in the process of parodic deflation. It should not go unremarked, however, that many of the factual formats have themselves become so characterized by stylistic excess (for instance, by making ever more preposterous performance demands on their participants) that it becomes ever more more difficult to distinguish the mock version from the genuine article.

The role of technology

This initial assessment of recent developments within the domain of factual/documentary programming would not be complete without a brief consideration of the role played by technology, since a number of significant changes have been shaped, if not made possible by the availability of new types of recording and editing equipment. It is important to remember, however, that these specific developments have all been taking place in the context of much broader changes. As a result of the transformation in communications technology we are now living in an increasingly 'wired world' in which we have access to a vast range of interlinked informational and entertainment based services. These services are rapidly merging and amalgamating, to the extent that there is now increasing convergence between once separate media forms. As one commentator has observed:

> New media based on computer technology hover around the borders of the medium we have hitherto defined as television. Digitization and fibre-optic technology are paving the way to a convergence between television, telecommunications and computer industries, so that it is unclear whether we are watching old technologies overlap or whether we are witnessing the birth of completely new types of media. (Holland, 1997: 247–61)

All this is beginning to impact on our traditional understanding of 'the screened image', as the multi-media technologies and the new digital systems bring audio-visual material to us in a variety of forms. To an increasing extent, still and moving images are made available via the Internet, enabling broadcasters to alert their audiences to a wide range of additional resources and materials to complement the programmes they transmit. Viewers are now beginning to develop an appetite for this kind of expanded service provision, to the extent that producers of serious, multi-part series nowadays feel almost duty bound to set up a dedicated web site.[4] With the softer, more entertainment-oriented forms of programming, the new technologies have arguably played an even more significant role in that they have actively contributed to the pleasure that audiences derive from being able to participate in these carefully contrived media events. The phenomenal success of *Big Brother* (Channel 4, 2000), for instance, was attributable in no small measure to the skilful way in which the begetters of the series deployed the full range of multimedia and interactive technologies (live web transmission, video streaming, internet chat rooms etc.) to activate and orchestrate audience response, particularly among members of the younger generation.

If multi-media technologies in general are beginning to have an impact on how audiences use or interact with factual/documentary material, it is the development in recent years of particular recording and transmission technologies which has led to some of the liveliest debate. For several years now, for instance, web cam technology has enabled individuals or groups to project images of themselves and their domestic spaces to a potential audience of millions. There has been much conjecture about the cultural significance of the web cam phenomenon, from the perspective of both producers and receivers, but one explanation is that it reflects a more general blurring of the distinction between the public and the private sphere. For their part, producers of web cam material, as well as satisfying any exhibitionist aspirations, may be motivated (like producers of reality programming) by the hope of financial gain through advertising and sponsorship deals. With those who consume such material, there is evidence to suggest that, though their principal motivation is voyeurism, there may be other factors in play. The fact that events are relayed in real-time and that the technology allows for interaction with subjects (e.g. via live text chat) brings a different order of reality, a heightened degree of authenticity to the experience. An additional psychological explanation may also be sought in the very mundanity of what is being projected. As one observer has commented: 'The plotless action is calming – the opposite extreme from TV drama' (Ciprian, 1998: 3).

Producers of factual TV entertainment have not been slow to seize upon the voyeuristic appeal of web cam-like material and live web cam footage has become an important component of reality shows and game-docs such as *Big Brother* (Channel 4, 2000) or *Smart Hearts* (Channel 4, 1999). Likewise edited web cam extracts are now incorporated into 'real-life' programmes in order to enhance their reality appeal (see Chapter 3). It might also be claimed that consumers' growing familiarity with web cam material has sharpened awareness of what is involved in producing and sustaining a performance. Much of the debate has centred on questions relating to the authenticity of this performance. Web cam and other types of surveillance cameras may be unobtrusive to the point of of virtual invisibility, but the subjects' knowledge of their presence is always going to have some determining effect on the behaviour of those who are thus surveyed. In the same way, those who agree to have their every move registered by special batteries of cameras and microphones for the purposes of a *Big Brother*-type entertainment exercise know that they are, in a very real sense, tailoring their performance for the benefit of an imagined audience. The point I am seeking to underline here is that the success of the reality game-docs owes just as much to the culture of self-exposure as it does to the technologies by which those once private or personal domains are opened up to larger public scrutiny.

Perhaps the most significant impact that new technology has had on factual programming in the 1990s, however, has been the development of highly portable recording equipment. This has enabled film makers to operate increasingly as participant observers and to produce footage which creates a sense of vicarious presence. Those reality shows, for instance, which provide dramatic eyewitness accounts of police arrests or other incidents where the emergency services are called into action, derive much of their appeal from giving to the viewer the illusion of potential involvement in dangerous or disturbing events. By the same token, the various indications that hand-held recording devices are being used (camera wobble, problems with focus and framing, poor sound etc.) have acquired a sign-like status, suggesting a form of direct and active involvement in a sequence of unfolding events.

The development of miniature cameras and microphones which can be secreted about the person of an investigative reporter has likewise extended the range of factual programming since the early 1990s. A whole series of 'undercover' programmes have come on stream, with titles such as *Disguises* (ITV, 1993) and, more recently, the heavily promoted *MacIntyre Undercover* (BBC 1, 1999). At the heart of such programmes is the promise that – by patient and exhaustive investigative reporting – evidence will be gathered which will clearly reveal the extent of an individual's or organization's involvement in a shady or criminal exercise. Audiences will be able to witness how individuals literally condemn themselves out of their own mouths. While the attempt publicly to expose crimes and misdemeanours belongs to an honourable tradition of documentary and journalistic investigation, the use of hidden cameras to secure the incriminating footage and the promotion of such programmes on the promise that they will feature 'shocking exposures' has understandably enough led to charges of sensationalism.[5] Broadcasters may attempt to justify the use of hidden cameras on the strength of the compelling evidence they provide. What they are less willing to concede is that footage of this kind contains a strong voyeuristic element and that programmes like *Disguises* or *MacIntyre Undercover* can be sold to audiences more on the basis of their dramatic appeal than on their documentary credentials. The undercover investigator becomes an intrepid adventurer with whom the viewer is required to identify and the sense of drama and suspense is further heightened by the use of various tension-building techniques. Audiences are encouraged to ask whether undercover reporters will be able to maintain their disguise or whether their cover could be blown at any moment. The recorded action is edited together in such a way as to encourage parallels with fictionalized police investigations which viewers would be accustomed to finding in a similar slot in the evening schedules.

The images obtained by using cameras hidden about the reporter's person still, of course, bear all the marks of human agency – a fact that enhances their dramatic impact. In some respects the images obtained via secret filming techniques resemble those we find in the many types of surveillance footage which have begun to play an increasingly dominant role in contemporary factual programming. Surveillance images carry with them a different set of resonances, however, in that they appear to capture relatively unmediated views of a piece of unrehearsed reality being played out before the patrolling eye of the camera. As such, they are accorded higher credibility value, as witnessed by the increasing employment of surveillance cameras to detect and deter crime.

Certain changes have also been brought about by the wider availability and reduced costs of acquiring recording, editing and transmission equipment. This has, among other things, led to a significant narrowing of the gap between professional and non-professional practice.[6] The web cam, for instance, developed out of the capacity of home-based individuals to rig their domestic spaces with strategically located digital cameras linked to their PCs and then to broadcast their offerings to a much wider public via the web. There are some who believe that this narrowing of the gap between professional and non-professional realms which has been facilitated by the new technologies has introduced a democratizing impulse into TV's factual discourse (in the sense that it has opened up possibilities for voices to be heard or images circulated that are not totally subject to the supervisory control of the broadcaster). While one could cite one or two examples of where the democratizing potential of camcorder technology had been harnessed to open up new spaces within the factual domain (*Video Diaries* and *Video Nation* would be cases in point), these instances are few and far between. Mostly the new technologies have been exploited to strengthen the existing power base of established broadcasters.

The most significant impact of technological development has been, as already suggested, on the day-to-day business of programme making. Producers of factual programming themselves have been adept at exploiting the new possibilities afforded by advances in camera technology. By using small digital cameras they are able to achieve that intimate style of film making which lends itself to the confessional character of subjects' discourse. Likewise the strategic placement of those near invisible 'lipstick cameras' has enabled exchanges and events to be recorded which could not have been captured by more conventional means.[7] These advances have not just been in the area of camera design (e.g. the development of ever more sophisticated digital cameras). The development of relatively inexpensive non-linear editing equipment has likewise brought a series of cost and efficiency benefits to the business of programme production. It has also meant that, with certain types of factual/documentary project, single operators can be solely responsible for the conception, shooting and editing of factual programming material. (The programme maker Chris Terrill who was responsible for *Soho Stories* (BBC 2, 1996), *The Cruise* (BBC 1, 1998) and *Jailbirds* (1999) is someone who has made a name for himself as a lone operator.)

The fact that, thanks to technology, certain types of factual programming can now be produced at considerably reduced cost has, naturally enough, been welcomed by efficiency and cost conscious broadcasters. It has also led to the introduction of certain innovative production procedures which have, however, been criticised in some quarters for the alleged limitations they impose on what used to be called artistic freedom. In two series put together in the mid–1990s (*Russian Wonderland* (BBC 2, 1995) and *United Kingdom!* (BBC 2, 1997)) the initial filming was undertaken by single camera operators and the footage was handed over for further processing to a small editing team who then shaped the material according to broadcaster-determined criteria. This clearly illustrates a more commodified approach to programme-making facilitated by the availability of new technology. As I have written elsewhere about this case:

> Film-makers' particular concern is that this new way of working appears to demote them to being mere 'suppliers of footage' and to deprive them of any significant involvement in the crucially important editing process. This raises important questions about the authorial status of what is finally transmitted. (Kilborn, 1998: 211)

It is, in other words, not technology alone which has brought about the changes in working practices. The economic pressures on broadcasters have, if anything, had more of a determining influence in this respect. The new technologies have not only facilitated the way in which the events which constitute the 'raw material' of factual programming are recorded, they have also had an influence on the way that factual programme making is organized as a professional business. To be more specific: the availability of high-quality lightweight cameras and of affordable non-linear editing equipment has certainly enabled film and programme makers to develop innovatory styles of work, some of which have succeeded in commanding the attention of huge TV audiences. The generally lower costs of this equipment and the fact that smaller crews can be employed in the production of factual material has meant that certain types of factual product can now be put together far more cheaply than was once the case. In an age when closer attention is being paid to balance sheets than at any time in broadcasting history, the knowledge that low-cost factual programing which commands high ratings can be acquired at a fraction of the cost of producing or buying in relatively high-cost drama has resulted in a glut of factual material being commissioned and inserted into prime-time schedules.

Notes

1 This explains why the popular factual formats have often met with such derision at the hands of established documentarists such as Paul Watson who think that the rise of the pop-doc represents a threat to work which has a more serious and thought provoking agenda.

2 In the genre of television news programming, for instance, Channel 5, the UK terrestrial broadcaster which began transmission in 1995, pioneered a style of news

presentation whereby newscasters no longer were seated behind conventional desks but stood, or perched on a high stool, as they addressed their audience.

3   The American sociologist Erving Goffman throws some light on this phenomenon in his suggestively titled book *The Presentation of Self in Everyday Life* (1969). In the preface to this work he speaks of 'the way in which the individual in ordinary work situations presents himself and his activity to others, the way in which he guides and controls the impression they form of him, and the kinds of things he may and may not do while sustaining his performance before them' (Goffman, 1969: 9).

4   In the case of blockbuster television series it has almost become de rigeur to provide additional contextual material and analysis via a dedicated web site. With *Cold War* (CNN, 1998), for instance, the dedicated web site included all the annotated programme scripts, details of the relevant sources for all the historical 'facts', the dates and locations of all interviews – and suggestions for further reading.

5   At the time *MacIntyre Undercover* was transmitted, broadcasters were becoming especially nervous about charges relating to the faking of documentaries and the use of false guests in talk shows (see also Chapter 5). There was therefore considerable sensitivity about whether the series would raise difficult questions about invasion of privacy and the legitimacy of secret filming techniques for sometimes questionable ends.

6   It has also led to the recognition among ordinary members of the public that their home videos may have high commodity value when offered to network TV programme makers putting together programme packages largely based on amateur video material.

7   Programme makers also make extensive use of footage captured by surveillance cameras. The inclusion of surveillance footage, especially black-and-white images, in various styles of reality programming will often carry with it echoes of anxiety or apprehension, as there is a general perception that cameras have been positioned to record the activities of miscreants.

2 The changing factual landscape

In Chapter 1 we saw how formats with a strong entertainment component had begun to dominate the factual/documentary landscape. This present chapter will be looking into the particular conditions out of which these formats sprang, as well as considering the charge that they have led to the dumbing down of factual/documentary provision. The extent to which these developments were prompted and influenced by changes occurring in the wider media environment and within individual broadcasting institutions will also be considered.

Though UK broadcasters have declared themselves pleasantly surprised by what they hail as the unprecedented ability of reality formats to generate so much audience interest, the capacity of certain genres to excite the public imagination (broadcaster-speak for 'attract high audience ratings') has been a recurrent feature of broadcasting history. Broadcasters have always been adept at the art of breathing new life into old genres and the success of the various strands of reality programming is no exception to this rule. The trick has always been to produce formats which encourage particularly strong forms of viewer involvement. The hugely successful quiz shows and game shows of the 1950s and 1960s, for instance, provide classic examples of programme categories which appeared to give high profile to the contributions of ordinary members of the public who were allowed to participate. These were TV genres which enabled viewers to enter into particularly strong forms of identification with characters and situations introduced and thus heightened their sense of involvement in what was essentially a piece of made-for-TV entertainment. Likewise broadcast soap opera – which for decades now has featured so prominently in broadcasters' prime-time schedules – was introduced out of the shrewd calculation that the serial mode of presentation was ideally suited to the domestic conditions of TV reception. Soap opera consumption could become part of the 'flow' of everyday life and could attain the status of a routine event. The point being made here is that the new generation of reality formats follow in the tradition of television's continuing need to refashion its programming provision in accordance with what are perceived to be emerging audience 'tastes'.[1] On closer inspection, however, these new formats will reveal themselves to have borrowed extensively from established formats, in particular by introducing features which will secure viewers' involvement by persuading them that the events being played out on screen have a special relevance to their individual real-life experiences.

Making the case that the new reality formats have more in common with TV genres of yesteryear than many programme makers might be willing to concede cannot disguise the fact, however, that there are certain features of this particular broadcasting phenomenon which have their origins in the rapidly changing media environment of the late twentieth and early twenty-first centuries. More than at any other stage in TV's relatively short history, programme makers now find themselves in an intensely competitive broadcasting environment in which they are placed under constant pressure to come up with new audience-grabbing formats. They are also required to operate under strict economic constraints. Production or acquisition costs of programme material are carefully measured against likely or actual consumer take-up, and this determines the kind of projects which gain preferment. The fact that production costs for many of the types of programming discussed here have generally been significantly lower than for comparable programme categories has proved to be a powerful incentive in encouraging broadcasters to support the development and commissioning of 'cheap and cheerful' reality formats.[2] In Britain, for instance, there is evidence to show that the apparently irresistible rise of the docu-soap in the late 1990s was at least partly connected with the failure of certain established formats (the sit-com and the police drama series) to generate the audiences considered appropriate for the early or mid-evening schedule. The docu-soap's success is thus as much attributable to space opening up in a broadcaster's schedule as it is to the audience developing a taste for a new type of programming.

The barbarians at the gate?

In spite of the digital revolution that has led to a vast increase in the number of available TV channels (some of them specializing in the delivery of factual material) there is a persistent belief that the various reality formats which have emerged in the last decade or so are symptomatic of a more general cultural decline. In the eyes of the cultural pessimists who fear that the barbarians are already at the gate, the reasons for this decline are not difficult to discern. They lie in the pressures imposed on broadcasters, operating in an increasingly commercialized media environment, to lower the quality threshold in order to provide suitable material for viewers seeking relatively undemanding slices of diverting entertainment.[3]

The label most often used to express the idea that we are experiencing a marked cultural decline is 'dumbing down'. Like many other labels employed to describe developments in the socio-cultural sphere, it is notoriously imprecise. Since the early 1990s, however, it has been applied to a wide range of artefacts and phenomena and has been frequently mobilized to indicate the user's disapproval that cultural life is being increasingly subject to commodifying forces (Mosley, 2000: 1).

In the eyes of those who believe that we are relentlessly exposed to the forces of dumbing down, all the promises of diverse cultural provision in an age of informational plenty are little more than promotional hype. What these complainants perceive to be the sad reality is a systematic process of 'levelling down', where in the words of one commentator, 'intellectual nourishment of all kinds is nudged embarrassingly to the sidelines in the blinkered quest for ratings' (Brooker: 2001: 52). What is hailed by some to be a democratizing attempt to widen access and introduce greater diversity and choice is revealed, on closer examination, to be merely a commercially inspired attempt to capture the attention of consumers by adopting a Lowest Common Denominator approach.[4]

Others of a more optimistic persuasion take the contrary view, maintaining that all the doomsday pronouncements about cultural debasement have to be seen in far more relative terms. The optimists claim that, thanks to technological advances, TV viewers are now able to access a vast informational storehouse (even though the storehouse may contain more than its fair share of dross). According to this line of thinking, the image of the vulnerable, passive media consumer has been supplanted by the model of the technologically empowered individual who has acquired a high degree of media savviness. Media savviness suggests a heightened awareness of the strategies employed by broadcasters to command viewers' attention. In some quarters this savviness is celebrated as being an indication of the changing relationship between what in the new media order are often referred to as 'users' and 'service providers'. Increased user knowledge of how products are fashioned, together with individuals' seeming capacity to use the media for their own ends, is viewed by some as a 'long-overdue concession to democracy and inclusion' (Fox & Ryan, 1999: 2). Media savviness may also suggest a readiness on the part of some individuals or groups to participate more directly in various forms of media discourse and debate. This usually manifests itself in the desire to lay claim to the legendary fifteen minutes of TV fame, but occasionally, as we will discover in Chapter 5, it has meant that 'ordinary' individuals have been able to seize the initiative from media professionals in more radical ways.[5]

When debating the issues surrounding dumbing down, then, most commentators are concerned to weigh up the potential cultural losses against the possible gains resulting from widened access and the shunning of elitism. In spite of all the optimistic pronouncements about audiences' ability to exploit the potential afforded by the new technologies, many observers are of the firm conviction that the forces of dumbing down have already left a permanent blight on the cultural landscape. Television – or more accurately the particular forms of heavily commercialized television which have gained the ascendancy in the last couple of decades – is generally seen as one of the principal offenders in this regard. Television stands in the dock accused of being the medium that has actively contributed to – if not actually set in train – the process of cultural decline (sometimes for no better reason apparently than it has allegedly diverted people's attention away from other more challenging pursuits). No one has written more incisively on this issue than the American scholar Neil Postman. In his much quoted work *Amusing Ourselves to Death: Public Discourse in the Age of Show Business* (1985) Postman evokes a nightmare vision of a world in which television has become a wholly commodified medium totally dedicated to entertainment delivery. Rather than stimulating or provoking debate, television has, to Postman's way of thinking, become a domain where logical thinking and critical thinking are actively despised. Television has become an inhibiting rather than liberating force, whose sole purpose is to divert rather than enlighten. Increasingly, therefore, we are condemned to live in a sound-bite culture where the captivating image counts for more than the well-researched presentation, where the ability to perform on camera counts for more than the capacity to produce reasoned argument and where the inherently serious genres of news, current affairs and documentary are fast becoming just another entertainment category (Postman, 1985: 155–6).

Postman's bleak vision of a wholly entertainment-oriented broad-casting sphere is a cautionary reminder of what might await us once a media system becomes dominated by marketplace concerns. This critique is, however, based almost wholly on the heavily commercialized US model of broadcasting.[6] Other systems, arising out of a different set of historical and economic circumstances and not (yet) as beholden to the commercial imperative, have resulted in different kinds of broadcasting provision. In Europe, television has, generally, been much more determined by public service models of broadcasting. Thus, while it is true that the impact of globalizing forces has led to television the world over looking more and more alike, broadcasting in nationally or regionally defined spaces still bears the clear imprint of specific traditions and preoccupations. Nowhere is this more apparent than in the attitudes that broadcasters have displayed towards various types of factual/documentary material.[7]

Adapting to the challenge of a new broadcasting age

Broadcasting has been fundamentally transformed over the 1980s and 1990s. From the imposition of new management structures to the stream-lining of production techniques, from the introduction of new-style com-missioning systems to the beefing-up of programme sales divisions – there is hardly any aspect of the industry that has not been subject to far-reaching change. During this period broadcasting has become an increasingly glo-bal affair, as well as becoming an ever more business oriented operation, with individual companies becoming, to an increasing extent, parts of much larger multi-media conglomerates seeking to extend their portfolios or to gain some other form of territorial or economic advantage.

These times have brought with them considerable uncertainty. Prod-uct suppliers (aka programme makers) have become ever more beholden to the dictates and requirements of television executives as the latter seek to (re)position their respective channels in an increasingly crowded mar-ketplace. Programme makers operating in the broadly defined area of 'docu-mentary production' have, arguably, been forced into more compromises than those involved in other forms of programme production. As I have commented elsewhere:

> Given the new commercial imperatives to which virtually all broadcasting systems have been subjected – documentary film makers are having to adjust

to a climate which some feel is far less conducive to what once appeared to be fundamental objectives of the documentary form. For these film makers the new broadcasting ecology represents a hostile environment with fewer opportunities for hard-hitting, socially progressive interventions. (Kilborn, 1996: 141)

As with any other period of change, the times have been especially challenging for long-established service providers such as the BBC and ITV for whom the 'comfortable duopoly' conditions in which they had lived for almost three decades have now become a distant dream. For both these organizations, the old certainties relating to their function and identity have simply evaporated. In the words of one concerned observer:

> Broadcasting has entered a period of enormous upheaval, one which poses enormous challenges ... It also signals the advent of an era of uncertainty for our established broadcasters, an era in which they may find their traditional sources of revenue under increasing pressure as the audience starts to fragment. In this new digital age, the vitality and security of public service broadcasting is likely to be seriously threatened by those who believe it has a diminished role to play in the brave new world. (Puttnam, 1998: 6)

Before looking in more detail at how individual broadcasting institutions have adjusted their factual programming provision to requirements of the new media age, the following section presents a more general context for what has been happening in the sphere of factual/documentary production.

The producers

The question of how the new competitive broadcasting environment has impacted on the commissioning and transmission of factual/documentary material will be returned to a little later in this chapter. First we will consider what implications the changed priorities have for the film and programme makers involved in the uncertain business of making a living out of factual/documentary programme production.

The first point to make is that, over the years, most producers committed to the making of 'serious documentary' work (i.e. work which explores aspects of the contemporary or historical world in a striking or thought-provoking way), have had a difficult relationship with television. Television is considered to represent a relatively hostile environment for many documentarists. All too often, so the argument goes, they are required to compromise themselves by tailoring their work to television's very specific requirements, whether this be the dictates of a particular programme slot or whether they have to bow to the demands of having a celebrity presenter to front the programme in question. Work that falls, even marginally, outside the closely defined limits that television imposes stands very little chance of being commissioned or screened. Work that is provocative or disturbing (e.g. in its depiction of violence in a war torn region or in the way it may challenge the political consensus) will often not find its way onto our screens. Nowadays it is also generally the case that work that has not been specially commissioned for television will stand very little chance of being aired.

Those who work in the broadly defined area of 'independent film production' (as opposed to those who work for independent companies specializing in programme production for television) have always sought, by all the means at their disposal, to preserve their integrity by creating spaces for themselves outside the heavily commercialized and harshly competitive world of television. The number of opportunities for documentarists to operate freed from the shackles of television are, however, severely limited. This is especially true of the situation in Europe. In the United States there is still a relatively vibrant independent documentary film sector which provides for a measure of innovation and experimentation outside the much more cost and ratings conscious world of television (Corner, 2000: 682).

To suggest, on the other hand, that those documentarists who have become dependent on television have somehow sold out to the enemy is to present the situation in overly black-and-white terms. It is simply that they have to work harder now than at any previous time in television's history to gain access to the few spaces for serious documentary that television has available. Measured in these terms, television is thus not the declared enemy of documentary. It is rather that the programming requirements of the medium have never been entirely conducive to fostering work that represents the best in documentary endeavour. Those involved in documentary production have thus always, one suspects, had to struggle against the forces of conservatism present in most broadcasting institutions (witness the furore over Peter Watkins' *War Game* (1965) or the various institutional battles fought over the making or screening of controversial drama-documentaries). The difference between then and now as far as

we gotta do what we gotta do

boom

programme makers are concerned is that the programme-making business has become a deal more precarious than it once was. Everything is much more market-driven, with the consequence that a large part of the professional life of today's programme makers is now taken up with the quest to secure funding for future projects. Nowadays, as well as having to acquire a much wider range of programme making skills than was formerly the case, documentarists are required to hone their persuasive skills at pitching programme ideas to the all-powerful commissioning editors of broadcasting institutions and also to develop a keen eye for selling their work in an increasingly internationalized marketplace.

One gains a good idea of just how cutthroat the world of factual/ documentary has become by considering the views of those who have specialized in the business of buying and selling documentaries. The work of independent documentary sales agent Jan Rofekamp, for example, involves acting as an intermediary between film and programme makers and the representatives of TV channels wanting to acquire their products. As he reflects back on the far-reaching changes that have taken place over the 1980s and 1990s, Rofekamp acknowledges that, when he began work in the early 1980s, the documentary sales business was relatively straightforward:

> Our clients were a group of friendly and well-organised Public Television stations which existed in every major country. It was relatively easy to sell to them. The borders of the licensed territories were clearly defined. (Rofekamp, 2000: 8)

With the changes that occurred in broadcasting in the early 1990s, however, the work of the sales agent quickly became more complex. The arrival of the new cable and satellite distribution systems, together with the emergence of a number of players with global outreach brought considerable volatility into the market for factual/documentary programming. In particular, the emergence of the so-called thematic channels (e.g. The History Channel, National Geographic) with their very specific programme requirements, had the effect of segmenting what had hitherto been a clearly defined market. Slowly but surely the cable and satellite operators began to drive down costs, since – just as we have seen with powerful multinational supermarket chains – their combined weight meant that they were able to dictate terms to their respective suppliers. The consequence of this was that, to an increasing extent, factual/documentary film making became a matter of satisfying the demands of quite specific markets.

From the point of view of the documentary sales agent, the television world quickly divided into two camps, which Rofekamp identifies as First and Second markets. The First Market encompasses the 'principal terrestrial public and private channels in each country', a constituency which includes the well-established public service broadcasters as well as relatively new entrants such as Canal Plus and La Sept/ARTE. The type of material required by the First Market includes 'high profile [films)], treating international subjects, impeccably made, internationally promotable, award winning, edgy, strong story or character driven documentaries'. The Second Market, by contrast, operates according to a different set of principles and is primarily driven by the requirements of the cable, satellite and digital channels. While from the point of view of the documentary salesperson, supplying the needs of the First Market may have its particular attractions (the kudos that comes with supplying the needs of the quality end of the market), satisfying the demands of the Second Market has, if anything, acquired even greater importance. As Rofekamp observes:

> The enormous increase in worldwide interest for documentary and the greatly reduced costs of filmmaking equipment has caused hundreds of new producers to enter the buying and selling arena. While available slots for their documentaries are significantly on the rise in the low paying Second Market, there is almost *no* increase in the independent doc slots in the First Market ... Further impacting this problem is the fact that in some cases even the First Market no longer pays enough to cover all the costs for high quality docs. (Rofekamp, 2000: 9)

The problems facing film/programme makers are therefore all too clear: how at a time of great uncertainty and volatility in the documentary market to secure the funding to continue to make thought-provoking, challenging and authored films, when the demand for such films seems, if anything, to be on the wane. Given what has been happening on the world stage in recent times, one might plead there was greater need than ever before for high-profile documentaries engaging with international subjects, but the economics of contemporary broadcasting would appear to militate against them.

In the present broadcasting climate, then, most factual/documentary film makers have been forced into some kind of compromise as they become progressively more dependent on their television paymasters. This affects both the subjects they choose and the manner in which they are able to tell their stories. Thus, in the UK, even those who have aspirations to produce serious or challenging documentaries have been forced into the recognition that it is topics with a strong national flavour which are more likely to be commissioned. By the same token the film maker who wants to break free from a particular stylistic mould in the attempt to make a personal statement is likely find that the opportunities for getting this type of work funded and screened are severely limited. In the new broadcasting age it is the marketplace which dictates and this is a sphere where risk taking and experiment tend to be actively discouraged in favour of the tried and tested homogenous products which are in tune with audience expectations. There are good reasons for agreeing with Jan Rofekamp when he reaches the following conclusion:

> Controlled, formatted, indigenous and low cost documentary productions is where we are headed. And since there are many young and eager men and women who are willing to work for little money for what looks like a ticket into the industry, it appears there will be no shortage of personnel for these productions. (Rofekamp, 2000: 10)

The erosion of public service broadcasting (PSB)

What made Rofekamp's work as a documentary sales agent much more demanding in the 1990s were the changes occurring in the domain of public service broadcasting, the sector on which he and his colleagues in the field of documentary production had once been so reliant. Throughout the history of television it has been the public service channels who have continued to support the 'cause' of documentary, to the extent that the level of a station's commitment to documentary has sometimes been taken as an indicator of its public service credentials. In surveys produced in the 1990s which compared the number of documentaries being broadcast in different EU states, it could be shown that the countries with the longest standing public service tradition showed proportionately more 'serious' documentaries. In one 1994 survey, for instance, Britain, the Netherlands and Germany came off particularly well, while in countries such as Italy and Spain documentaries had largely disappeared from prime-time viewing (Kilborn, 1996: 142–3). An earlier and possibly more significant survey carried out in 1991, which monitored documentary programing of fifty-three TV stations in fourteen European countries (including PSB broadcasters) had established that documentaries constituted, on average, a mere 4 per cent of a station's output (*ibid.*)

While documentary work may never have bulked all that large in the schedule of any one broadcaster, public service broadcasting has, by common consent, certainly contributed to the nurturing of the documentary tradition. For more than four decades, following the end of the Second World War, documentary was one of the categories of programming most clearly identifiable with public service broadcasters' remit to inform, educate and entertain. In line with their commitment, PSB broadcasters were able to set up relatively well-resourced documentary production departments, whose output was regarded as making an important contribution to a channel's PSB profile.

Following the major changes that have occurred in the media environment in the last two decades, public service channels have been forced into a radical reappraisal of their role, in terms of their organizational structures and also with regard to the relationship with their respective audiences. Organizations like the BBC have been actively encouraged to incorporate a number of private sector practices into their operations in order to become leaner, fitter and more efficient outfits. Likewise most PSB organizations have had to give thought to fashioning a new identity for themselves, one which reflects their own changed role in the new media order, but also one that takes into account changes that have been occurring in the wider society. The earlier idea that broadcasting should first and foremost have an educational role had perhaps inevitably led to broadcasters adopting a patronizing, we-know-what-is-good-for-you stance. Such frankly elitist attitudes have now, for the most part, given way to more enlightened ways of thinking which recognize that, in the new, multi-channel environment, audience expectations and patterns of viewing have undergone radical and irrevocable change.

While few observers regret the passing of some of the more 'stuffy' elements of public service broadcasting, misgivings continue to be expressed about what losses might be incurred if the ethos of public service broadcasting continues to be eroded. Will the commercial pressures on PSB broadcasters lead to the inevitable tabloidisation of news, current affairs and documentary provision? Will the persistent demand for more accessible types of programming result in an overall qualitative decline? In the attempt to to provide answers to these questions, a brief summary follows of how UK broadcasters have sought to adapt their factual/documentary provision in response to the challenges of the new media age.

The changing context of factual/documentary production in the UK

All those working in the television industry in the UK and elsewhere have had to accept that they are operating in a rapidly changing world (Holland, 1997: 3–7). Not only have the programming requirements of broadcasters changed, but also the conditions under which programme material itself is produced have been significantly transformed. Some of these changes have been brought about by the new technologies but others have resulted from the development of new working practices. Nowadays programme makers also have to operate under increasingly tight budgetary constraints and are having to adapt their working methods accordingly. Programme makers are, in short, having to get used to tailoring their films to narrowly defined, broadcaster-imposed specifications. As one industry insider has dryly observed:

> Most documentary film makers have come to terms with the reality of made-to-measure films. There is still a place for those who believe they are creative artists but the opportunities for exhibition remain severely limited. (O'Sullivan, 1994: 21)

The transformation of broadcasting in the last decade or so has also led to some radical restructuring in the television industry. To an increasing extent factual/documentary programming is no longer produced in-house but by independent production companies (Kilborn & Izod, 1997: 23) who compete with each other to provide material for the slots that broadcasters need to fill. As such, factual programme making becomes more and more a broadcaster-led exercise, in which an increasing number of programme makers feel that they are now slavishly beholden to the networks' commissioning editors.

All this is a far cry from the situation which existed in UK broadcasting just a generation previously where, for better or for worse, programme making was firmly entrenched within established institutions. This arguably gave greater consistency and focus to the work produced and also ensured that sets of programme-making skills could be more easily passed on from one generation to the next. Today's generation of programme makers lead a more precarious existence.[8] Quite often the necessary programme-making skills have to be acquired 'on the job' rather than in the course of an institutionally supported apprenticeship. All this reflects the undeniable fact that programme making has become an intensely competitive business. Production companies are required to operate to ever tighter deadlines and budgets have in many cases been reduced.

Factual/documentary programming is also nowadays measured by a different set of criteria in terms of the function it is required to fulfil. To an increasing extent it is called on to 'perform' like any other form of programming. Moreover, while space is still found in the schedules for the large blockbuster series which can be sold on the worldwide market, the opportunities for one-off investigative documentaries requiring extensive research have significantly decreased. At the same time the borderline between the 'information' genres (news, current affairs and documentary) and the entertainment genres is becoming progressively more blurred.

All television channels have had to adjust to the harsh, market-oriented realities of the new broadcasting age. The following section will provide a brief sketch of how UK broadcasters have, since the 1990s, restructured and adapted their factual and documentary output in the light of changed scheduling priorities.

ITV network

Of all UK terrestrial channels ITV – or Channel 3 as it sometimes likes to call itself – is the broadcaster which, in recent times, has experienced perhaps the most far-reaching changes. No longer operating as part of a 'comfortable duopoly', it has been transformed from a public service institution financed principally out of advertising into a wholly commercial enterprise. As part of the transformation, ITV has also been subject to radical changes in its corporate structure. All these changes have left their mark on the programming portfolio of the channel, no more so than in the sphere of factual/documentary programming.

The 'landmark' event which ushered in the changes at ITV was the 1990 Broadcasting Act. As a result of this legislation the ITV Network was fully commercialized and the regulatory regime under which it operated was considerably relaxed (Horsman, 1999: 2–3). This legislation, together with the relentless commercial pressures as the network sought to manage its dwindling audience share, paved the way for the slow but inexorable decline of serious documentary on ITV.

While some have regarded the qualitative decline in ITV's factual/ documentary provision as perhaps inevitable in the light of its new profit oriented mission, the fact remains that ITV companies were still under an obligation from the ITC (Independent Television Commission) to continue to include examples of serious documentary in their schedules. The fact that ITV companies appeared to be reneging on their franchise promises by radically curtailing their output of serious documentary work sounded alarm bells in certain quarters. Throughout the 1990s ITV's documentary output was subject to close critical scrutiny and during this period the self-appointed watchdog organization Campaign for Quality Television (CQT) produced a series of highly critical reports chronicling ITV's fall from grace as far as documentary provision was concerned. The 1998 CQT report *Serious Documentaries on ITV,* for instance, suggested that, in terms of both quality and quantity, documentary on ITV had suffered a serious decline:

> For more than 20 years ITV earned a world-wide reputation for producing major documentary films on matters of public interest in a format which also interested the viewing public. Now that tradition is under serious threat ... What the ITC [Independent Television Commission] describes as 'serious documentary coverage' has been cut back to the point where it is barely viable to produce. And having been allowed to wither by ITV itself, serious documentaries are now sown so thinly, – so randomly – throughout the network schedules that it is all but impossible for the audience which used to watch them to know when they might appear. (Campaign for Quality Television, 1998: 2)

In spite of ongoing attempts by ITV executives to rebut the criticisms about the qualitative and quantitative decline of serious documentary programming on ITV, there is plentiful evidence to show that, as a consequence of the relentless pressure to deliver audiences to advertisers, ITV controllers have been resorting more and more to diverse forms of factual entertainment (including the docu-soap) to maintain its already reduced audience share (Brown, 2000: 2–3).

Another factor affecting the decline of serious documentaries on ITV was the internal restructuring of the organization which took place in 1993. One of the results of this restructuring was the setting up of a Network Centre. Prior to the establishment of the Centre, responsibility for the production and airing of networked documentary work had been that of individual ITV companies who had developed highly regarded strands of documentary programming such as *First Tuesday* (Yorkshire Television), *Viewpoint* (Central Television) and *Disappearing World* (Granada Television). Work screened in these strands generally had high production values and was characterized by the thought-provoking manner in which it approached its subjects. The existence of these well-established documentary units, where producers, technicians and directors developed good, long-term relationships, was also beneficial in another sense in that it provided an excellent training ground for young film makers who could be taught the ropes by more seasoned documentary hands.

The creation of the Network Centre effectively put paid to these arrangements and rapidly brought about the demise of these strands, as ITV sought to reposition itself in the broadcasting marketplace. Documentary film makers who had learned to value the contributions made by these strands were more than a little distressed when it became clear they would fall victim to the new programming philosophy. It was also recognized that the loss of these strands also had wider implications for the whole status of television documentary. This is nicely illustrated in an exchange of open letters between Rod Caird, film maker and one-time executive producer of the ITV series *Disappearing World* and Stuart Prebble, then head of factual programmes at ITV.

In the initial letter Caird reflects on what he sees as the wider significance of ITV's decision to axe the series:

> The series [*Disappearing World*] has been around for 26 years, producing about three films a year. The films are made as a partnership between film-makers and anthropologists, in far-flung places, and often the stories are to do with the subtle relationships between people, rather than the more straightforward narratives of cops and robbers. There is no host, no famous personality to tell a story and draw in an audience ... *Disappearing World* is the very antithesis of what is seen today as the successful documentary proposal – a domestic subject involving preferably policemen or somebody else in uniform, solving an emergency. I don't mean to be dismissive of factual programmes which deliver big audiences. We all make them and watch them. But please beware the temptation to regard them as fulfilling all the audience's needs in the documentary area. (Caird, 1993: 18)

Here in a nutshell is the critique that many observers have made about ITV's factual output as it geared up to face the new commercial challenges brought about by the 1990 Broadcasting Act. From now on the sole criterion for commissioning and airing documentary/factual programmes would be their audience-pulling potential. Prebble, himself a documentary and current affairs programme maker of some repute, attempts to allay Caird's fears by suggesting that, even in a much more competitive environment, excellent projects such as *Disappearing World* will always stand a good chance of being commissioned. On the other hand, Prebble is forced to concede that the criteria for determining what is 'deserving' have themselves shifted. As he spells out in his response:

> In order to be part of [a] series, a programme idea will either have the potential to draw a larger than average audience or, more probably, it will have the potential to make waves ... It means nothing that is bland, nothing of interest to only a tiny minority. It also means nothing that is in the schedule just because it has been around for a long time. (Prebble, 1993: 6)

The message to aspiring documentarists could not be clearer: in order to survive as a programme maker in the heavily commercialized world of today's broadcasting, factual programme makers will have to adjust to the entertainment-led requirements of ITV schedulers. As Prebble puts it:

> ITV has been put by the Government into an environment which is more commercial and difficult than ever before. The choice facing us is simple; we either remain competitive, which means reaching desirable numbers and types of viewers, or we go out of business ... So every programme of every kind has to justify its place in the schedule. Documentaries are no exception. (*Ibid.*)

Subsequent events have shown Prebble to have been quite accurate in his assessment of ITV's future, especially in the way it has resorted to the deployment of pop docs as a vehicle for building audiences in peak-time.[9] Thus, while in the period immediately following the establishment of the Network Centre, there was still a residual ITV commitment to serious documentary (in the shape of a documentary strand *Network First*, the slot in which serious ITV documentaries were accommodated), this commitment became far less tangible from 1995 onwards, as competition from terrestrial and satellite broadcasters began to eat into ITV's core audience. The decline could be measured not just in quantitative but also in qualitative terms. As the authors of the CQT report comment:

1995 would be the last year ITV debated any serious attention to *Network First*. Thereafter the series – the only slot on ITV to be devoted to 'serious documentaries' – would suffer the dual attack of a major cut in the number of films commissioned together with a gradual reduction in budgets. (Campaign for Quality Television, 1998: 9)

From now on ITV developed what was effectively a new policy regarding factual/documentary programming. Popular factual programmes – especially those highlighting crime and domestic issues – were increasingly deployed in peak-time as a way of attracting large numbers of viewers. Such programmes were high on dramatic incident and short on any more sober analysis of the contemporary world. Typical of the programmes which began to feature ever more prominently were series which focused on the seamy and more squalid aspects of social and inter-personal relations. Series which promised lurid and titillating revelations with titles such as *Neighbours from Hell, Divorces from Hell,* or *Nannies from Hell* from now on set the tone for ITV's factual provision.[10] Programmes such as these were strategically inserted into the peak-time schedule where they drew audiences of up to 11 million viewers. Occasionally – as in one extended sequence of a *Neighbours from Hell* programme (April, 1998) which dealt with a deeply disturbing case of racial harassment – serious social issues were touched on. For the most part, however, these programmes were conceived as slickly packaged entertainments. Pandering to lowest common denominator tastes and calculatingly voyeuristic in their often ghoulish revelations, they had more than a little in common with the peep and freakshows of yesteryear (see Dovey, 2000).

ITV's factual programming will be discussed further in Chapters 3 and 4. In concluding these reflections on how ITV adjusted its documentary/factual programming to the needs of the new broadcasting age, two final points can be made. First, following the 1990 Broadcasting Act, ITV programme planners have used 'performance' criteria to determine whether a factual programme merited inclusion in the peak-time schedule. In practical terms this has meant that the more demanding or serious type of documentary has either been squeezed from the schedule or driven to a more marginalized position. Not surprisingly, therefore, ITV has continued to be criticised by the Independent Television Commission for the deficiencies of its factual programming. In one of its recent performance reviews of ITV, for instance, the ITC delivered the following judgement:

> Human interest stories, CCTV and surveillance footage, consumerism and lifestyle provide the bedrock for a lot of the factual output, with a blurring of the distinction between features, documentaries and current affairs in topics and treatments. (Cited in Morrison, 2000: 1)

Doubtless in response to this and similar criticism, ITV did in 1999 reintroduce a new clearly branded, serious documentary strand (*Real Life*) into its schedule, but the general populist drift of factual programming on ITV is clear for all to behold. Second, even judged by the performance criteria it was using to determine the type of factual programming it commissioned and aired, ITV was not particularly successful at developing new strands of popular programming that were bold and formally innovative, or in any way breathed new life into factual formats. Series introduced in the second half of the 1990s such as *Neighbours from Hell* and *Hollywood Women* may have pulled in large audiences, but did so, as already noted, on the strength of their voyeuristic appeal. Particularly galling in this respect must have been the discovery that it was their rivals at the BBC who were fast becoming the acknowledged brand leaders in the development and selling of new lines in popular documentary. As we shall see in Chapter 3, it was the BBC which was responsible for developing the formally innovative docu-soap. Shrewdly scheduled in peak-time slots, docu-soaps such as *Airport* and *Driving School* proved that the Corporation was able, in one sense, to beat ITV at its own game and to force ITV into ignominiously having to play catch-up by cloning some of the formats developed by its non-commercial rivals.

The BBC

In the UK it has been two institutions (the BBC and Channel 4) who, following ITV's effective withdrawal from the field, have carried the responsibility for maintaining a balanced diet of factual/documentary programming. Whether it stems from public service obligations enshrined in the BBC Charter or in Channel 4's case from their original programme-making remit, both organizations have always had a strong commitment to the factual/documentary genres. This continues to be reflected in their respective schedules in spite of certain kinds of 're-balancing' which both have had to practise in recent years in response to the changing media environment. This point is emphasized since some critics neglect the broader picture when reaching damning judgements about falling standards.

As all broadcasters have geared up to meet the challenges of the multimedia age, the BBC has been forced into a major reappraisal of its traditionally perceived role. Still committed to providing a 'quality' broadcasting service, BBC executives have not always found it easy to reconcile the BBC's traditional public service role (representing all that is deemed to be valuable in the cultural life of the nation) with its need to compete in an increasingly globalized broadcasting environment. The challenge has been how to square the BBC's old public service mission to provide broadcast services that bring a measure of cultural enlightenment with a new more consumer-oriented role. Some idea of the difficulties encountered by the BBC in effecting this transition is provided by the valedictory reflections of the former Director-General John Birt as he prepared to step down from office in Spring 2000. In an article significantly entitled 'The BBC is a civilising force and it must be protected', Birt identifies the move into the digital era as representing possibly the greatest challenge to the BBC.

> [Digital] will move us from the world of scarcity, where only a small number of channels could broadcast, to the world of plenty. Anyone will be able to make and to publish their own programmes … In a total digital world, no-one will wait about for a programme of their choice to be transmitted, they will want all programmes on demand, at a time of their choosing. (Birt, 1999: 18)

Behind this upbeat assessment of the new multi-media digital world there lurks a fear, however, that certain powerful players will emerge who will exercise excessive control over the various digital gateways. To Birt's mind, if the gateway controllers are not brought under some kind of regulatory control, then we are likely to see a marked decline in the quality and diversity of programming provision. While not specifically invoking the doomsday barbarians-at-the-gate scenario, Birt sounds some serious warnings about what we might anticipate in an unrestricted digital era:

> Another risk of the digital age is that the worst excesses of print may be imported into the new media … Our culture may be degraded by the instant availability in new media of the raucous, the vulgar and the sensationalist … There is a risk to our national culture. We have already seen in this century the emergence of a global culture which is essentially American. (*Ibid.*)

The BBC, naturally enough, is seen as a bulwark against such barbarizing tendencies. Birt's remarks also illustrate, however, the difficulties encountered by a public service provider in reconciling its status as major cultural institution with the need to 'make its way' in a consumerist age. Forever being reminded (especially by its commercial rivals) of its cultural responsibilities, the Corporation has had to show that it is capable of reconciling this established role of being a provider of quality 'domestic' services with that of becoming a player in the global media market.[11]

In the current broadcasting environment the task of reconciling these two objectives has proved more difficult to achieve than Birt would have us believe. Much of the programming produced for airing on the mainstream channel BBC 1 in the period when Birt was Director-General could be said to have been informed by a distinctly populist agenda . It was during this time that the BBC became more and more reliant on entertainment-oriented factual programming to boost its ratings and to prevent the channel from slipping below the unofficial share target of 30 per cent. While few would argue that the channel had descended to the point of being 'raucous, vulgar and sensationalist', many commentators feel that the BBC has been forced into too many compromises in its programming policy (Dugdale, 2000: 4–5).

The major challenge for the BBC in the 1990s has been how to negotiate its entry into the digital, multichannel age without reneging on its public service commitments. In the factual/documentary arena the constant refrain has been how best, across the spectrum of its two terrestrial channels, to maintain its traditional reputation for quality programming with the need to cling on to what is deemed to be a respectable audience-share. As already observed, this has involved the Corporation in a precarious balancing act. Already in the early 1990s it had become apparent that BBC 1 was becoming more populist in its scheduling strategy. In the early years of the new millennium these tendencies have become still more marked and it is perhaps no surprise that even BBC 2 (the channel once reserved for serious, demanding documentary work) should also be seen to be including a mixed diet of popular and serious documentary work in its bill of fare (Brown, 2001: 8–9).[12]

The truth is that, like all other major broadcasters, the BBC – in order to justify its continued existence in an age of ever widening consumer choice – has been forced to diversify its services in order to ensure that the multiple publics that now make up its audience are adequately served by the programmes on offer. Part of the Corporation's strategy has involved the creation of specialist satellite and digital channels, which can make use of the vast store of programming material (including many documentaries) that the BBC has accumulated over the decades. A new digital channel (BBC 4) has now been launched which has a broad cultural remit. Likewise the BBC has continued its work with the Open University, but has also opened up a new Learning Zone. All these moves might be seen as wholly consonant with the BBC's public service commitments. Other developments which have taken place in the same period, however, cast doubts on the 'quality commitment'. Some critics contend that, in order to maintain, or even raise the level of funding made available through the licence fee, the Corporation has downplayed the extent to which its mainstream channel, BBC 1, has moved significantly downmarket. There has, so the critics allege, been an increasing tendency for the BBC to trawl in those waters where its commercial competitors felt they had secured sole fishing rights. As one commentator has observed:

> There is a stubborn belief within the TV industry and among advertising buyers that whatever BBC policy makers say, the practitioners running BBC 1 are hypocrites, hell-bent on competing for market share. (Brown, 1999a: 10)

The war of words about the role and function of the BBC will continue to be waged in the coming years, as competition for audiences becomes still more intense and the funding mechanisms of public service broadcasters are subject to ever greater scrutiny. As Gavyn Davies, the new chairman of the BBC, has quickly come to recognize since taking office in 2001, the Corporation is under greater pressure than ever before to fulfil multiple goals. It needs to continue to provide programming that will command the attention of viewers concerned to use television for recreational as much as for educational purposes. At the same time it needs to maintain its reputation for the making and airing of quality programming (epitomized by challenging and serious documentary work) which can be highlighted when the time comes to renew the Corporation's charter.

Channel 4

Most observers are agreed that Channel 4 has, over the 1980s and 1990s, made a significant contribution to TV documentary programming, with respect both to the quality and the range of work commissioned and trans-mitted. Channel 4 has had a longstanding commitment to documentary, a commitment that was enshrined in its original broadcasting remit which requires the channel to display 'experiment, innovation, originality and diversity'.

One should make clear at the outset that some of the work commis-sioned and screened by Channel 4 can indeed be counted amongst the highest achievements of documentary film making. One might single out particular series such as Phil Agland's wonderfully evocative and insight-ful study of life in modern China *Beyond the Clouds* (1994) or the often provocative films screened in the *Cutting Edge* strand. The channel has also provided, especially in the first decade of its existence, diverse oppor-tunities for film and programme makers in the independent production sector. The channel's Independent Film and Video Department in the 1980s (especially the *Eleventh Hour* strand) also played a significant role in nur-turing the work of UK documentarists by providing them with funding possibilities and also sustaining them in the belief that documentary could be a forum where hitherto unheard or suppressed voices could be heard. In its early days, then, Channel 4 remained true to its promise that it would be bold and innovative in its programming, that it would be prepared to take risks in its treatment of controversial and taboo subjects and that it would appeal to tastes and interests not generally catered for by the main-stream channels.

The reputation that Channel 4 gained for the challenging quality of much of its programming is principally attributable to its broadcasting remit. There was, however, a happy coincidence between the time of its launch and the rapid changes which were occurring in British society in the early years of the channel. As Sylvia Harvey has noted:

> The development of the new channel beyond the moment of its legislative conception was to be fashioned by a culture both more pluralistic and more stratified than that of the two preceding decades: a greater variety of ideas and lifestyles, sharper extremes of wealth and poverty, more ferocious po-litical and ideological disagreements, together with a general lessening of public interest in official politics. (Harvey, 2000: 106)

What enabled Channel 4 to be so refreshingly different from other broad-casters was a funding mechanism that did not put it under the same pres-sure as other channels. For almost a decade it was funded out of an agreed proportion of ITV advertising revenue; and though the channel carried on-screen advertisements, it did not have to sell its own airtime. This meant that the channel could build up a portfolio of 'alternative' programming and occasionally take the kind of risks that mainstream broadcasters could not entertain. Thus, while the BBC already in the late 1980s was beginning to tilt some of its factual/documentary programming in the populist direction, Channel 4 could still, with some justification claim that it was upholding the core values of 'experiment, innovation, originality and diversity'.

A significant shift in the way that Channel 4 conducted its affairs came, however, in the wake of the 1990 Broadcasting Act. From now on the channel was required to sell its own airtime and this immediately forced it into a far more competitive relationship with other channels, even though a safety netting arrangement was put in place with ITV to safeguard Channel 4's TV advertising revenue (see Harvey, 2000: 116). These changes have, in the mind of many critics, left their mark on the both the type and the range of Channel 4 programming. The channel has, allegedly, lost some of the edge which characterized much of its early programming output. It still courts controversy with some of its programmes, but often this seems to have more to do with the risqué character of the subject matter than in the stirring of genuine debate. As Michael Jackson, who later became Head of Channel 4, but was still at the BBC when he made these remarks, observed in a 1996 speech to the Royal Television Society:

> Am I alone in thinking that the pursuit of demographics – in particular young, lager-drinking, upwardly mobile men – has led to a sapping of Channel 4's originality? … Treating the audience simply as categories of consumers is the worm in the bud of any television channel. (Cited in Beckett, 2000: 2)

Developments in Channel 4's programming strategy in recent years do indeed suggest that the channel is, at very least, putting a different emphasis on certain parts of its original remit. It is still striving to be a broadcaster in tune with the times, but it has set its sights much more resolutely on the youthful audience. The channel still rejoices in its capacity to break with stultifying convention, but sometimes in ways that lay it open to charges of voyeuristic titillation. It is still, in the words of one of its regional controllers, 'concerned to address its audience on the assumption that they are smart, insightful and media-savvy' (Cosgrove, 1999), but it seems to many observers that the means by which this is being achieved are all too predictable. The occasional documentary excursion into chronicling the sexual shenanigans of youth might be defended (on the grounds of extending the thematic range of factual/documentary programming), but when a disproportionate number of programmes are devoted to subjects relating to sex and pornography, one begins to suspect that the commercial imperative is gaining the upper hand.

Certainly in the second half of the 1990s programmes specifically targeting the youthful audience became a noticeable feature of Channel 4's programme provision. And even though, unlike BBC 1 and ITV, the channel held back from jumping on the docu-soap bandwagon, the increasingly youthful orientation of the channel is plain for all to see. Late night Channel 4 programming frequently includes titillating 'explorations' of how Britain's youth disports itself in foreign holiday resorts (*Ibiza Uncovered* and *Caribbean Uncovered*) or frank, no-holds-barred explorations of the sex industry. In this respect it does appear to be moving closer to some of its broadcasting rivals than may have been envisaged in its original broadcasting remit. Some critics are of the opinion that the channel has in one sense 'sold out' on its way to becoming more of a mainstream broadcaster. Even some of its erstwhile supporters are now resigned to the fact that Channel 4, as it moves into comfortable middle-age, may have become too conformist and lost something of the rebellious edge it once had. In the words of Anthony Smith, a founding father of the channel:

> [The channel] contains none of the experiment with which it began … It has become professionalized in the wrong way. It doesn't have a mission to be anything other than another television channel. (Cited in Beckett, 2000: 3)

In the early years of the new millennium, Channel 4 is still, however, a broadcasting force to be reckoned with. It has been concerned to redefine its public service broadcasting remit, while at the same time giving due weight to the styles of programming that reflect the values of an increasingly aspirational and fun-loving society (epitomized in the highly successful series *Big Brother*). It also still has a commitment to producing those more demanding types of programme which challenge received wisdom or establishment values in a way not paralleled on any other channel. In the words of its present Director of Programming, Tim Gardam:

My job is the management of ambiguity … We are not there, as are BBC and ITV, to pour the ratings of one show into the next, desperately seeking to distract the audience from looking for something new by offering them yet more of the same … We are probably an uneven channel; we can lurch from idea to idea, sometimes magnificently, sometimes embarrassingly. But it is in the interweaving of the accessible and the challenging, the funny and the demanding that our critical and our commercial success rests. (Cited in Lister, 2001: 8)

Summary

This chapter has illustrated how established terrestrial broadcasters have tailored or refashioned their factual/documentary provision to the require-ments of the new media environment. While these are the channels which have been responsible for some of the more significant developments in the field of factual/documentary programming the new cable, satellite and digital providers are also beginning to make their mark in that they are creating considerable volatility in the market for factual and documentary programming.[13] The arrival of the new channels may not, in itself, have transformed the factual landscape, but their presence has certainly had an influence on the commissioning and scheduling policies of the major broad-casters. Already we are witnessing some of the repercussions of this in the form of the decisions made by certain mainstream channels to 'relocate' some of the more challenging types of documentary work onto one of the organization's digital channels. Soon after the start-up of BBC 4, for in-stance, it quickly became obvious that documentary work which would have formerly been shown on the terrestrial channel BBC 2 was now being accommodated on the Corporation's new digital channel, thus allowing the former to become that much more of a mainstream provider. In an increasingly competitive multichannel environment, developments such as these will continue to occur as new channels jostle for viewer attention and certain types of factual/documentary programming reveal themselves to be powerful weapons in the armouries of channel schedulers.

Notes

1   In much the same way as the more popular soap opera narratives have become part of the cultural life of the nation, so the new reality formats have produced a level of

public interest, involvement and excitement which – for all the complaints about dumbing down – have to be accorded considerable cultural significance.

2   One of the ironies here is that, in purely generic terms, the distinctions between 'factual' programming and popular forms of of dramatic fiction have become progressively more blurred.

3   The view that television has become a vehicle for encouraging instant forgetfulness or a state of unthinking inertia carries with it echoes of the Frankfurt School critics who, writing in the 1920s and 1930s, believed that the mass media had an essentially trivialising and debasing influence, principally because those who had a controlling influence over media output were more concerned with the making of personal profit than with the raising of public awareness (see also Thompson, 1995: 7).

4   Though frequently linked with the supposedly malign influence of the mass media, dumbing down is seen to extend to many other cultural spheres, including those of painting, sculpture, music and architecture. As one cultural observer has pithily commented, 'The relentless dumbing down of British culture is debasing the notion of excellence. Good, intelligent work still emerges, but bogus "democratic" values are threatening to drown us in dross' (Glancy, 1998: 50).

5   This savviness also includes a heightened awareness of the conventions and strategies used by programme makers in the attempt to engage viewers' or listeners' attention. (see also remarks on 'mockumentary' in Chapter 6).

6   It should not go unremarked that such a system has also shown itself capable of producing some of the best examples of internationally acclaimed television programming, including such jewels as *Friends* and *The Simpsons*.

7   One might even go so far as to suggest that a broadcaster's attitude towards the broadly defined documentary genres acts as a kind of qualitative barometer in the rapidly changing world of contemporary broadcasting.

8   Programme makers often complain that whilst most of their energies are expended in satisfying the market's demands for the 'softer' type of factual product, they still harbour lingering ambitions that they will be able to afford to commit time and energy to a serious well-made documentary.

9   Prebble is uncannily prescient in one other respect. In a final barbed comment to his former colleague he reminds him that 'very few producers of factual programming have spent much time bemoaning the passing of a disappearing world; instead the new competition has stimulated them to new levels of creativity'. Three years later the producers of a much heralded ITV documentary *The Connection* (1996) were to take these remarks all too literally in creatively shaping a documentary about drug smuggling and not disclosing that large sections of their account were fabricated (see Chapter 5, pp. 131–5).

10 The pattern for the new populist strain of ITV documentary had been set in 1993 with the commissioning of the three-part series *Hollywood Women*. Though succeeding in garnering a large audience in excess of 9 million viewers, the series attracted much criticism from the ITC for its titillating, down-market tendencies.

11 The BBC has, among other things already launched a 24 hour news service and several revenue-generating digital channels. It has also entered into new partnership

arrangements with commercial operators such as Sky.

12 Small wonder that at the 2000 *Guardian* Edinburgh International TV Festival the current Director-General of the BBC, Greg Dyke, referred to BBC 2 as having a 'split personality'.

13 Just as in the world of magazine publishing the tendency has been towards ever more specialized publications, so in television niche providers have begun to colonize the territory of mainstream broadcasters. The general tendency is towards a 'publisher' model of broadcasting.

3 Playing the 'reality' card

In Chapters 1 and 2 we have seen how changes in the media environment during the 1990s had begun to leave their mark on factual/documentary programming. Depending on one's point of view, these changes either created exciting new opportunities for factual entertainment or, alternatively, sounded the death knell for those more serious forms of documentary work which claimed to be culturally enlightening rather than thinly disguised entertainment vehicles.

One of the most noticeable features of the tranche of programming sometimes referred to under the generic label 'reality TV' is that much of it displays distinct hybrid traits (Roscoe, 2001: 17). This reveals the extent to which programme makers, driven as they are by the need to produce popular formats which deliver audiences to broadcasters, have adopted what might be seen as a tactic of limited risk. By taking elements from established programme categories and by combining them in a new *mélange*, programme makers are able to claim certain innovatory qualities for the resultant product. Hybridizing is not always, however, inspired by hard-nosed business calculations. It can be a productive device for creatively breathing new life into tired genres. As John Corner has observed:

> Although quite directly commercially driven in many cases, the releasing of new depictive energies which often follows boundary-crossing has been a clear gain which may well outlast its core cynical audience. (Corner, 1996: 181–2)

Much of the boundary-crossing to which Corner refers has involved the employment of various techniques commonly used in popular dramatic fiction. What can be emphasized here, however, is that the kind of generic exchange practised in the new reality formats almost always relies on the popularity of a tried and tested genres. What has not been picked up by media critics is that, such has been the market penetration of the diverse factual formats in the 1990s, some of *their* generic features are being effectively re-imported into fictional programming categories. Thus we have witnessed fictional police drama series such as *The Cops* (BBC 2, 1998) which occasionally had the feel of a docu-soap. Likewise some of the basic scenarios of docu-soaps seem to have provided inspiration for producers of dramatic fiction. The activities of builders which were the focus of the docu-soap *Builders* (BBC 1, 1999) are fictionally revisited in *Grafters* (ITV, 1999), while the trials and tribulations of tour guides or holiday reps captured in docu-soaps such as *Holiday Reps*, (BBC 1, 1997) or *Chalet Girls* (ITV, 1998) are reprised in popular drama series such as *Sunburn* (BBC 1, 1999).

What many of the new reality formats have in common is the type of relationship they seek to establish with their audience. Film and television texts have always, of course, sought to position their audience by providing particular perspectives from which to view a series of on-screen events. The new factual formats, however, seem to acknowledge this act of positioning far more openly and make this the subject of ironic, knowing commentary. Sometimes this takes the form of a more or less playful relationship being established with the audience, as the programme maker seems to take the viewer more and more into his or her confidence (see also Chapter 6). At other times it involves the audience being invited to participate in the sequence of on-screen events as they unfold, in the full knowledge that the events have, to a greater or lesser extent, been contrived. In other words, the new reality formats take a very different stance vis-à-vis the audience to the one favoured by traditional documentary. The prevailing spirit is one of chumminess and camaraderie. There is also a sense in which we are made to feel that those who appear as on-screen protagonists actually represent the interests and preoccupations of the audience. Viewers relate to these persons both as characters in a special made-for-TV event *and* as real individuals with flesh-and-blood characteristics. Rather than being allowed to remain at a safe, critical distance, viewers are drawn in to the world that these real-life performers inhabit. It is the high degree of viewer involvement which they encourage that is, arguably, the key to the great success of some of the more recently developed reality formats.[1]

It is only fair to point out, however, that – as signalled at the start of this chapter – the arrival of the new reality formats has not been greeted with universal acclaim. Misgivings have been expressed about the way in which observational techniques developed by traditional documentary have been allegedly hijacked for the purposes of 'mere entertainment'. Doubts have also been voiced about the legitimacy of encouraging members of the public to produce performances specially tailored for the camera (though this of course immediately raises the question about the extent to which documentary, throughout its history, has also required a form of performance from its contributing subjects.) The new formats do, however, raise a series of ethical issues relating to such matters as the invasion of privacy and the gaining of consent of those who agree to participate (Hibberd et al, 2000). Some indication of the gravity with which the issue of privacy is treated is provided by a 1999 ruling by the US Supreme Court in Washington which sought to restrict the activities of camera crews as they attempted to capture dramatic footage of individuals being chased or arrested by police (Campbell, 1999: 8–9). From the TV producer's point of view, the near certainty of being able to sell these images to a programme maker specializing in putting together reality programme packages made it a potentially highly profitable exercise. The Supreme Court recognized, however, that the rights of individuals (and of family and friends who were being made guilty by association) were in some cases being infringed or overridden in the quest for a highly prized commodity: the dramatic footage of the arrest. The practice of 'riding with the cops' which began in the US and has long since spread to Europe and elsewhere is now, at least in the US, subject to rigorous constraints. Following the Supreme Court ruling, camera crews are now prevented from joining in a police raid of a house or property without first obtaining the owner's permission. The issue of collusion or complicity between programme makers and institutions whose activities they chronicle will be returned to later in the chapter. For the time being we can reflect briefly on the origins of 'reality' programming, before moving on to examine the reality formats which have come to the fore during the 1990s.

Old wine in new bottles?

To think of reality programming as a late twentieth and early twenty-first century phenomenon is to misunderstand the nature of the experience being communicated. From the earliest days of the moving image film makers have sought to capitalize on the undoubted frisson that an audience feels when confronted by apparently 'real life' events up there on the screen. The audience's excitement at seeing those flickering silent images of workers exiting the factory in the early actuality sequences produced by the Lumière brothers shows how powerful this illusion of reality can be.[2] Robert Flaherty's dramatically enhanced account of Inuit life in *Nanook of the North* (1922) which evokes in the audience that quintessentially documentary experience of 'Being There', on the other hand, provides another illustration of how events can be manipulated according to the narrative requirements of a film maker with very set ideas on the picture he wishes to convey (Rothman, 1997: 1–20). In the case of *Nanook of the North* Flaherty manoeuvres his lead character into situations which purport to give us insight into how Inuits conducted their lives, but which also clearly bear the marks of dramatic orchestration. This is not a world removed from the way contemporary docu-soap producers set up situations which are dramatically enhanced for the benefit of a TV audience.

Documentary's claim to be offering a 'window on the world' to its respective audiences of cinema, and later television viewers also finds echoes in some of the debates surrounding latter-day reality formats. Purists may well rail against the audacity with which contemporary programme makers invade personal and private space in the interests of producing captivating footage, but the issue of documentary's intrusiveness has been around since the genre's infancy (Nichols, 1991: 186–90). As one programme maker has recently observed when commenting on what he called the anthropological tradition in documentary:

> *Big Brother*, with its laboratory layout, [is] in its own way, just documentary-making by another route. The audience tuned in to see a type of reality – real human beings behaving in unusual circumstances, just as Flaherty's audience did. (Clark, 2000: 42)

Even the penchant, discernible in many of the contemporary factual formats, for reconstructing historical episodes and events is by no means a recent phenomenon. In the early days of documentary, film makers often had to resort to re-enactment techniques because of the limitations imposed by the ponderous, non-portable equipment. In the course of documentary's later development techniques of dramatic (re)construction have been used for a variety of purposes, including the 'reconstituting' of unrecorded events and the production of 'speculative' versions of hypothetical events (see Chapter 6, pp. 164–9).

What the new reality formats have provided, in short, is not so much of a radical departure from traditional factual/documentary discourse. As in other forms of artistic or creative endeavour, there may not be that much that is entirely new under the sun. Formats which appear at first sight to be bold and innovative prove, on closer examination, to rely in no small measure on producers' ability to adapt conventional techniques to the new breed of entertainment-oriented reality formats.

Formatting reality: patterns of development

In talking or writing about the phenomenon of 'reality TV' or 'reality programming' one is soon made aware that one is in fact tackling a relatively broad generic category. Both terms have been used to cover a broad range of popular factual formats and have, for this reason, probably outlived their critical usefulness. As I have written elsewhere:

> One moment the term 'reality television' is being used to refer to slice-of-life observational modes of documentary film making, the next it is being used to describe types of fictional drama rooted in real life programming. (Kilborn, 1994b: 423)

For this reason it is more useful to refer to 'reality formats' or 'factual formats', especially as the term 'format' both underscores the commercially driven need of broadcasters to produce work according to established formulae and draws attention to the crucial importance of packaging in the development of a programme concept.

A & E formats
Broadcasters first became aware of the potential of this type of material in the 1980s when, starting in the US, a brand of popular factual entertainment emerged which was marketed under the label of 'reality television'. The main focus of this category was on the work of the accident and emergency services who could always be relied upon to provide the kind of drama and excitement which purveyors of factual entertainment were looking for. Arranging by whatever means (either as invited or uninvited guests) to be present at police raids, fires, traffic accidents, air and sea rescues and wherever other acts of heroism and bravery might be encountered, producers of these early reality shows gathered the raw footage which they then proceeded to edit together into entertainment packages for the prime-time TV audience. Depending on the requirements of individual broadcasters, different types of show were produced, but the basic ingredients of the Accident and Emergency (A & E) strands remained the same:

- footage of the event (usually shot by a single camera operator, but sometimes by a member of the emergency team)
- re-enactments of the rescues or raids, often made using structures and conventions borrowed from fictional forms of TV or film drama
- interpolated 'live' studio discussion where A & E officers are introduced to those they have rescued or otherwise assisted.

The other recurrent feature – some would call it a basic generic requirement – of these early A & E formats – was for an anchorperson, usually a well-known figure from the sector of TV news and current affairs, to introduce the individual action snippets and, if necessary, to comment on their significance. In the case of programmes destined for transmission by public service broadcasters, this would frequently necessitate drawing attention to the lessons that needed to be learned (in terms of accident or crime prevention) from the events that had just been so graphically depicted. While the earnest, public service injunctions are a recurrent feature of many of these shows, most of them also contain a strong voyeuristic element. By so graphically depicting the disturbances which can suddenly erupt from the apparently quiet surfaces of life, these shows also play on audience fears of their own lives being subjected to similar cruel twists of fate. Just as disaster movies seek in their final, leave-taking sequences, to reassure audiences that, after all the mayhem, harmony has been returned, so too these A & E formats work hard to put viewers' minds at rest that order has been reinstated. This is achieved either by getting the avuncular anchorperson to voice words of reassurance following the mayhem which the viewers have just witnessed or it may involve focusing on the competence and efficiency displayed by the emergency services in restoring, however briefly, order to a seemingly chaotic world.

Some idea of how successful (measured in terms of audience ratings) these action-centred A & E formats have been can be gleaned from the fact that they are still, at the time or writing more than a decade later, a regular feature of broadcasting schedules. Like most other TV genres, however, these formats have undergone a series of structural and thematic developments in order to address broadcasters' new scheduling needs. A sub-genre of A & E programming with titles such as *Storm Force* (C4, 1998) has emerged, for instance, which focus on natural disasters (avalanches, volcanoes, hurricanes). Meanwhile another group of shows with titles such as *Police, Camera, Action* (ITV, 1997) and *Motorway Life* (ITV, 1999), relying extensively on surveillance footage or video material recorded by the police or other emergency services, offer viewers the voyeuristic pleasure of being able to gloat at various forms of motorway madness.

As these A & E formats have developed, the constant endeavour has been to come up with variants that will catch the attention of the channel-hopping viewer. There is evidence to suggest that broadcasters are seeking out ever more sensational events or occurrences to capture the attention of the action-hungry viewer. It also goes without saying that the heavy action-orientation of these shows immediately increases the chances of selling them to the worldwide TV market. The constant desire to extract maximum commercial potential from these formats is also evidenced in how they are scheduled. Mindful of their general popularity with viewers, schedulers will sometimes group individual reality programmes to form a solid 'reality wall'. On the evening of 6 April 1999, for instance, ITV's mid to late evening schedule was wholly devoted to factual entertainment. Beginning at 8 p.m. with *Parking Wars* (motorists' daily battles with parking attendants) the evening continued with *Motorway Life* (drama and mayhem on the motorway), and *Family Feuds* ('Five families whose lives have degenerated from squabbling to all-out war'). Maintaining this theme of disruption and disturbance, the evening culminated with *Holidays from Hell* ('What happens when the holiday of a lifetime turns into a nightmare') and *Pleasure Island* ('a fly-on-the-wall series about what's been dubbed the sexiest resort in the world').

Docu-soaps

The emergence in the late 1980s and the early 1990s of the largely action-centred reality formats and their popularity with audiences naturally enough encouraged the development of other factual formats. The second half of the 1990s saw what appeared to be the irresistible rise of the docu-soap. As the term implies, docu-soaps were essentially a hybridized format, combining certain structural and narrative features of soap-opera with elements of observational documentary. What docu-soaps offered the viewer was a different type of reality entertainment, an antidote to the fast-moving reality TV formats. They were more gently paced and much less centred on dramatic incident. Their attraction for viewers lay in the way in which producers were able to combine traditional documentary features (e.g. eliciting people's views as they go about their day-to-day occupational or professional activities) with a set of narrative components which encouraged them to be read as just another form of soap.⌐

From 1996–2000 docu-soaps experienced unprecedented ratings success and were a conspicuous presence in the schedules of the major networks. By the turn of the century, however, a marked viewer fatigue had set in and the number of docu-soaps commissioned and aired was drastically reduced. Broadcasting executives had, by their own admission, become over-reliant on the docu-soap to retain audience attention. There was also a feeling in some quarters that irresponsible commissioning had so flooded the market that the initial vigour of the docu-soap format had been quickly dissipated. Suffice to say that the docu-soap, having achieved rapid ascendancy in the sphere of factual programming, has now taken its place alongside all the other reality formats which jostle for our attention.

Reality game-docs

The success of the docu-soap had made producers aware of the still un-tapped potential in factual formats with a strong emphasis on the notion of 'real-life performance'. Casting around for a new type of programme that would 'excite the public imagination' (broadcaster-speak for 'jack up falling ratings') producers carefully analyzed the structuring features of earlier shows and came up with a hybrid format which skilfully amalgam-ated features of the action-centred reality formats with other elements drawn from the game show, talk show and docu-soap. Sometimes referred to as 'reality game shows' (Roscoe, 2001: 16) (the best-known to date have been *Big Brother* and *Survivor*) these new factual formats have, for all the criticism to which they have been exposed, been able to achieve the status of 'landmark' television events. They have shown themselves capable of generating the same intense forms of viewer involvement that character-ized audience response to the supersoaps of yesteryear such as *Dallas*. Pos-sibly their most significant contribution to the development of the factual programming genre has been their clever exploitation of the new tech-nologies which has enabled producers to launch multi-media promotional campaigns and made it possible for audiences to have interactive involve-ment, thus creating a strong sense of viewer participation.

Reality game-docs claim a certain reality status for themselves by focusing on a series of 'real-life' exchanges between a group of carefully selected individuals gathered together in a highly contrived, made-for-TV environment and required to respond to a number of challenges dreamed up by members of the production team. Some of the reality game-docs may make nods in the direction of observational documentary, but the core of their appeal lies in the opportunities they provide for especially intense forms of audience participation. They never make any serious claim that they are attempting to throw revealing light on 'real-life' issues. What they provide are entertaining diversions in which everything that happens is imbued with a high degree of postmodernist playfulness, but at the same time what is being enacted on our screens makes for a particularly compelling viewing experience. As Conrad Green, one of the producers of the British version of *Big Brother* puts it:

> At the core of it [*Big Brother*] there's a unique tension, a triangle of control. It's the only format I can think of where no one controls it. Normally in a TV programme, either the participants control it because they are completely in charge of their destiny; or the producers totally control it because it's a gameshow with strict rules; or the audience controls it with a clapometer or phone-vote talent contest. But in *Big Brother* you have this brilliantly formatted balance of power at the core of it, where I as a producer can intervene only to a certain amount; where the people in the the house can determine their fate only to a certain point; and the audience control things, but not completely. So there's this strange triangle of control which makes everyone feel they participate in it much more. (Wells, 2001: 2)

Reality game-docs are, for better or for worse, examples of contemporary television par excellence. At one level we, as viewers, are being invited to witness a number of individuals who have agreed – or better, have been shrewdly selected – to participate in a televised elimination game, where one contestant pits his or her wits against another. At another, we are being encouraged to make judgements about the game-players' performance ability (how well they adapt to developing situations and how good they are playing themselves). Finally there is the participatory hook: the opportunity of becoming involved in the various voting-off procedures, of sharing in the media hype and in taking part in the the peer group chat that is one of the major attractions of these shows.

Reality game-docs also speak to their audiences in not dissimilar ways to some of the more successful soaps. Like soaps, they secure a high degree of audience involvement by drawing viewers into a series of highly contrived 'real-life' scenarios. Also like soaps they encourage that form of distanced and sceptical viewing in which all the narrative and manipulative ploys being practised by the show's producers themselves become the subject of ribald commentary among members of the participating audience.

While it is possible to discern a general pattern of development in the onwards march of factual formats (from the early action-centred A & E programmes to the more recent performance-oriented shows), it is more difficult to differentiate clearly marked phases. So intense has been the fervour with which production teams have sought to develop new formats and concepts, that – as one surveys the factual TV landscape since the late 1980s – the impression one is left with is of constant swirling and churning motion, as generic boundaries are regularly traversed and as ever more creative ingenuity is deployed in dreaming up scenarios which will allow 'real-life' performers to strut their stuff on the television stage. There are certain elements, however, which have remained constant in what might otherwise be seen as a period of decisive change in the field of factual/ documentary television. The first of these has been the high premium placed on entertainment in all the recently developed formats. The second has to do with the nature of the relationship these formats, generally speaking, seek to cultivate with their intended audience. What characterizes these formats, namely, is a much more open acknowledgment that viewers will have become familiar with the styles, approaches and conventions being employed in these entertainment vehicles. Perhaps the clearest indication of this is the extensive use of playful humour and self deprecating irony in the narrational commentaries that are an integral feature of many of these formats.[3] By employing such modes of address, programme makers are seeking to establish that more 'knowing' relationship with the audience. The popularity of the new formats with audiences arguably has a good deal to do with the viewers' delight and appreciation at *not* being addressed in the sometimes patronizing ways of old but being spoken to in a generally lighthearted and conversational tone. That much of the ironic humour should be directed at the products churned out by today's television industry (see remarks on mockumentary in Chapter 6, pp. 175–83) is but a further illustration of the knowing, tongue-in-cheek relationship that factual producers have succeeded in forging with their audience.

Let a thousand hybrids bloom ...

The constant attempts by broadcasters to 'stretch the factual envelope' and to present each new factual format as being significantly different, in style and approach, from all that had gone before cannot disguise the extensive cloning and borrowing that has occurred as programme makers have sought to keep their product lines moving. This hybridizing impulse is discernible across the whole spectrum of recent factual programming. It not only entails the fusion of different elements from established factual/documentary formats; it also involves extensive cross-genre borrowing. There are, for instance, some remarkable parallels between the new reality formats (including the docu-soap) and TV talk-shows (see Livingstone & Lunt, 1994: 37–43). In TV talk-shows a pivotal role is played by the host or hostess whose function it is to elicit contributions from studio guests and generally to be seen as an organizing, if not commanding presence. An additional dramaturgical requirement of a host is, by carefully timed tactical interventions, to play off guests or contributors, one against the other, in the interests of enhancing the show's dramatic appeal. A further function of the host in the more confessionally-oriented programmes is to perform the role of mediating agent, gently assisting the guests to unburden themselves of the emotional trials and tribulations they have been through. The parallels with the reality and docu-soap formats are here quite striking. Structurally both formats depend on the contributions of a number of 'ordinary people' (people like you and me) integrated into a carefully packaged piece of diverting entertainment. In the case of reality TV shows, there will frequently be an on-screen presenter acting as host and commentator. One of their primary functions is to introduce the sequence of reality clips which form the basis of the show. With docu-soaps it is the narrator figure who, likewise, takes on the anchoring role. Docu-soap narrators, with their generally chummy, up-beat and warm-toned style of address, perform a similar guiding function to talk-show hosts, in spite of the fact that they are only present in the disembodied form of the voiceover.

Perhaps the most obvious instance of cross-genre borrowing in the broad category of of reality formats lies, however, in the requirement for participants and contributors to deliver confessional performances. This requirement may acquire the highest level of priority in the talk-show where guests may sometimes feel they are entering the equivalent of a confessional box. Docu-soaps and reality game-docs have, however, likewise incorporated the confessional imperative into their textual frameworks. Docu-soap protagonists entrust confidences to the camera, using similar styles of conversational address to the ones adopted by talk-show guests. Likewise game-doc performers know that part of the employment contract is to share personal intimacies with fellow housemates – and by extension with the millions of viewers hanging on their every word and gesture. It would be going too far to suggest that the docu-soap and reality game-doc formats are merely talk-shows by another name. The fact remains, however, that much of the ratings success of the hybridized formats rests on programme makers' ability to build into the format design a confessional component which assists in the creating the illusion of an intimate bond between on-screen subjects and members of the TV audience.

A slippery slope?

Just as talk-shows (especially those emanating from the United States) have in recent years been subject to the criticism that the talk was becoming ever more toxic and the shows more sensationalist, so too have producers of reality TV formats been accused of indulging in similar lowest common denominator tactics in their efforts to capture viewer attention. In the late 1980s, the intense competition in US broadcasting had led to some channels, especially the small cable operators, developing a form of reality programming which – because it homed in voyeuristically on the victims of traffic accidents and of crimes of violence – won for itself the name of 'ghoul TV'.[4] Television's demand for this type of material also led to the unsavoury phenomenon of the 'video vulture', a late twentieth-century version of the news hound, someone who was willing to stalk the streets or shadow members of the accident and emergency services in the hope of being on-hand to record material which they could then sell to the highest bidder (Kilborn, 1994b: 426–7).

In most parts of Western Europe we have been spared the excesses of the more voyeuristic types of reality TV. Elsewhere, however, in an increasingly deregulated broadcasting environment, some broadcasters have developed reality TV formats which are sensationalist and voyeuristic in the extreme. The example of *Ratinho Livre*, a programme transmitted by the small Brazilian TV station Record is a case in point. Taking its cue from some of the more 'action-oriented', knock-about shows developed in the United States (the name of Jerry Springer comes to mind) *Ratinho Livre* provides a cautionary example of where factual entertainment can land when it attempts to push back the boundaries in the shameless pursuit of ratings. Described by one observer as 'half chat show, half freak show' (Bellos, 1997: 20), the show relies on a steady stream of poor, disaffected and usually impoverished Brazilians being ready to come forward and expose some of the worrying realities of life in modern Brazil. Occasionally they will be encouraged to mete out physical revenge on those they consider responsible for their woes. In other words, like many other forms of reality TV, the producers of *Ratinho Livre* are really only concerned to encourage the more dramatic manifestations of disaffection on the part of their participants. They make no attempt to provide any kind of explanatory context which might throw light on the origins of such angry outpourings. The criticism to which the show's producers are exposed, of course, is that such a programme contains only a thin veneer of social concern and that the ex-politician Ratinho who presents the show and appears to be championing the cause of the exploited is himself part of an equally exploitative process as the TV station in question seeks to lure viewers away from rival channels.

If *Ratinho Livre* provides one example of reality TV where the freak show element dominates, a show that has been aired recently on Russian television provides a salutary example of a type of programme that can be spawned in a media environment freed up from earlier regulatory constraints. *Road Patrol* is a show developed in the mid–1990s by Russian programme makers with a clear sense of the opportunities provided by the new commercially driven television market.

Like so much television programming produced in the 1990s *Road Patrol* provides a good illustration of how television executives develop a format in order to exploit a market opening. Russian television viewers had, until the early 1990s, been fed on a diet of material which sought to underline Communist achievement and to decry the glitzy superficiality of capitalist society. Frequently serious if not preacherly in tone, it sought to avoid the dramatic excesses of Western-style television. Now, in just a few short years, the pendulum has apparently swung to the opposite extreme. Like many of the early A & E shows, *Road Patrol* masquerades as an attempt to raise awareness about the need for greater citizen vigilance in the increasingly dangerous post-communist world. These educative aspects belie the true intention of the series which displays all the classic characteristics of ghoul TV. As one observer has commented:

> Broadcast four times a day, seven days a week, *Road Patrol* is one of Russia's most popular programmes – attracting viewers with its voyeuristic intrusion into the disasters that strike the capital every day. In 15-minute snatches, an assortment of murders, crash deaths and apartment infernos are flashed across the screen ... The hysterical grief of victims is recorded. Dead bodies are shown in close-up on prime-time television. This is not a show for the squeamish, but its success is immense. (Gentleman, 2001: 6)

Road Patrol's detailed chronicling of death, disaster and various types of violent encounter are clearly targeting the audience's voyeuristic inclinations. The producers of the show may defend it on the grounds that the material presents an awful warning to the unwary and weak-minded, but – as with so much A & E reality programming – the bottom line is the ghoul appeal of the graphic depictions of carnage and mayhem.

~ Creating and selling the reality experience

The promise that all the early, and some of the later reality programmes make to their respective audiences is that viewers will be swept along on a 'roller coaster' of real-life action. What viewers are offered is the prospect that, from the comfort and safety of their domestic havens, they will be able to witness an astonishing range of daring deeds, fatal encounters, acts of bravery, whether these reality bites be of the dramatic, fast-moving variety (police chases, traffic accidents etc.) or whether the focus is on the more mundane, humdrum and quirkier aspects of human experience (programmes which often rely on home movie footage submitted by viewers).

The common feature of all these reality formats is that all of them, to a greater or lesser extent, have commodified reality. In other words: programme makers, having discovered the great selling appeal of 'real-life' action and performance, are now making a sustained and systematic attempt to exploit the 'reality' phenomenon. In the early days of television 'ordinary people' were conspicuously absent from the television screen. Occasionally they might be invited to deliver brief cameo performances, as a lippy contestant in a quiz show or making a vox pop contribution to a news or current affairs programme. By and large, however, television was the domain of the professional performer and opportunities for lay individuals to appear on any form of programme were severely limited (Hibberd et al, 2000: 13–15).

All this has changed quite dramatically since the 1980s with the discovery and development of the reality formats which purport to offer viewers some relief by bringing them back to the 'world of reality' after having exposed them so relentlessly to the glitzy world of artifice which had become TV's major stock in trade. Returning the viewers to the real is, however, revealed to be just another television strategy for diverting their attention from 'real life' issues. It may seem that the reality TV packages are offering some antidote to the glossy, plastic world evoked by TV fictions, but on closer inspection they are revealed to be anything but tales of the ordinary. As the critic Jay Rosen has commented:

> What all of these [shows] share is an interest in hyping the 'real' – real crimes, real desperadoes, real arrests, real suffering by real-looking people … [A] show like *Cops* is not a world beyond the image, but a process by which imagery simply appropriates the look, the feel, the very name of the real … Television has a tendency to loosen the viewer's sense of reality, so that the outside world seems not more violent or threatening, but more insubstantial, more fleeting – more like television in *form* rather than content. Reality programming may be a kind of adjustment within the television universe, a response to the medium's own tendency to reduce the world to a mere procession of pictures. (Rosen, 1990: 38)

This constant hyping of the real has the effect of making reality into a commodity like any other, in the sense that it is shaped and offered for sale like any other consumer product. The sights and scenes from the real world, the reality snippets, become a resource that can be deployed in various ways. Captured by the lens of the amateur or professional film and video maker, these reality sequences are carefully fashioned by teams of highly skilled operators into a commodity which, given its high action count, can be profitably traded in the TV markets of the world.

The objective of those commissioned to produce reality programming is to come up with the kind of programme package that makes its primary appeal by virtue of the fact that the filmed or re-enacted events are rooted in the world of actuality. Just as important, however, are the techniques and strategies employed for absorbing viewers into the action and for aligning them with one or more of the featured protagonists. Many of the techniques for absorbing the viewer into the dramatic action (especially in the case of the scenes which have been dramatically reconstructed) have been borrowed from film and television fiction. At the same time, however, producers are clearly out to exploit the reality status of what is being depicted. Viewers are persuaded that the on-screen events they are witnessing call for a different order of emotional and imaginative response than the one which might be forthcoming with modes of programming centred on wholly fictional characters and events. For instance, the programmes belonging to the first A & E phase of reality programming work very hard to convey the sense of 'Being There' as a way of securing maximum audience involvement. One quickly recognizes, however, that the strong illusion of presence and actuality is dependent on the deployment of very specific stylistic and structural devices. Wobbly, blurred images; poor sound and constant attempts at reframing are just some of the markers by means of which reality television makes its claim on our attention (much as Direct Cinema had done several decades previously).

Particular types of narrative organization are also favoured. One frequently encounters a tripartite structure, for instance, whereby a relatively static initial sequence in which the presenter or anchorperson sets the scene gives way to short snatches of dramatic action, and these in turn are followed by a quieter after-the-storm recovery phase in which emergency workers reflect back on missions successfully accomplished or where survivors share with us memories of their near brushes with death or disaster. Other recurrent techniques to convey or reinforce the impression that the viewer is being engulfed by the real include the attention-grabbing credits sequences. The popular American series *Cops*, for instance, whets viewers' appetite by means of an opening set of credits featuring slickly edited moments of drama from earlier shows. In addition, the voiceover commentaries which accompany these shows make great play with the fact that events are recorded on the wing, in specific locations and as and when they happen. As the opening sequence to *Cops* has it: '*Cops* is filmed on location as it happens'. Throughout the programme, the commentary will then seek to reinforce this actuality idea, in order to remind viewers that they should apply appropriate non-fictional frames of reference in their response to what they are witnessing.

Whose reality is this anyway?

The other question which has frequently been asked of the early reality TV formats is: 'Whose reality is it anyway?' In the A & E reality formats, for instance, one might reasonably claim that viewers gain a highly selective, and for this reason partial view of the emergency team's function and responsibilities. So intense is the focus on the drama and action surrounding, say, a police arrest that the whys and wherefores of that arrest are effectively left out of account. Only rarely is one given any explanatory context for the actions one is witnessing and hardly ever is the question of the legitimacy of the arrest raised. Likewise with most A & E shows, viewers are almost invariably positioned behind or alongside the police or the emergency services. This encourages the belief that they are acting authoritatively or bravely on our behalf. In a world where uncertainty lurks around every corner these representatives are – in both narrative and ideological terms – the agents who will be able to restore some semblance of order to a disordered world. The precise manner in which this restoration is accomplished, however, presents a view of the world in which the forces of good are seen to triumph over evil in ways which owe more to certain popular mythologies than to the lived experience of contemporary citizens. All too often, order is returned by the simple expedient of cuffing a suspect following a police raid.[5] The A & E reality formats also give high priority to cases in which members of the emergency services are cast in more or less heroic mould. The chronicling of a number of failed missions or botched rescues could provide a more accurate, authentic reflection of reality, but reality formats are governed by a different set of imperatives than that of documentary chronicling. Viewers need to be provided not only with the diverting entertainment of vicarious involvement in successful rescue missions. They also have to be given a measure of reassurance that the 'powers that be' are assisting in the quelling of the tide of lawlessness or will be on hand when any other form of natural or manmade disaster threatens.

The point being emphasized here is that these broadly defined A & E formats seek to position their audiences in quite specific ways. Programmes like *Cops* , for instance, rely heavily on securing what could be called the 'affiliative involvement' of an audience. This is achieved by aligning viewers alongside law-enforcement officers as they track and arrest presumed criminals and felons. In this relatively black-and-white world where questions of possible mistaken identity are not allowed to intrude on the dramatic spectacle of raid-and-arrest sequences, the viewer becomes in effect an ideological partner (or accomplice) of the police. In another tranche of reality programming which I will call 'collaborational' (represented by programmes such as *Crimewatch UK, Crimestoppers* or *America's Most Wanted*) the viewer is offered a slightly different subject position, one which allows for a more active and collaborative form of involvement. The proposition, or underlying assumption here is that law enforcement agencies need the constant support of the publicly minded citizen, indeed that it is one of the citizen's civic duties to assist in tracking down those who have offended against society's codes.

The American scholar Jessica Fishman has suggested that these two distinct categories of A & E reality programming, characterized here as positioning their viewers affiliatively or collaboratively, mobilize two distinct types of popular myth. The first category is where viewers are being invited to admire the efforts of law and order agents in their battle to keep the disturbing forces at bay and where 'power and authority … are typically bestowed upon an elite few' (Fishman, 1999: 268). According to Fishman, it is a 'progressive myth' which is here being brought into play. Where, on the other hand, there is the prospect of some form of participatory involvement by ordinary people in the law-restoring process, it is a 'populist myth' which is being deployed. It is Fishman's contention that the 'crime busting' reality formats consciously draw on one of these two myths:

> In reality-based crime television's *progressive myths*, official agents are the heroes; their arena is a rarefied one of advanced technology and specialized knowledge; and the narrative highlights their seemingly immediate successes. In reality-based crime television's *populist myths*, everyday people are the heroes; civilian surroundings constitute their arena; and the narrative is one in which order unravels and justice depends upon the public's collective anti-crime efforts. (Fishman, 1999: 270, my emphasis)

In many forms of reality television featuring the work of the police there will, as already suggested, be considerable overlap between 'progressive' and 'populist' myth deployment. In programmes such as *Crimewatch*, for instance, even as the active collaboration of the populace is being elicited, the presence in the studio of uniform-clad police officials and the references to their efficiency and resourcefulness could be seen to be activating that other myth which highlights the role of more paternalistic or authoritarian forms of institutional control.

Applying these mythic terms of reference to the various categories of reality programming we are currently examining, one is certainly struck by the frequency with which the populist myth is being actively incorporated into the narrative framework of individual programme types. One of the distinctive features of the long-running series *Crimewatch UK*, for instance, is its appeal to the authority of the ordinary person. The appeal takes the form of active soliciting for information, with viewers being encouraged to divest themselves of knowledge they may possess in order to help the police track down presumed deviants and malfeasants. Programmes in this category also work hard to persuade the viewers that their contributions count. The celebrity hosts who normally anchor these programmes are not only slick, professional performers; they are also to some extent representatives of the popular voice, enthusiastically reporting back to the audience what results have been achieved through members of the public responding to earlier calls for information and assistance. As a further conscience-pricking stimulus to collaboration, programmes like *Crimewatch* will also include sections which highlight the fate of victims of crime. Finally, as a tangible reminder of the possibility of participatory involvement, there are regularly interpolated studio shots of those manning the phone lines and fielding the incoming calls from viewers with information to impart.

To the extent that *Crimewatch* appears to be reaching out and seeking to involve viewers in the fight against crime, it certainly seems to be activating the populist myth. This impression is arguably reinforced by the image of the police which the programme seeks to project. In a series like *Cops* police are shown in action-mode and will occasionally be seen resorting to strong-arm tactics in the fight against crime. With *Crimewatch*, on the other hand, police officers have been displaced from their operational environment of street patrol, squad car or police station and thrust into the alien world of a television studio. Most of them appear in uniform, but some seem rather ill-at-ease in this relatively unfamiliar setting.[6] The very fact that the police representatives are seen communicating with the public in this way and that they will sometimes show signs of nervousness or uncertainty might, in one reading of these programmes, be regarded as reinforcing the populist myth. The audience's perception of those all too human frailties behind the institutional mask might strengthen the viewer's conviction that some form of collaborative involvement is needed.

In assessing the manner in which the different crime-centred reality formats key into various myths relating to law and order issues, one also has to recognize that most forms of contemporary factual programming exhibit sufficiently hybrid tendencies to make it likely that in a single programme different kinds of subject positioning are being undertaken. Or, using mythological terminology, in a programme like *Crimewatch* even as the populist myth is being mobilized and the supportive involvement of the viewer-citizen is being sought, the presence in the studio of uniformed police officers and the repeated references to their cool efficiency and re- sourcefulness could be seen to be activating that other 'progressive' myth, the one that emphasizes the role of the police as protectors and their occa- sional need to resort to more authoritarian forms of social control.

The other issue one needs to address which is prompted by this dis- cussion of myth relates to the image of institutional authority which is being projected by these A & E reality formats. While it could never be claimed that, given the diverse funding and regulatory mechanisms under which it has operated, television has, at any point in its history, had a truly radical agenda, there have been certain moments when it has succeeded in exposing flaws and shortcomings in the practices of society's institutions. Roger Graef's series *Police* (BBC, 1982) did alert viewers to some serious deficiencies in police procedures, while Peter Watkins' powerful drama- documentary *The War Game* (1965) showed up the gross inadequacies of civil defence planning at the time. Developments in broadcasting in gen- eral and in factual/documentary programming in particular since the early 1990s have, however, made it less likely that overtly critical programmes will be produced. With the A & E reality formats, certainly, the image of the police and of the other emergency services is relatively benign. Also with crimestopper series such as *Crimewatch* the image of the police which emerges is almost wholly flattering and complimentary. Criticism of po- lice operational strategies simply does not belong to the series' remit. The programme makers are, it could be argued, too dependent on maintaining a good working relationship with those who are their principal, if not sole source of information to start throwing doubt on police working meth- ods. By the same token the police themselves recognize that they stand to gain considerable public relations mileage from their association with the

Crimewatch programme. In the words of two critical commentators:

> As for the police, apart from undoubtedly achieving some results (though obviously on a minuscule scale in terms of the total incidence of crime), the main benefit, at a time of mounting public concern about crime, lies in the widely diffused sense that something is being done about the problem. *Crimewatch* offers a generally useful public relations context in which the police are portrayed in an unambiguously positive and sympathetic light. (Schlesinger & Tumber, 1993: 31)

This readiness of institutions or organizations to cooperate with programme makers with at least half an eye on the public relations benefit to be derived from such exposure is a phenomenon that one has encountered ever more frequently since the early 1990s. The growing number of 'softer' factual formats (those which manifestly do not have an investigatory, revelatory agenda) is, in part, responsible for this. Once institutions began to recognize that most broadcasters were primarily concerned to produce relatively lightweight factual entertainment, rather than to expose institutional shortcomings, there has been no shortage of volunteers to cooperate in new programme-making ventures.

Dramatizing the real

One aspect not yet mentioned in this overview of reality formats is the extent to which many have had recourse to various types of dramatic reconstruction. Actuality footage shot as events unfold may be the most highly prized asset, but where it is not available, producers will usually have to resort to some form of re-enactment. Just as in the broader debate over drama-documentary (Paget, 1998; Rosenthal, 1999), so with reality programming there has been much discussion as to how reconstructions should be handled. There is, for instance, always a concern that, in today's competitive broadcasting environment, the desire to produce captivating footage will lead programme makers to take unwarranted liberties with the 'facts as we know them'. As I have written elsewhere:

> [There are] fears that in their desire to create maximum dramatic effect, producers will begin to distort the very reality they claim to be representing. In particular they will blend fact and fiction in such a way that makes it impossible for the viewer to decide how much is based on factual evidence and how much is ... imaginative fabrication. (Kilborn, 1994b: 431)

The dramatic reconstruction of incidents and events certainly leaves the way open for various kinds of fictional embellishment, and it is this which has led to expressions of disquiet that the boundaries between factual and fictional genres will become progressively more and more blurred. The use of dramatic reconstruction will be explored further in Chapter 6, but it is worth commenting here on the use of re-enactments in some of the early A & E reality formats.

With programmes such as *Crimewatch* the use of dramatic reconstructions could still be defended on the public service grounds that the intention was to provide memory-jogging re-enactments which might assist in apprehending criminal suspects.[7] With other A & E reality formats which came on stream in the course of the 1990s, however, it became clear that reconstructions were principally being used to advance the claim of the programme to be dramatically entertaining rather than factually enlightening. The BBC series *999*, for instance, which was first screened in 1992 and which was closely modelled on the American series *Rescue 911*, was regarded as something of a watershed in that it marked a decisive move on the part of the Corporation in the direction of factually-oriented entertainment. On the surface, and in the promotional material that accompanied the programme's launch, *999* claimed to be casting revealing light on how the emergency services operate and to show what risks they undertake on the public's behalf. A due measure of public service gravitas was introduced into the proceedings by employing a senior news and current affairs presenter, Michael Buerk, to anchor the programme. For all these attempts to highlight the programme's public service credentials, the series *999* is manifestly driven by an entertainment agenda. Re-enactments of dramatic rescues are the series' principal stock in trade and no efforts are spared to extract maximum dramatic tension from the reconstructed events. To these ends a series of techniques familiar from film and TV drama (fast editing, mood music and devices to build narrative tension) are regularly deployed and viewers are drawn into the screened events almost as if they were watching a Hollywood action movie. In the words of one *999* producer:

> We are using all the available film techniques to make engaging films that include non-documentary drama techniques. Once you would have done it in a straight documentary way, but this is a way of making factual television more accessible to a big audience. (Powell et al., 1992: 32, my emphasis)

Dramatic reconstructions have continued to be a regular component of many of the more action-oriented reality formats. A particularly favoured device is getting a survivor of a dramatic or near-death experience to set up the event for the viewer, then to screen the reconstruction and finally to add in some post-trauma reflection from those who have lived to tell the tale. The pay-off here is that a powerful connection can be established in the audience's mind between the dramatic presentation of the re-enacted events and the persona of the on-screen survivor. It also enhances the 'real-life' claims of these shows, since the very presence of the survivor provides living confirmation of the veracity of the events we are witnessing in the re-enactment.

Performing the real

With the A & E formats developed in the later 1980s there was still a predominant sense that the sights and sounds which were being recorded for our edification and entertainment were drawn from what was recognizably the socio-historical world. There were still traces of that long-standing documentary ambition to produce a mediated representation of the world 'out there'. One could, in other words, still make a clear distinction between the domain of the chroniclers (here the TV programme makers) and the world they were seeking to represent. As television, however, has interposed itself more and more on the world 'out there', there is a sense in which that earlier distinction between separate worlds has become progressively clouded. Factual programme makers are nowadays not so much concerned with the observational chronicling of events as the staging and shaping of events for viewer consumption. Producers of factual programming might still claim they were attempting a warts-and-all exposure of reality in all its joyful and quirky manifestations, but as more and more reality shows began to crowd in on the TV schedules, it became increasingly apparent that producers' principal concern was to win viewers over to a world that television itself was creating. This trend was already discernible in the United States in the late 1980s. As Jay Rosen has commented:

> With its growing list of reality shows, television purports to bring us closer to the real world. But *closure* is a better description of its aim: to offer a world in which every desire we have, including the desire to transcend television, can be programmed back to us as TV. (Rosen, 1990: 38)

As TV factual programming developed through the 1990s, this trend became ever more pronounced. To an increasing extent 'reality' became something that needed to be formatted according to television's designs and specifications. Television's intervention in – and shaping of – the 'real world' became the norm rather than the exception; indeed one of television's promises to its viewers was its ability to mould and manipulate the world of actuality to its own designs. Even the terms 'real' and 'the real world' began to acquire additional connotations, as factual TV producers rushed to cash in on the public appetite for reality. This was not so much an exploration of reality, as a remaking of the real in approved televisual formats. Television had by this time become such a powerful force in the land that it was able to persuade an increasing number of lay individuals to participate in the newly emerging reality formats, the primary appeal of which was seeing how 'ordinary' people responded when placed in a series of highly contrived situations. For the broadcasters there were a number of conspicuous benefits in adopting this approach:

1   The new reality formats, depending as they did on specially contrived situations, gave programme makers much greater control over the events which formed the raw ingredients of the programming. The control extended to key concerns such as the setting-up of the event, the selection of real-life performers and the manipulation of storylines.

2   Though the new forms of contrived factual entertainment featured 'real-life' individuals in starring roles, the events depicted were, to all intents and purposes, essentially televisual productions (in both senses of the word). Those who agreed to participate did so on television's terms. Their status was no longer that of testimony-giving documentary subject, but that of television performer.

3   There was a shared recognition between programme makers and performers that the parties were meeting each other half way in the production of these diverting entertainments. For the programme makers there was the knowledge these 'performances of self' could be a sure hook to secure viewer attention. For the volunteer participants there was the pleasing prospect that their involvement in a high-profile media event could be fame-and-fortune bringing. Indeed many of those who volunteered their services did so in open

acknowledgement of the fact that this form of television exposure would result in them acquiring celebrity status.

The emphasis on the performance ability of subjects is most discernible in the game-doc formats such as *Big Brother* which achieved such prominence in the later 1990s. It was, however, already present in embryonic form in the wave of docu-soaps which came to the fore in the mid–1990s. Here too we are confronted by entertainment-oriented pieces, which may nod nostalgically in the direction of traditional forms of observational documentary but which also anticipate the more performance-oriented reality game-docs. Docu-soaps provided, if you will, a training ground for the increasing number of individuals who craved the celebrity that television could bestow. By the same token, the success of specific docu-soap series depended, in no small measure, on the ability of producers to spot the performance potential in individuals belonging to the professional or occupational group undergoing the docu-soap treatment. The success of a docu-soap was therefore largely dependent on programme makers' ability to tease sustained and persuasive *performances* out of their usually all too willing subjects.[8]

The consciousness that individuals are performing for the camera has taken on a new order of significance with the reality game-doc formats which have largely superseded the docu-soap. Here, the emphasis on performance is so strong that it becomes a moot point as to whether one can accurately describe them as reality- or actuality-based. Indeed the shows make a special point of detaching the participants/contestants from everything that could remind them of the 'normal' lives they have been required to put temporarily on hold. Once detached from their everyday realities, the main task for contestants is to enter wholeheartedly into the playful spirit of the show, even though the playing of the game still has its more challenging side, in that the players will have to display various types of physical and mental prowess, not to mention low animal cunning, in order to survive.

With the reality game-docs, the made-specially-for-TV qualities are also openly celebrated as one of the major sources of the shows' appeal. These shows (of which *Big Brother* and *Survivor* have hitherto been the best known examples) are also much more 'in-your-face' than the earlier reality formats. They allow the TV audience to peer in voyeuristically on other people's lives in a way that carries strong reminders of the fairground freak show. For the watching audience, part of the appeal of watching these programmes is seeing how the game-players set about bonding with each other as required by the rules of the survival game. At the same time, however, given the various voting-off procedures which also are an essential part of this game, participants are pitched in competition with each other, as each seeks to stake his or her claim to remain in the game. Acts of betrayal are, in other words, par for the course in reality game-docs! This introduces an additional measure of drama and suspense to the proceedings – not unlike the one that spectators of earlier gladiatorial combats presumably experienced – as viewers begin to anticipate which contestant will be the next to suffer the ignominy of rejection and defeat.

The more successful of these reality game-doc formats all bring together the above mentioned elements in various combinations, though the locations chosen for event enactments differ quite significantly. *Survivor* offers viewers the exotic appeal of a tropical island location, while *Big Brother* requires its housemates to share the claustrophobic confines of a specially designed building.[9] All these shows, however, have this much in common: they all make no bones about the fact that they are conceived as pieces of diverting TV entertainment. Those who volunteer their services as participants in these programmes are also under no illusion as to what is expected of them. From the outset it is made clear to would-be participants that, if they succeed in getting through the initial audition process, they will be expected to maintain a high level of performance, in which their ability to emote, react, interact, argue, commune and much else besides will be put to the severest test. For all those involved in these game-doc ventures, it is abundantly clear that all this is being conducted solely in the interests of TV entertainment. The programmes do not make any extravagant ethnographic or sociological claims, though producers will sometimes make much of the fact that their shows can be psychologically enlightening in that they reveal how individuals respond in unusually demanding situations. Some shows reinforce this element by recruiting a resident psychologist to comment on subjects' success at coping with the demands placed upon them. The principal attraction of such shows, however, is still seen to be the provision of a voyeuristic experience, in which part of the appeal is witnessing the humiliation of others.

Even though shows like *Big Brother* may be thought to have ushered in a new era of factual TV programming, there is nothing that is *essentially* new in terms of the basic programme content. One can, for instance, draw a direct line between the reality game-docs of the late 1990s and those much earlier exercises in TV voyeurism of the 1950s such as *Candid Camera* in which members of the public found themselves the subject of television's leering gaze. The game-docs also carry echoes of those more recent dating shows such as *Blind Date* (ITV, 1985–) where those with a craving for media exposure are also drafted in to another television venture in contrived reality.

Other categories of programming that emerged in the 1990s and laid some claim to being documentary in their aspirations might also be regarded as being precursors of the later reality game shows. One such series which masqueraded as a piece of social anthropology while barely concealing its populist intentions was the six-part series *The Tourist Trap* (Channel 4, 1998). This programme combined game-show and documentary elements in almost equal measure in what the producers trusted would be an enticing package. Four groups of (initially) unsuspecting holiday-makers are offered a free holiday at a Mediterranean resort in exchange for their being filmed for what they are told is a promotional documentary. The tourists are, however, not aware of the trap into which they have fallen. Every move they make is being filmed by batteries of concealed cameras and microphones and, in addition, several actors have been hired to play the role of stooges whose job it is to add some spice to the proceedings. As with some of the later survivor formats (e.g. *Castaway*, BBC 1, 2000), the producers of *The Tourist Trap* make the somewhat spurious claim that it would be sociologically enlightening to see whether the four national groups (in this case Germans, Brits, Japanese and Americans) perform in accordance with perceived national stereotypes when confronted with a series of 'challenges'. While most critics were not overly impressed by a series which so openly played on cultural stereotypes, *The Tourist Trap* did, in some senses, put a marker down for those other contrived reality formats which would soon flood the television market. Depending as it does on hidden camera techniques to register the reactions of the participants to the ever more ludicrous situations into which they were placed, *The Tourist Trap* prefigures that whole repertoire of factual programmes where contestants are filmed, this time knowingly, in situations contrived by the format developers.

Staging reality events

The feature that is common to most of the more recently developed reality formats is that they all, to a greater or lesser extent, depend on the staging of an event (see also Chapter 6). Situations or scenarios are contrived and volunteer 'real-life' performers are sought who – sometimes for considerable lengths of time – are willing to take time out from their everyday occupations and pursuits in order to participate in these made-for-TV shows. Many ideas have been tried in order to get the right balance of ingredients for these contrived reality formats, but the most successful, in audience ratings terms, have all revolved around the castaway motif. Like so much else in contemporary television there is nothing essentially new about the idea in itself. Literature and film provide countless variations on the castaway theme. Clearly the idea of being uprooted from one's normal environment and placed in a strange, exotic or potentially dangerous location strikes a strong imaginative chord in all of us! Many of these tales are accounts of endurance and survival and this is an element that has been picked up by the recent crop of game-docs. These late twentieth and early twenty-first century television variants on the castaway archetype will almost always give an entertainment-oriented spin to the traditional tales of survival. In the series *Castaway* (BBC, 2000), *Survivor* (ITV, 2001) and *Temptation Island* (Channel 5, 2001), for instance, the basic set-up remains that of a group of selected volunteers confronting the challenges of living for a period in remote, inhospitable or exotic conditions, detached from the alleged comforts of civilization. The conditions of exile can vary quite radically according to the prescribed format of the individual programme. In *Castaway*, for instance, the participants knew that, once they had been selected for what the series producers referred to somewhat disingenuously as a 'sociological experiment', they would (barring serious illness or some environmental catastrophe) be together for a whole year. With *Survivor* and *Temptation Island*, on the other hand, the participants knew from the outset that if they did not pass muster with the audience and their fellow contestants, they would be voted off the island. Members of the audience thus have a controlling influence over who goes and who stays.[10]

The basic calculation behind all the castaway and survivor series is that the tight confines of the situation, the shrewd mixing of volunteer participants and regular allocation of tasks and challenges will all combine to generate a series of responses and interactions which are food and drink to producers of TV entertainment. One should, of course, at no time underestimate the degree of manipulation and control being exercised by the show's producers. Whether or not programme makers admit it, the participants are all dancing to their tune. Producers of these shows will certainly leave no stone unturned to ensure that, first, participants are manouevred in such a way as to increase the likelihood of dramatic exchanges occurring and, second, every opportunity is exploited for the fuelling of press and media speculation about the likely turn of events. As Germaine Greer has shrewdly observed:

> Reality television is not very real. The situations are contrived and the protagonists handpicked … It's always the case that although the people who volunteer for reality shows may all be exhibitionist, someone who is careful to remain unwatched is pulling their strings. (Greer, 2001: 1)

Big Brother

Of all the reality game-doc formats to date none has acquired anything approaching the cult status of *Big Brother*. Here producers have been conspicuously successful in creating a reality brand which, more than any other, has captured the public imagination in a way that more sceptical observers would not have thought credible. Detractors of the show may rail against the way in which it encourages a voyeuristic response, but they cannot deny that the originators of *Big Brother* have produced a format which provides a television experience which is refreshingly different from all that television had had to offer hitherto. Indeed, a crucial factor in the success of *Big Brother*, and that of other reality game-doc formats, is the unerring accuracy with which they home in on how the contemporary audience, and particularly the members of the younger generation, use television.

Analyzing the structure and content of the *Big Brother* show, there is nothing about its individual components to suggest that it would experience such runaway success. The fundamental concept of the show is itself unexceptional in that it takes the form of a game-like contest for survival in which participants are eliminated until only one remains.[11] The key to the show's success, however, lies in the manner in which the producers have been able to build it up into a major media event. Much is made, for instance, of the selection of the contestants and how they found their way

onto the show. This reinforces the status of participants as 'real-life' individuals, thus strengthening the identificatory bond which viewers may feel
with them. (It is, after all, common knowledge that tens of thousands of
viewers have applied for a place in the *Big Brother* house. The contestants
are therefore, in some sense, acting vicariously on the viewers' behalf.)

The other fundamental element in *Big Brother*'s winning formula
has been the scope it provides for participants to indulge in various types
of performative and often humorous interplay. Those chosen to appear in
the show have already come through a rigorous selection process with great
care being given to choosing individuals who will not be fazed by the various performance demands placed upon them. There is a recognition on
the part of the contestants that they are all dramatis personae on a television stage specially rigged and designed to encourage the lively interpersonal exchanges on which this type of show feeds.[12] The tasks and challenges
which are doled out by the unseen 'Big Brother' figure are mere contrivances to afford the audience the delight of witnessing the participants indulge in entertaining, party-game antics and of measuring their success at
bonding together as a group. For the audience one of the particular pleasures of becoming involved in *Big Brother* is measuring participants' success at getting on with fellow housemates, while at the same time being
required to compete against each other for the privilege of staying on in
the show.

In identifying the principal structural features of *Big Brother*, one
also has to underline the key significance of the stage on which everything
is played out. The house domain, that contained environment in which
participants are effectively imprisoned for the duration of the show, is
manifestly a televisual construct, totally isolated from the world 'out there'.
Big Brother does away with any pretence that the chosen setting is anything
more than a hastily erected backdrop for a particular form of television
entertainment. The building – viewed from the outside – is revealed to be
little more than a glorified container or studio set. This emphasis on the
house-dwellers' detachment from 'normal', everyday life is a feature which
recurs in many other reality game-doc formats. What distinguishes *Big
Brother* from the other survivor shows is that the distance between the two
worlds, the real world from which the players emanate and the constructed
one in which they are temporarily confined, is cleverly incorporated into
the format design. The occasional shot of the house from an outside vantage

point will reinforce this sense of the physical separation of the two worlds. All the liminal movements of the housemates as they enter or leave the house are invariably the subject of speculation and excited debate. One might even go so far as to suggest these dramatic exits and entrances represent an Alice-in-Wonderland-like move between the fantastical world of television and a real world which is obsessively concerned with becoming part of an all-enveloping media event.

While all the above mentioned elements combine to make *Big Brother* an enjoyable enough piece of factual entertainment, what has enhanced its claim to have special significance in the annals of TV broadcasting is the clever use it has made of interactive technology. *Big Brother* was one of the first shows to capitalize fully on those technologies which allowed viewers to key into the programme at any hour of the day or night – whether it be via web site, chat lines, video- and audio-streaming, or simply by downloading the *Big Brother* ring-tones onto one's mobile phone – and in so doing become a communicant in an all-enveloping media event. It is by exploiting the range of interactive possibilities, by generating a sustained buzz of excitement around a contrived media event and by creating the illusion that the audience are calling all the shots that *Big Brother*, and shows like it, have been able to attain such landmark status in the history of contemporary television. As one critic has observed:

> These new hybrids have created opportunities for audiences to engage with these forms in new ways, either through convergence or through the construction of new viewing positions. The fact that performance is so central to these forms is one way in which a new dynamic between text and viewer has been opened up. They speak to an audience which is acutely aware of the constructed nature of the 'reality' on offer, and which is prepared to join in the performance of the real. (Roscoe, 2001: 18–19)

A new form of soap?

For all their proven ability to generate a 'new dynamic between text and viewer' the reality game-docs also employ tried and tested positioning strategies to engage the audience's attention. One of the principal appeals of *Big Brother*, for instance, is that – just as with with earlier peepshow-type programmes such as MTV's *The Real World* and the BBC series *The Living Soap* (BBC 2, 1992) – viewers can enjoy the voyeuristic titillation which comes from being able to tune in to a series of intimate exchanges between relative strangers. And as they lap up *Big Brother*, audiences may also be reminded of the ways in which they engage with other types of TV programming. It is as if these reality formats, in a highly knowing manner, are keying in to audiences' generic knowledge of a wide range of television practices. Not only are viewers expected to be conversant with the conventions governing the staging of this type of media event; they are also aware that many other reference points are being provided which can potentially enhance their viewing pleasure. The fact that Germaine Greer could refer to *Big Brother* as 'soap opera come to life' (Greer, 2001: 2) is instructive in so far as it suggests that viewers, in responding to the programme, may very well be encouraged to apply similar frames of reference as they do when watching their favourite soap. This includes the ability to accord the text a multivalent status i.e. be able to engage with it at more than one level. Thus, viewers may, at one level, treat the unfolding drama as having a degree of credibility in much the same way that they see elements of real-life experience reflected in soap opera narratives. At another level, however, they are sufficiently media literate as to be aware that everything being played out before them has been contrived to meet their perceived entertainment needs. To this extent they are able – like many soap opera viewers – to take a more relaxed and distanced view of events, treating everything they see and hear either with a degree of scepticism or even as some elaborate game (Kilborn, 1992: 83). Viewers are, of course, encouraged to apply soap opera frames of reference, because game-docs are so palpably structured and presented as if they were another form of soap. Game-doc participants are encouraged to indulge in gossipy, soap-like forms of interchange. Also, just as in soaps, there is a relatively high incidence of close-up shots to allow us to scrutinize character reaction. And as far as narrative structuring is concerned, there are also parallels between the two genres in that game-docs, in order to maintain narrative pace and interest, also constantly switch the focus of attention from one group of characters to another. Likewise at the end of each episode game-doc producers will almost always utilize one of the cliffhanger or tease devices familiar from TV serial drama. In other words, just as in soap opera, the constant attempt is to create dramatic entertainment out of what is, after all, a highly unpromising and potentially boring situation.

The point which needs to be reiterated with respect to *Big Brother* and all the imitations to which it has given rise is that they are manifestly not concerned with capturing the weft and the warp of 'real-life' historical experience as traditional documentaries claim to do. Reality here is quite literally being staged. And as with any stage performance, no efforts are spared to ensure that what is being served up is an audience-friendly product. To these ends, just as producers of some Hollywood films will use pilot screenings to measure audience response to certain characters or to particular twists and turns in the narrative, so those responsible for developing the original Dutch version of *Big Brother* used similar techniques to gauge audience appreciation of characters and storylines. Producers regularly tuned in to *Big Brother* chat rooms to get an indication of how certain characters were coming across and used this information to tweak storylines or give higher profile to one character at the expense of another (see Wells, 2001: 2–3). By the same token, when it came to the editing of material, techniques appropriated from narrative fiction (including soap opera) were used to ensure that sufficient pace and variety were introduced into what could otherwise have been a highly pedestrian sequence of events.

Cloning and selling reality formats

Whatever cultural significance one attaches to *Big Brother*, there can be no question that it represents a major milestone in the development of factual TV programming. Here was a media event which had the same kind of global resonance as *Dallas* more than a couple of decades previously. And just as *Dallas* had led to widespread attempts to produce cloned versions of the original, so too the success of *Big Brother* and of other reality game-docs led to frenetic activity among programme makers to come up with cloned products that would enable them to cash in on the public's new-found appetite for this form of entertainment.

Just as with the slightly earlier docu-soap boom (see Chapter 4), which led to a veritable feeding frenzy among UK programme makers, so too with reality game-docs: many of the major TV networks sought to jump on the bandwagon either by producing – under licence from Endemol the Dutch originators – their own version of the *Big Brother* series or by coming up with cloned versions based on some of the *Big Brother* ingredients. The production of these new reality formats has become a multimillion dollar global industry with individual companies vying with each other to produce variants on that basic concept of having a group of 'real-life' participants corralled in controlled, contained environments while their every move is monitored by batteries of strategically positioned cameras. Producers have displayed considerable ingenuity in developing these formats. Attempting to generically sub-divide programmes is difficult, since most combine many of the same ingredients, but it is possible to make a broad distinction between shows that highlight the idea of challenge and adventure in which separate teams compete against each other and, on the other hand, those programmes which base their appeal more on observing the developing relationship between the corralled participants. The American series *Survivor* (which finished its US run by attracting an audience of more than 50 million) best exemplifies the first category, while the archetype for the second sub-set is *Big Brother*.

Cloned versions of the *Big Brother* and *Survivor* formats have, predictably enough, come thick and fast, though it is worth noting that there was a hiatus in the commissioning of certain reality formats following the events of 11 September 2001 when some broadcasters felt that the public's appetite for the more cynical and humiliating reality shows would be diminished. (In the event it has proved to be all too brief a hiatus.) Space does not permit a detailed examination of the many cloned varieties which have emerged, but – again as might have been anticipated – many display distinctly downmarket tendencies. Some, such as *Temptation Island* (Sky TV, 2001) have introduced a decidedly tawdry element to the 'survival' concept. Young and apparently happy couples are whisked off to an idyllic island resort and there they encounter various well endowed stooges (of both sexes) whose task it is to put temptation their way. Here sexual titillation, voyeuristic excess and the tease element (who will have the strength to withstand such temptation?) all combine to produce a particularly heady mix. (Small wonder that certain American advertisers, fearful of being associated with such a programme declined to advertise their products in the commercial breaks of the series.)

Other programmes have taken an element from an existing show and developed it into the central idea of a new series. Earlier reality formats, for instance, had used stooges to add a little more spice to the proceedings (see p. 77). *The Mole* (Channel 5, 2001) makes the stooge the central part of narrative interest in that it focuses on contestants' attempts to work out who is the mole planted among them bent on sabotaging their efforts to win a prize. Likewise *Popstars* (ITV, 2001) took the form of an elimination contest, where young wannabes competed against each other for the prize of pop glory and lucrative recording contracts. Other reality strands, by contrast, have picked up on the idea of emerging relationships between participants and made that the central lynchpin of the show. The American dating reality show *The Bachelor* (ABC, 2002), for instance, centres on the attempts of a partner-seeking male to select a mate from more than a score of prospective candidates.

The business of developing, licensing and selling reality formats has now become so big that a number of production companies specializing in the genre have been set up. Of these one of the largest and most successful is Endemol, originally a Dutch company but now with branches in most major countries. Endemol was responsible for developing *Big Brother* but has gone on to develop an impressive portfolio of other reality formats. In the course of the year 2000 the company came up with the following variations on the familiar reality theme: *Money For Your Life*, described as a 'no-holds-barred video diary'; *Chains of Love*, a series in the same vein as *Temptation Island* but this time allowing participants to choose four members of the opposite sex to whom they were chained for a whole week in a *Big Brother*-type surrounding; and *The Bus*, a road movie version of *Big Brother* in which the contestants move from town to town on a bus and where they 'interact with members of the public and modify their behaviour according to media coverage' (Endemol press release).

As should have become abundantly clear by now, much of the success of these programmes depends on producers' ability to generate sufficient pre-launch publicity to suggest that the show in question is an unmissable media event. Much thought and effort goes into the publicizing and promotion of these shows and a range of programme-specific strategies are devised to stir the public's interest. These will include all the conventional means (pre- launch trailers, press releases, interviews with leading characters) (Meech, 2000: 103–10), but will nowadays extend to the building of web sites, the setting up of chat rooms and the use of various interactive technologies (Roscoe, 2001: 17–18).

An additional promotional technique (especially for the survivor reality game-docs) is to produce carefully edited sequences, or even whole programmes, given over to the selection and induction of participants. The underlying idea of *Shipwrecked* (Channel 4, 2000) was that a small group of young people should be marooned for three months on the remote island of Moturakau, two thousand miles off the coast of New

Zealand. The search for a suitable cast of volunteer castaways was featured in the introductory programme to the series which showed how the original five hundred applicants were reduced to the final sixteen participants. Likewise with the heavily promoted BBC series *Castaway* (BBC 1, 2000), where a group of volunteer castaways spend a year on an inhospitable Hebridean island, the first four episodes were devoted to the selection process. Viewers were encouraged to conjecture which of the volunteers might get through to the next stage, what physical and emotional demands would be made on them and how well equipped they might be for facing up to the rigours of island life under the continuous scrutiny of the camera eye. What was of course *not* shown, on the other hand, were the potentially far more revealing discussions between key members of the production team concerning the structuring of the whole event: how the choice of specific participants might generate certain types of dramatic conflict, how the known likes and prejudices of the target audience might be reflected in a particular mix of characters and how the needs of certain embryonic storylines might be served if certain casting decisions were made.

Summary

Factual programming on television has demonstrated a marked tendency towards the commodification of the real. Such are the economics of contemporary broadcasting that it seems highly likely that factual programming will continue to develop along these lines. We will undoubtedly witness a further growth in hybridized reality formats, ever greater use of interactive technology to promote and extend active audience involvement and, last but not least, more and more examples of 'reality staging' where ordinary members of the public are drafted in to perform roles in specially created, made-for-TV scenarios. The idea of 'reality staging' will be returned to several times in the course of Chapters 4, 5 and 6. However, to conclude this chapter we will briefly reconsider the institutional and economic conditions out of which these swathes of reality programming emerged.

Without a shadow of a doubt the primary driver in these matters has been the demand of broadcasters for more accessible forms of factual programming to fulfil specific scheduling needs in ever more competitive times. Economics has played a significant role in these developments, in so far as more and more channels have been forced into adopting low-cost solutions to programming provision as audiences have fragmented and advertising revenues have generally declined. The reality formats discussed in this chapter have proved to be a valuable asset to cost-conscious broadcasters who have been more than happy to play the reality card as long as audience figures have remained reasonably buoyant and costs of programme production and acquisition have been proportionately lower than for other genres on which they had previously relied.

The fear is, of course, that the entertainment imperative will continue to impose such a baleful influence that the more challenging forms of documentary work will suffer further erosion. Critics of this persuasion argue further that, as a consequence, any residual hopes that television will be able to exert a 'civilising influence' will be lost (Dunkley, 2000: 20). This may be attributing too much power to the medium of television. Ultimately, the constant playing of the reality card by a generation of TV schedulers tells us more about the state of television than the state of civilization. With this in mind, the remainder of this book will continue to explore the changing forces in television which led to particular developments in factual programming. It is small wonder – given the tight constraints under which producers now operate – that programme makers have generally adopted low-risk strategies in the development of new programming formats. Initiative, in programme making terms, is now more often than not defined as the ability to take elements from tried and tested genres and to recombine them into attractive new hybrids.

One of the best examples of this cross-genre raiding is the docusoap which, in almost equal measure, combines elements of the talk show, soap-opera and observational documentary. Developed in the UK in the mid-1990s, the docu-soap enjoyed unprecedented success for roughly a four-year period (1996–2000). During this period docu-soaps were virtually omnipresent in the early evening schedules of mainstream broadcasters (especially BBC 1). It is to this particular phase in the development of popular factual programming that we turn in the following chapter.

Notes

1   John Corner refers to the quality of 'nosy sociability' (Corner, 2000: 687) cultivated by docu-soaps, in which characters interact with each other and with the audience just as they would in the familiar setting of a soap opera.

2   The fact that the sequences were also offered as an entertainment package, as if they were part of fairground spectacle, also gives an indication of the potential commodity

value of such material.

3   The use of ironic commentary is part of a more general move towards greater self-reflexivity in much of today's TV programming (Kilborn & Izod, 1997: 239).

4   In some cases producers were even able to persuade those who had survived such traumas that they could derive some therapeutic gain from reenacting their experiences for the benefit of the camera, using the dubious argument that public disclosure would be good for them (Anderson, 1995: 160–2).

5   With respect to arrest sequences in A & E reality programming, it is noticeable that individuals caught in compromising situations often show a remarkable capacity to produce a suitably tailored performance for the camera (as if this represented a small consolation for the embarrassment or discomfiture suffered).

6   For the audience this sense of slight unease is possibly reinforced by the viewers' own sense of surprise at seeing police displaced from the locations in which they are normally to be found in the world of TV crime drama.

7   While every effort is made to ensure that these crime reconstructions are handled sensitively, producers of *Crimewatch* would find it hard to deny that they are trading on the public's voracious appetite for dramatic and suspenseful footage. The dramatic re-enactment of crimes is now, of course, a TV genre in its own right and real-life crime dramas have become a regular feature in most mainstream schedules.

8   Discerning the performance potential in subjects is by no means an entirely new phenomenon. Documentary film makers have always, to a greater or lesser extent, indulged in the careful screening and auditioning of subjects.

9   The *Big Brother* series screened on Channel 4 in the summer of 2002 attracted considerable publicity after one disenchanted housemate succeeded in escaping the confines of the house.

10   Allowing the audience to pronounce judgement on the performance of the participants in this way bears distinct echoes of those TV talent shows whose history can be traced from the 1950s (*Opportunity Knocks*, ITV) right up to the present day (*Pop Idols*, ITV, 2002; *Fame Academy*, BBC, 2002) where viewers have also been able to determine the fate of contestants.

11   In spite of the temptation to draw parallels between the manner in which participants are evicted and the hiring-and-firing activities of profit oriented Western society, *Big Brother* – and shows like it – still remain essentially televisual events. To interpret them in any other way would be to attribute too great a significance to the power of television and to underestimate viewers' capacity to engage with the medium on its own terms.

12   The layout and furnishings of the specially designed *Big Brother* living space differ according to the particular national variant of the show.

4 Performing the real: the rise and fall of the docu-soap

Before the arrival of the brasher, more playful reality game shows such as *Big Brother* and *Survivor*, the form of actuality-based programming that had enjoyed unexpected, if rather short-lived success was the docu-soap. This chapter considers the conditions which proved so conducive to its meteoric rise. It also explores in some detail the structuring principles of a sub-genre which relied very heavily on ingredients drawn from established TV formats. Docu-soaps encapsulate many of the elements which broadcasters (and audiences) have come to regard as essential features of popular factual entertainment. They place high premium on audience accessibility; they make no bones about the fact that they are principally conceived as light entertainment vehicles, and last but not least they cleverly exploit the appeal of seeing 'real-life' individuals indulging in various types of performance activity, this time not in a contained, made-for-TV environment but in the context of their everyday working situations.

Docu-soaps still carry with them echoes of more traditional forms of documentary, but it was arguably those features drawn from popular TV genres such as soap opera and the talk-show which led to them catching on in the way they did. As we shall see, however, docu-soaps in many ways represent the response of a group of alert, enterprising programme makers to TV schedulers' requirement for a form of actuality-based programming which could be relied on to generate large, appreciative audiences at peak-time. As docu-soaps established an ever firmer hold over UK programme schedules in the period 1996–99, however, it was not long before the first voices of disapproval and dissent began to be heard. The proliferation of docu-soaps was regarded as providing still more evidence of television's downmarket slide. Likewise there were fears that the format would simply encourage those chosen to appear to indulge in 'amateur dramatics' (Morrow, 1998: 172). Perhaps more seriously, misgivings were raised that, if the format became more established, it would have the effect of further marginalising those more deserving forms of consciousness-raising documentary. In the words of one observer:

> Docu-soaps are seen as a quick fix by commissioning editors and schedulers. they deliver large audiences at a fraction of the cost of quality drama. Everyone wants them. But there's a danger that in the rush to deliver more and more, quality will slip and standards will not be maintained.
> (Mulholland, 1998: 7)

Broadcasters quickly sprang to the defence of docu-soaps, suggesting that their warm reception by audiences was indicative of a more general revival of interest in factual formats (Willis, 2000: 102). Much was also made of the fact that the popularity of the docu-soap showed how a genre was able to reinvent itself. This flew in the face of those gloomy predictions of only a few years previously, that documentary on TV was a seriously endangered species. Even the accusation that docu-soaps were nothing but lightweight entertainment vehicles, incapable of even 'scratching the surface of understanding' (Watson, 2000: 10) was refuted by pointing out that docu-soaps were not per se generically predestined to be light, frothy and insubstantial in their treatment of their respective subjects. Suggestions were also made as to how the format could be adapted to serve a more serious purpose, even though it was conceded that the entertainment priorities of the genre would always militate against more probing forms of sustained investigation.

A short history of docu-soaps

The rise of the docu-soap owes much to broadcasters' recognition that popular factual entertainments had considerable audience-building potential. Like all other television genres, however, docu-soaps developed out of a particular set of circumstances affecting TV production and scheduling during a specific phase of broadcasting history. As discussed in Chapter 2, the mainstream channels in the UK were going through major periods of adjustment as they geared up to face the challenge of a new broadcasting age. For ITV this signalled the virtual disappearance of serious documentary on ITV 1. For the BBC, as public service values were steadily eroded, it involved a major reappraisal of the role of documentary programming, resulting in a higher premium being placed on the notion of accessibility than hitherto. For some critics this simply meant that the BBC was caving in to commercial pressures and accordingly dumbing down its output. Others of a more optimistic inclination felt that the new broadcasting environment would give programme makers the necessary stimulus to broaden the range of their work and develop new factual formats and approaches. Serious documentaries of the traditional variety would still bulk large in the BBC's overall provision, but these would be complemented by new styles of entertainment-oriented factual programming designed to appeal to a wider audience. It was this readiness to contemplate more popular forms of the factual which paved the way for the docu-soap. Some indication of the extent to which the winds of change were blowing through the corridors of the BBC at this time is gained from remarks made by the then editor (later head) of documentaries at the BBC, Paul Hamann. Interviewed by a journalist in 1991, Hamann was clearly under no illusions as to what would be required of factual/documentary programming in the coming years. In his own words:

> Good documentaries will get good audiences and I don't see any reason why they shouldn't have good slots. *What I want to do is to beat the pants off my colleagues in light entertainment and drama.* (Jwarg, 1991: 146, my emphasis)

The types of factual/documentary work which Hamann and his colleagues at the BBC encouraged were, among others, those which took elements from tried and tested formats and combined them into vigorous new hybrids. In the case of the docu-soap we are clearly dealing with a hybrid format in that, as the name suggests, it combines certain qualities of observational documentary with structuring features of soap opera. But while the docu-soap has been hailed as an entirely new and distinctive programme category which became extremely popular in the second half of the 1990s, its origins can be traced back to earlier attempts to marry together documentary observation and dramatic presentational modes. Paul Watson's ground-breaking series *The Family* (BBC 1, 1974), for instance, provides an example of a programme which, at least as far as its structuring principles are concerned, anticipates the later docu-soap. Watson uses a serialized presentational technique to introduce us to the members of a working-class family, the Wilkins, from Reading. Following standard soap opera practice, each of the twelve episodes brings an update of what has been happening to the family in the time since we last encountered them. Individual family members were also encouraged by Watson to open up to the camera in a manner which provides a distinct pre-echo of later docu-soap confessionals. The audience thus became absorbed in the unfolding drama just as they would with a wholly fictional soap opera.

Watson was accorded considerable critical acclaim for *The Family* on the grounds that the series succeeded in graphically depicting the strains and stresses of working-class life in 1970s Britain, in the same way that Craig Gilbert's 1971 documentary *An American Family*, a twelve-part series made for PBS, had chronicled family life in the United States. Equally significant for our present concerns, however, are some of the criticisms which were raised about Watson's work. These related in particular to the serial mode of presentation which Watson adopted. This meant that the interview material to be incorporated into later episodes was still being filmed as earlier episodes were being transmitted. Critics felt, with some justification, that as as members of the family became aware of how they were 'coming across' as television personalities, they consciously began to shape their behaviour according to the roles they imagined they were being called on to perform. Performance criteria thus became the dominant measure for the contributions they were disposed to make, in exactly the same way that later generations of docu-soap stars were to tailor their own performances in accordance with the perceived entertainment requirements of the genre.

Watson's later series *Sylvania Waters* (BBC 1, 1993), another fly-on-the-wall account of domestic life, again contains many pre-echoes of later docu-soaps (even though Watson himself has always gone out of his way to deny that there are any connections between this work which he considers a 'serious film about serious issues' and docu-soaps which he derides as cheap and irrelevant (Watson, 2000: 10)). Like *The Family*, *Sylvania Waters* provides a highly selective and skilfully edited account of family life, this time in an Australian suburban household. Noeline and Laurie, the couple in question, are both larger-than-life nouveaux riches individuals, with a penchant for giving free vent to their opinions and feelings. As such they would certainly not been out of place in one of the later docu-soaps which put such high premium on the notion of performance. When it was first screened, the series caused much controversy, partly because the stars of the show, Noeline and Laurie, felt that in the process of editing, they had been wickedly caricatured and partly because it was felt that the series projected such a distorted picture of Australian family life. The series did, however, provide an early indication of the direction in which factual/documentary programming was moving, away from fly-on-the-wall observational styles and towards more authored, entertainment-oriented approaches. As Watson commented at the time:

> This is not the Wilkins … This is not wobble-scope fly-on-the-wall. This is
> rather more mannered. This is *The Simpsons* for real – the big speeches and
> the big actions. (Selway, 1993: 67)

In making *Sylvania Waters*, then, Watson was clearly – and legitimately –
using a degree of poetic license in exposing some of the unsavoury truths
about family life. Shrewd editing helps to heighten the dramatic impact of
some of the family exchanges and one can frequently detect Watson's authorial presence in the way that the narrative unfolds. The leading characters, Noeline and Laurie, may themselves have a highly developed capacity
for self-projection and they may also have had a sense of what the film
maker was looking for, but it is still down to Watson's skill as a documentarist
that he has been able to produce an entertaining and insightful account,
which has something of the quality of a real-life soap. Small wonder then
that journalists at the time picked up on this, referring to *Sylvania Waters*
as a 'soap-vérité or even as soapumentary' (Dale, 1993: 17). Nor is it perhaps surprising – as is revealed by the following quote – that the epithet
'docu-soap' should have been used (to my knowledge for the first time) to
describe the hybrid qualities of the series:

> The series has the combined appeal of a compelling soap-opera, the irony
> and comedy of satire and the hard currency reality of documentary. *You
> might call it docu-soap.* (McFadyean, 1993: 13, my emphasis)

Other series produced in the early 1990s might also be regarded as having
paved the way for the later wave of docu-soaps. *The Living Soap* (BBC 2,
1993–94), a series closely modelled on MTV's *The Real World*, is one such
example of a series which deliberately blurred the boundaries between
documentary and soap. It followed the lives of a group of students who
shared a house in Manchester and who had agreed to have their activities
filmed in exchange for free accommodation and doubtless the opportunity of becoming media celebrities. Part of the producers' unwritten contract with the students was that they (the students) would in effect become
characters in a real-life soap.[1] It was, for instance, not unknown for producers to provide advice as to how emerging rivalries in the student household might be dramatically developed. It is this contrived nature of *The
Living Soap*, together with the use of some of the structuring principles of
television drama, which clearly identify it as a precursor of those many

types of reality staging which came thick and fast later in the decade (see also Chapter 6). It is these same aspects which also allow us to designate *The Living Soap* as a piece of lightweight factual entertainment, in contrast to Watson's *Sylvania Waters* which is still sufficiently probing in its engagement with the real world to earn for itself the label 'documentary'. *Sylvania Waters*, for all the dramatic entertainment that Watson extracts from this closely observed study of the joys and tensions of family life, can still be read as a study of a recognizable social reality (that of an established group of closely-knit family members interacting and squabbling with each other) whereas *The Living Soap* is the product of a wholly manufactured situation, specifically designed to be part of a TV entertainment package. It is simulated rather than documented reality. This recognition that in this modern technology-driven age representations have come to create rather than reflect reality has been eloquently described by critics such as Jean Baudrillard. In a very real sense, the staging of reality has become the accepted order of the day. As one observer commented at the time *The Living Soap* was being broadcast:

> It is now widely understood that reality as it appears on TV is a produced or invented discourse rather than something out there to be captured or discovered. What counts is no longer representation, but the simulation of reality. (Beard, 1993: 35)

Attempting to combine the harder edge of documentary with the softer qualities of soap opera was something on which other production teams were also engaged in the early 1990s. As already intimated, it was around this time that the BBC began to explore ways of broadening the base of its factual/documentary output by producing formats with strong entertainment appeal. In-house producers were encouraged to develop ideas for factually-based programmes which would represent a departure from the staid, sober documentaries with which the Corporation had been traditionally associated. Jeremy Mills, then a BBC producer but later to become head of the highly successful independent production company Lion Television (a company which initially specialized in docu-soap production), recalls two series which he made for the BBC in the late 1980s which established the distinctive character-based approach which was to become the classic hallmark of later docu-soaps. *The Vet* (BBC 1, 1989) and *The Doctor* (BBC 1, 1990) were both series which relied on 'getting up close' to working professionals as they went about their daily business. Though focusing on just one character (in contrast to the larger cast of performers normally required by fully fledged docu-soaps) both the aforementioned series have many docu-soap features. Both constantly switched perspective between the working environments and the private domains of their subjects and both placed strong emphasis on the character and personality of their chosen participants. *The Doctor*, for instance, combined scenes in which we follow an experienced GP on his rounds with others in which we got to know him as a person. There was also an attempt to work in some material which engaged with issues of wider sociopolitical relevance, such as what it was like to work in the ever more pressurized National Health Service. Furthermore, in putting the material together to produce an accessible documentary, Mills and his team resorted to a series of techniques which were clearly more derived from television drama than from documentary. Mills speaks of creating individual storylines and deploying these in such a way as to produce a sense of an unfolding drama. In his own words:

> In *The Doctor*, for instance, we had certain story lines that went across the whole series, whilst there were others that were contained within an individual episode. (Interview with the author, London, 1998)

The point to be made, therefore, is that, several years before the docu-soap burst upon the scene, experiments were already afoot to develop forms of observational documentary that made extensive use of techniques borrowed from other forms of TV story telling. What accelerated the arrival of the docu-soap in the form we have come to know it, however, were those key changes in the broadcasting ecology which we have identified in Chapter 2. As we have seen, it was during the early 1990s that broadcasters operating in the public service domain became locked into an intensely competitive relationship with their commercial rivals. It was this increased competitiveness which brought about a climate which favoured the development of formats such as the docu-soap.

Nowhere were these changed priorities more apparent than in attitudes to scheduling and commissioning. In the 1980s, it was – as Jeremy Mills reminded me when I interviewed him – still common practice for in-house producers at the BBC to make a programme and then wait for a suitable slot to be found for it in the schedule. In the 1990s, however, as broadcasters began to experience the chill winds of a competitive market culture, programme making became a far more schedule-led operation.

Particular programming needs were identified to fulfil specific scheduling requirements and those in charge of scheduling began to wield ever greater influence in determining the types of programming that would be commissioned, especially for the prime-time slots when competition was at its most intense.

The needs of TV schedulers are part of the explanation why docusoaps came so rapidly to the fore in the mid–1990s. Their rapid proliferation resulted both from the general need for lighter, more digestible forms of factual entertainment and from a particular set of circumstances which affected the BBC's programming provision at the time. Until the mid–1990s, BBC schedulers had been able to rely on a combination of established formats to deliver the required ratings for the core period of the mid-evening schedule. The effects of increased competition, manifested in a dip in overall audience figures, had resulted in a need for new work to be commissioned which could, at no higher cost, win back viewers currently being lost to rival channels. It was at this point that programme planners at the BBC, recalling the success of the earlier factual series *The Vet* and *The Doctor*, commissioned an in-house team to produce one or more factual series which would combine techniques of observational documentary with those of popular dramatic fiction.

This call for a form of character-centred, factually-based entertainment resulted in the commissioning of two series which effectively set the gold standard for future docu-soap production. *Airport* (BBC 1, 1996) was a six-part series set in London's Heathrow airport, while *Driving School* (BBC 1, 1997) focused on the trials and tribulations of people preparing for their driving test. Both series deployed very similar techniques in the way that they approached their respective subjects and both depended for their success on producers' skill at identifying a number of personable, larger-than-life characters, most notably Jeremy Spake, the irrepressibly camp Aeroflot supervisor in *Airport* and Maureen Rees, the wonderfully warmhearted learner-driver-from-Hell in *Driving School*. Jeremy Mills who had a production involvement in both these series, has the following revealing observations to make about the function of characters in *Driving School*:

> The series was structured round characters who didn't have big stories to tell, but rather round big characters with small stories to tell … In the past we'd thought you really had to have a really big story to hold the attention of an

audience, but now we realized quite slight individual stories could be worked into an entertaining narrative mix. (Interview with the author, London, 1998)

Producers did, of course, have to show considerable resourcefulness in triggering the 'small stories' from their chosen characters. They were aware, for instance, that they would have to be far more interventionist in eliciting responses from subjects than would have been customary in more traditional forms of documentary. Recalling the approach he adopted in putting together material for *Airport* and *Driving School*, for instance, Jeremy Mills remarks:

It's not observational in the traditional sense ... it's more interfering and anticipatory ... you have to be able to predict the sort of response characters will have to a particular situation and you have to come up with appropriate trigger questions, – questions you will have to ask to get those wonderful one-liners that make it funny or explain the narrative. (Interview with the author, London, 1998)

Airport and *Driving School* both acquired seminal significance in the development of the docu-soap and their success led, almost immediately, to the commissioning of other factual series which married a soap-like mode of presentation with subjects known to be especially dear to the hearts of the consuming TV audience. *Children's Hospital* (BBC 1, 1996–), for instance, focuses on sick children in hospital and on the medical staff who tend to their needs. The programme has proved to have considerable longevity and might be regarded as having slightly more serious aspirations than some of the 'softer' varieties of docu-soap. As the producer of the 1998 series observes:

We are making serious and considered documentary films. That we have been able to tackle some rare and difficult cases in the current series is an indication of of the trust and understanding we have built up with the hospital authorities. (Household, 1998: 28)

Children's Hospital has traditionally occupied a prime-time slot in the evening schedule and in order to maintain its popular appeal has made extensive use of storytelling techniques familiar from the world of fictional medical soaps. Likewise the deployment of segmented narrative (interweaving storylines) ensures that the required balance is maintained between scenes which touch on darker themes and brighter ones in which courage triumphs over adversity.

Another cluster of programmes which could be classified as docu-soap in style and approach are those which have sought to capitalize on the obsessive British interest in pets, their ailments and those who care for their welfare. *Animal Hospital* (BBC 1, 1995–) with the avuncular Rolf Harris cast in the role of resident Master of Ceremonies is one long-running series whose ratings success has paralleled that of *Children's Hospital* and which deploys the same storytelling techniques. Likewise *Vets School* (BBC 1, 1996) which chronicled the final stages of vets' training and *Vets in Practice* (BBC 1, 1997–2002) have proved that relatively lightweight forms of character-centred factual entertainment focusing on animal welfare topics can be among the most bankable categories of TV programming.

Of all these vets-and-pets shows it is perhaps *Vets in Practice* which is the most docu-soap in its orientation. Just as with all successful docu-soaps, *Vets in Practice* attempts to achieve a satisfactory content blend by combining scenes which depict the young vets' professional interactions with animals and their owners with other sequences which focus on their much less confident forays into the world of human emotions and interpersonal relationships. Thus, while we may occasionally be alerted to more serious issues relating to animal welfare and veterinary practice, any 'messages' which these programmes may contain will always be of subsidiary importance to the texts' primary task: to deliver a piece of lightweight factually-based entertainment which makes few demands on its audience. It is in this respect instructive to consider the extent to which *Vets in Practice* uses narrational techniques borrowed from fictional drama. It is certainly no coincidence that for some commentators*Vets in Practice* contains distinct echoes of television dramas such as *All Creatures Great & Small* (BBC 1, 1978–90) and the Australian soap *A Country Practice* (Channel 7, 1981–93) in which the human interest aspect, especially the relationships between media or veterinary practitioners and their patients/clients, is always to the fore (Kilborn, Hibberd & Boyle, 2001: 383).

In the final analysis, all programming in the docu-soap category is more character- than issue-oriented. In *Vets in Practice*, for instance, it is matters of human interest, particularly collegial and vet/pet-owner relationships, which remain the focal point of narrative interest. A good illustration of this is provided by the manner in which those responsible for advertising the programmes highlight particular features. Here, for instance, is the promotional sales pitch for an episode of *Vets in Practice* broadcast in

September 1997. (Note in particular the identification of three interweaving storylines!):

> Late summer brings a chance for Trude Mostue to take a well earned rest when she goes back to Norway to see her family. Meanwhile Emma Milne performs a cow caesarian while she waits to hear whether she has got her dream job, and in Devon her boyfriend, Joe Inglis, treats an injured fox. (Radio Times, 27 September–3 October, 1997: 106)

The meteoric rise of the docu-soap in the period 1996–2000 is matched only by the speed with which it descended to earth again. The reasons for this are not difficult to discern. They have partly to do with the fact that potential subjects for docu-soap treatment were rapidly depleted, as more and more producers tried to jump on the docu-soap bandwagon. The unexpected popularity of series such as *Airport, Driving School* and *Vets in Practice* had, as suggested, led to a veritable feeding frenzy amongst programme makers, as rival channels sought to come up with their own docu-soap offerings. It was not long, however, before a certain audience fatigue set in and commissioning editors began to look to other forms of factual entertainment to fulfil their scheduling needs. As far as the BBC was concerned, there was also a recognition – as the decade drew to a close – that though they had scored some notable ratings successes, they had also begun to rely too heavily on this particular format. In the period October 1996–October 1998, the BBC had clearly established itself as market-leader in docu-soap provision and during this time had screened no fewer than thirteen docu-soap series (as opposed to just four shown on other terrestrial channels (Bethell, 1999: 15). It was at this point that misgivings began to be voiced about the Corporation's over-reliance on popular factual formats. BBC executives expressed misgivings that there had been an over-commissiong of docu-soaps and fears were expressed that this might have negative implications for those more challenging forms of 'serious' documentary with which the BBC had been traditionally identified (Kilborn, in Hibberd et al., 2000: 115–16). Critics were also, with some justification, beginning to complain that the widespread cloning of material was resulting in a generic loss of vigour. The ITV series *Dover* (1997), for instance, was considered to be a pale, unsuccessful imitation of the BBC series *Airport*, while *Chalet Girls* (ITV, 1998) which focused on the activities of nubile young women working in the tourist industry was palpably an opportunistic reprise of *Holiday Reps* (BBC 1, 1997). Suffice to say that by the second half of the year 2000 docu-soaps were beginning to be a far less visible presence in the schedules of all UK broadcasters than they had been in the previous three years.

Docu-soaps: the basic ingredients

Unlike certain other reality formats (especially the reality game-shows) where producers have experimented with combining different sets of ingredients into a programme-specific mix, the docu-soap displays a relatively stable set of formal features. Asked once to list what he considered to be the ingredients of a good docu-soap, producer Andrew Bethell came up with the following:

> Take any aspect of British life – it could be shopping, parking, travelling, eating, pet-care or clubbing. Find a contained location where a manageable cast of characters will engage in these activities or, more importantly, interact with the Great British Public. Keep an eye out for the one or two characters who will become your 'stars' ... It's not essential, but in the first few episodes you will need at least one shouting match and the commentary, 'unfortunately all did not go well for Tracey ...' That's about it. (Bethell, 1999: 14)

Expressed in these lapidary terms, as a set of instructions for would-be docu-soap producers, Bethell's list of ingredients does indeed identify the main structuring features of this (sub-)genre, though it possibly underplays the amount of manipulative processing work that is required once these 'raw materials' have been gathered. Thus, while the docu-soap audience has come to expect that characters will be filmed in their day-to-day working environments, the actual docu-soap setting is always subsidiary to the primary business of docu-soap, which is to produce a diverting entertainment package in which dialogue and character interaction are always privileged over any attempt to reveal more about the workings of the respective institutions.

A sense of place

The starting point, however, for each docu-soap is the 'contained location' to which Bethell refers. It provides the stage where a group of individuals ('people like you and me') can be assembled and filmed interacting with each other, with clients or members of the public and perhaps most important of all, with the programme maker, one of whose roles is to act as confidant to the lead characters. A wide range of locations and workplaces have been targeted by producers of docu-soaps, though the principal selection criterion is whether it will provide a group of telegenic characters.[2] In this respect, locations in docu-soaps fulfil much the same function as they do in fictional soap. In both instances they provide a starting point or backdrop for a series of character-centred sequences which are skilfully woven into a piece of lightweight entertainment. Also, just as with soap opera, producers of docu-soaps make the reasonable assumption that viewers will derive a measure of satisfaction and reassurance from being invited to return to a location with which they have become increasingly familiar. This sense of familiarity is one of the keys to docu-soaps' appeal. Audiences are encouraged, by a variety of means, to share the perspective of the characters to whom they are introduced. This is achieved principally by concentrating narrative attention on a select number of characters to whom viewers relate in much the same way as if they were characters in a soap. Those chosen to play the starring roles in docu-soaps are well aware of what is required of them in this respect and some have become extremely adept at delivering the requisite performance, whether this takes the form of producing witty one-liners or by commenting ironically on the challenges they face in their respective workplaces (with special reference to the friction that can arise when work colleagues do not see eye to eye with each other or when they feel that unreasonable demands are being made on them by their superiors).

The emphasis, however, is always on the idiosyncratic responses of individual characters. Once we have been conducted into the spaces which they regularly inhabit, we remain, as it were, confined within those spaces, in much the same way as we are positioned by soap-opera narratives (see pp. 109–17). It is, arguably, this combination of voyeuristic intrusion into an increasingly familiar world and the warm conviviality which the characters within that world exude which lies at the heart of docu-soaps' appeal. This sense which audiences gain of being privy to confessional moments when characters open up and reveal aspects of themselves which they might otherwise have chosen to keep hidden is, likewise, the quality of docu-soaps which aligns them with the talk-show genre. As John Corner has perceptively observed:

> There is a sense in which many docu-soaps, with their careful cast of 'lead players' and their rich opportunities for spoken interaction within the

routine spaces of a particular (usually occupational) life world, are a form of location talk-show. (Corner, 2000: 687)

The entertainment imperative

It is important to underline this generic affinity with soap opera and talk-show, since it is clearly one of the reasons why docu-soaps have proved so popular with TV audiences. Docu-soaps are not issue-oriented in the way that traditional documentaries are. They manifestly do not have an investigative agenda, but are, rather, obsessively concerned with larger-than-life characters, with lively conversational exchanges and with occasional dramatic outbursts which are, however, almost always swiftly and amicably resolved. All docu-soaps have ultimately the same objective: to produce a mildly diverting entertainment more likely to provoke an amused chuckle than to produce new insights into the world and its workings. Thus, despite focussing on the experience of individuals in their working environments, docu-soaps studiously avoid addressing serious employment issues such as gender bias, work stress, abuses of power, unfair dismissal or terms and conditions of service. The main objective of any docu-soap is not to uncover institutional or organizational shortcomings, but to come up with a series of relatively innocuous stories based on the workaday experiences of ordinary people. This is not to deny that docu-soaps will occasionally provide some illuminating insights into workplace practices. It could be argued, for instance that series like *The Cruise, Holiday Reps* and *Hotel* did give audiences some sense of the social hierarchies and command structures of organizations or may have revealed some of the harsher realities beneath the superficial glamour of jobs where service workers cater for the needs of the leisure and pleasure seeking multitude. The insights thus provided tend, however, to be incidental and are not part of of a sustained argument or critique. The abiding concern of docu-soaps is to focus on the personalities that light up the workplace rather than issues which render life problematical. It should therefore come as no surprise to learn that a number of individuals who acquired leading roles as characters in docu-soaps have gone on to make successful television careers, especially in programme areas such as the talk-show and the game-show where personality projection is the main requirement.

The highest priority of docu-soap remains that of producing a mildly diverting entertainment in keeping with the requirements imposed by the mid-evening schedule where, more often than not, they have been located. Very occasionally docu-soaps have, however, set out to tackle issues of more serious import.[3] *Life of Grime* (BBC 1, 1999) for instance, addresses the issue of environmental health, by highlighting the endeavours of Haringey Council officials to maintain environmental health standards in the face of indifference or even active resistance on the part of some residents. The series quickly became fixated, however, on the battle between council officials and the lead character, an elderly Polish war veteran who had insisted on filling his house and garden with mountains of rubbish. Another attempt to use the docu-soap format to tackle an issue of considerable social (and political) importance was provided by Chris Terrill's generally well received series *Jailbirds* (BBC 1, 1999). This series focused on the lives of inmates in a women's prison. Though it employs the standard structuring and narrative devices of docu-soap (interweaving storylines and the playing-up of character at the expense of argument and debate), it did bring some poignant insights into the reality of 'life behind bars'.

The various attempts to employ the docu-soap format as a consciousness-raising device are, however, the exception rather than the rule. The norm for docu-soap presentations has remained that of the character-driven entertainment vehicle where viewers are encouraged to establish the same sort of empathic relationship with the lead characters as they would with characters in their favourite soaps. Thus, while viewers may be encouraged to believe they are being given privileged, 'behind-the-scenes' access to people's working environments, the primary concern of docu-soap producers is akin to that of tabloid journalists, namely to home in on the human interest angle of the stories they are covering. By the same token, the audience has come to expect that docu-soaps will be able to satisfy, at least in part, that intense curiosity we have in the more intimate aspects of other peoples' lives (a curiosity which lies at the heart of soap opera's appeal). Small wonder then that the experience of watching docu-soaps should so closely resemble that of viewing soap opera. Both share that sense of eavesdropping on often intimate exchanges, of becoming involved in the developing relationships between characters and of being party to those confessional moments when individuals entrust to their unseen audience their private anxieties or undeclared aspirations (see also Dovey, 2000: 23–4). Just as audiences form strong bonds of attachment to the leading characters in their favourite soaps, so too in docu-soaps it is the audience's growing sense of identification with characters which constitutes one of this sub-genre's principal appeals. This familiarity is not just confined to the characters; it also extends, as in soaps, to the locations which provide the setting for action and dialogue. These locations are, by and large, ones of which the majority of viewers will have direct personal experience (hotels, holiday resorts, airports to name but a few). Hence, producers of docusoaps do not have to indulge in elaborate scene-setting exercises, since the broad contours of the respective environments will be familiar enough to viewers. A few establishing remarks via the voice-over narration will generally be enough to orient the viewer to particular features of the location in question. Thereafter the return to that domain will be signalled by one of the same cueing devices as employed by continuity announcers when introducing the next episode of a soap: 'It's time to see what's been happening in the last few days to the inhabitants of Paddington Green'.[4]

A light, non-threatening mode

Given their entertainment priorities, docu-soaps are, above all, characterized by a lightness of tone. From the outset they make it clear to viewers that – unlike more traditional forms of documentary – they are not going to make heavy demands by getting us to follow an argument about the socio-historical world (Nichols, 1991: 3–31); they are rather inviting us to share the views and experiences of a number of engaging or quirky individuals with amusing anecdotes to tell or sometimes with scarcely credible life histories. For a genre that is so dependent on extracting performances from the lead characters, it is important that producers make abundantly clear to their volunteer participants that their contributions will form part of an entertainment-based show and will not be incorporated into a programme which has a more serious, 'documentary' agenda. Interviews conducted with participants in docu-soaps have indicated that, by and large, they recognize that what is expected of them is an ability to indulge in lively, entertaining and frequently inconsequential banter. By the same token they know that it is highly unlikely they will be pushed into discoursing critically on the structure of the organization to which they belong.

It is for this reason that docu-soaps do not carry the same potential threat for the organizations who 'let the cameras in' as would be the case with documentaries with a more investigative agenda. This has meant that organizations who agree to become involved in docu-soap projects have had relatively little to fear from this particular form of media exposure, since it is manifestly not going to entail a rigorous examination or searching inquiry. Thus, whereas in the past companies have often fought shy of giving access to documentarists, now publicity-seeking institutions will often beat a path to the programme maker's door. And while docu-soap programme makers do not in so many words guarantee participating companies that this form of television exposure will give them substantial free publicity, the fact that docu-soaps are so clearly located at the 'softer' end of the documentary spectrum has led most of the companies to throw themselves with some eagerness into the docu-soap enterprise. Producer Andrew Bethell has the following revealing comments to make about how he persuaded the owners of the Blackpool Pleasure Beach to let him make a docu-soap about Britain's most popular tourist attraction:

> When we began serious negotiations with the Pleasure Beach, we used the formula: 'It's a trade off. We can promise you a substantial prime-time audience. Seventy-five per cent of what they will see will be good news for all of us, 20 percent will be a bit uncomfortable for you and 5 per cent could cause you trouble'. (Bethell, 1998: 5)

A trade off that affords a risk factor of only 5 per cent is of considerable appeal to any publicity-seeking organization and other companies have not been slow to volunteer themselves for docu-soap treatment. *Airline* (ITV 1998–), for instance, a docu-soap which is centred on the activities of low-cost UK-based airlines, provides a good illustration of how companies have been able to capitalize on television's hunger for character-centred entertainment with a nominal documentary flavour. In the case of EasyJet, the subject of the 1999 series, the company's decision to allow the LWT production team 'almost total access to EasyJet staff' may have seemed a rather risky exercise in view of all the many problems that an airline faces in its day-to-day operations. The risks involved in allowing incidents to be filmed where passengers complained about flight delays or about some malfunction in the airline's operation had to be set against the quite extensive free publicity to be achieved. For EasyJet Managing Director Ray Webster therefore the decision to 'allow the cameras in' was part of a hard-headed business calculation:

> The business rationale is simple: we don't sell through travel agents, so all our customers have to come to us – 70 per cent to our web site and the rest to our call centre. Therefore we have to find as many ways as possible of

keeping the EasyJet brand name in front of the consumer. We spend millions of pounds on press and poster advertising each year but nothing on television, so the *Airline* series provides us with a useful way of getting ourselves onto the screens. (Webster, 2000, 5)

The fact that directors of companies and heads of public relations departments can view their involvement in docu-soaps in this way tells us a good deal about the characteristic blandness of the format. The organizations who agree to participate have few fears about damaging revelations. On the contrary, the majority of organizations approached expressed delight in being selected as a candidate for docu-soap treatment. The lack of apprehension means that most participants throw themselves with some eagerness into the docu-soap enterprise, safe in the knowledge that what is being sought from them is principally a performance.

Producing a performance

The mention of performance leads us to what is possibly the key ingredient of docu-soaps, namely the expectation on the part of the production team (and by extension the viewers) that docu-soap characters will deliver some kind of performance. An important distinction can in fact be drawn between the way in which subjects in traditional documentaries (with occasional prompting from the film maker) have their words and gestures recorded *by* the camera and microphone and the manner in which docu-soap characters are, in a very real sense, required to produce a performance *for* the camera.[5] This does not necessarily mean that characters in docu-soaps are encouraged to 'ham things up' for the camera; it does mean, however, that they develop a good 'nose' for the type of material in which producers are likely to be interested. Above all docu-soaps place high value on those apparently spontaneous utterances where participants, with a little gentle coaxing from their interview partner, will deliver judgements on their colleagues, will recount amusing incidents that have occurred in the course of their work or will simply start musing about life in general. Each docu-soap works hard to contrive situations where characters can unburden themselves in this way. Thus in the series *Holiday Reps* (BBC 1, 1997–98) a sequence in which a rep is seen patiently interacting with disgruntled or outraged holidaymakers is frequently followed by a scene in which the same rep, this time in more private, confessional mode, is heard voicing her frustrations about the impossible demands of the job. This constant oscillation between public and private worlds, between the filming of events carried out in the line of duty and the more subjectively tinged confessional moments has become part of the standard currency of docu-soap.[6]

So central is the need for the engaging and entertaining personality in docu-soaps that those who are selected to participate acquire, in effect, a license to perform. Mindful that their contributions are going to form part of an undemanding light entertainment package, characters are usually happy to participate in what is for them as much a playful as a serious exercise. It is certainly no coincidence in this respect that many of the leading characters 'discovered' by docu-soap producers have either already been professionally associated with the leisure or entertainment industry or belong to that increasingly large category of individuals who crave the celebrity status which nowadays only television seems able to bestow. The idea that those who participate in docu-soap projects have in effect become actors in a staged performance has resulted in criticism being levelled at producers on the following two counts: first, that in order to guarantee the delivery of a performance, producers of docu-soaps seem to be only really interested in homing in on the more extrovert types of character who are prepared to act up for the camera and secondly that docu-soap production will always involve some measure of collusion or complicity between programme makers and their subjects (Cathode, 1998: 35). Both these accusations are made, however, without taking sufficiently into account the interpretive processes and filtering activities which a contemporary audience brings to bear when decoding these texts. Viewers certainly have enough media savviness to recognize that at least some of the scenes will have been set up for their benefit and that the 'reality' they are being invited to contemplate has effectively been generated by the intervention of a group of programme makers. It is certainly not too fanciful to suggest that audiences, when they tune in to docu-soaps apply what one might call the 'Actuality Plus' frame of reference, in acknowledgment of the fact that producers will have dramatically and creatively enhanced the reality being projected. This would certainly be the case with *The Matchmaker* (BBC 1, 1999), a series about one of the UK's most exclusive dating agencies. Here the idea of staging is carried to new heights, as characters are seen lovingly shaping and polishing the 'performance' which will result in them landing their dream partner. Each episode of *The Matchmaker* exudes a performative excess, in which the audience is intended to delight.[7] In the case of *The*

Matchmaker the sense that we are witnessing specially orchestrated events is reinforced by the witty, self-deprecating commentary provided by Alun Jenkins, the eponymous matchmaker who delights in posturing as a super-hero, a self-proclaimed expert on love, while providing little evidence that he is able to come anywhere near these high ambitions. Once again, as with no small number of docu-soaps, one is confronted with a programme which – principally through its narrative style and mode of address – speaks to its audience in a very knowing manner. In the case of *The Matchmaker* this knowingness is also reinforced by the slightly over-the-top, theatrical style which colours the whole production and is wholly appropriate to the stories being told and the events depicted.

A special kind of relationship?

If docu-soap characters are expected to produce a performance, one also needs to be clear about what kind of performance this is. Performance often suggests the learning or rehearsing of a certain role and then acting out this role before a live audience or having it recorded on tape or film. Docu-soaps, on the other hand, demand a different type of performance in that what they require of their volunteer performers is an ability to indulge in apparently spontaneous performance activity at the prompting of a (usually) unseen third party. It is, of course, the case that over the years virtually all categories of documentary have relied on the co-operation of one or more subjects as a team of incoming documentarists seeks to chronicle events occurring in the lives of individuals or in the organizations and institutions to which they belong. The relationship established between the incoming group of film making outsiders and the insider hosts has been the subject of endless conjecture and speculation in writing on documentary (Nichols, 1991: 76–103), but it is clearly of crucial significance to most documentary ventures. There would, however, appear to be an important qualitative distinction between the producer–subject relationship in docu-soap and that encountered in more traditional forms of documentary. With docu-soap no real attempt is made by the programme makers to conceal the fact that they are actively intervening in the lives of those who have agreed to participate. One of the consequences of this is that there is frequently complicity or collusion between programme makers and their apparently all too willing subjects. More than even in those forms of interactive documentary where the presence of the film maker is also openly acknowledged, the relationship between film/programme maker and one or more of the lead characters attains major narrative significance.

The upshot of this is that, rather than downplay their part in the shaping of events, docu-soap programme makers will, on the contrary, often highlight the increasingly close relationship they are forging with their subjects. As already signalled in Chapter 1, recent advances in camera and microphone technology have assisted in the development of such relationships, as the availability of miniaturized, unobtrusive recording devices has made it possible for a single lone operator to do all, or most of the recording work. Docu-soap producer Chris Terrill is one such operator and the success of much of his work (*The Cruise* (BBC 1, 1998), *Soho Stories* (BBC 2, 1996) and *Jailbirds* (BBC 1, 1999)) is attributable to the way in which he has been able to set up an easy, non-threatening relationship with his subject and to make that relationship part of the developing narrative. At no point, however, is there any attempt to disguise the fact that this is an act of intervention on Terrill's part and that he, just like them, has a distinct role to play. One could even go so far as to say that the presence of the camera, the difficulties Terrill sometimes has to keep filming while conversing and interacting with his subjects and his constant attempts to manoeuvre himself into positions where revealing footage can be obtained (especially in *The Cruise and Soho Stories*) all become important and integral parts of the final text. As will be demonstrated in Chapters 5 and 6, it might even be claimed that, by making transparent some of the processes by which 'real-life' material is recorded and by acknowledging their interventionist and constructivist role, producers of docu-soap may well have encouraged debate about the amount of reality 'framing and staging' that occurs in all forms of documentary work.

Soap by another name?

If both programme makers and audiences have come to expect a high level of performance ability on the part of docu-soap subjects, we should never forget that the whole process of docu-soap production is geared towards another type of performance, namely that represented by the multi-episode TV programme in its final edited form. Docu-soaps, like any other form of programming, are carefully assembled according to a number of structuring principles which guide the programme maker at each stage of the production process. These principles are ones which resemble those which underpin soap opera narratives. Indeed the more closely one analyses docu-soap texts, the greater number of affinities there appear to be between them and their wholly fictional counterparts.

Thus, while the programme makers themselves may always seek to underline that docu-soaps are grounded in real-life experience, from another perspective they could be said to be constantly tilting in the direction of soap opera. Many of the structuring devices used in docu-soap are directly borrowed from soap opera, with the result that, when audiences tune into docu-soaps, they may well be applying soap opera terms of reference in their response. The fact that docu-soaps have by and large colonized the same spaces in the evening schedule as the wholly fictional soaps may also encourage audiences to read docu-soaps in this way.

Docu-soaps reveal their close kinship with soap opera in the following ways:

- they are frequently focused on a single location with which, as the action unfolds, viewers become increasingly familiar
- they introduce us to a central core of characters with whom viewers are able to establish the same kind of relationship as they would with their favourite soap characters
- they are screened in serial fashion, with material typically being packaged in half-hour episodes, and having the same kind of cliff-hanger and leave-taking devices as are employed in fictional soap
- they make use of a segmented mode of narrative presentation, with three or more storylines being interwoven within each episode.

This particular structuring device not only enables pace and variety to be injected into the narrative, but also arguably fosters the illusion that this is another form of soap.

A sense of place

One of the pleasures of soap opera viewing, it is generally agreed, is that of being enabled to pay a regular visit to a location that has acquired 'favoured location' status in the memory or imagination of the viewer (Geraghty, 1991: 13–14). Docu-soaps likewise work hard to persuade viewers that they are being conveyed to a place with which, as the series progresses, they will become increasingly familiar. Just as in any fictional soap, the combination of continuity announcements ('It's time for our regular visit to …'), snappy credits sequences and catchy signature tunes cue the viewer for entry into a world which may offer a considerable measure of reassurance (especially when the real world may appear increasingly incoherent and fragmented). These traditional scene-setting devices are usually comple-mented by a series of conventional establishing shots of the location we are about to enter. Thus in the case of *Hotel* we are treated to shots of the Adelphi hotel facade, while in *The Cruise* there are appetite whetting, night-time shots of the illuminated cruise ship. Such shots will be repeated inter-mittently throughout each episode as a reminder of where the action is being played out.

Viewers quickly become accustomed to the narrative conventions which docu-soaps employ, including the devices used to switch between storylines which will often also entail a locational move. Unlike fictional soap where the switch to a new location can sometimes be surreptitiously indicated within the overall narrative flow, the move between locations in docu-soap will almost always have to be marked in some more explicit way. More often than not, this is achieved via the voice-over narration, with viewer orientation being provided by phrases such as "Meanwhile back in the hotel reception area, A is arguing with B about ..."

Generally speaking, locations in docu-soap have a similar dramatic function to those in soap opera in that in both cases they provide a stage or platform for various types of character interplay and dialogue. In tradi-tional documentary the camera's contemplation of a building or landscape can – especially when underscored by some form of musical accompani-ment or voice-over commentary – acquire special narrative significance. Docu-soaps are, on the other hand, driven by a different set of impera-tives, and locations seldom have anything like the same significance. Docu-soaps are, in short, so character-dominated that locations will tend to acquire the largely backdrop status they have in soap opera.

A central core of characters
Just as soap opera relies on a central core of characters whose scripted performances maintain narrative momentum and thus ensure continuing viewer involvement, so docu-soaps depend on a cast of characters who – with appropriate guidance and prompting from programme makers – can have a similar impact on audiences as their fictional counterparts. Selec-tion of suitable characters is, for these reasons, a crucial part of any docu-soap production. One of the essential programme making skills is the ability

to assemble a group of characters who will not be fazed by the presence of the camera, but will be able – in interaction with other characters – to provide the lively, engaging performances on which docu-soaps so depend.

The characters who are singled out for starring roles in docu-soaps also have to exhibit another important quality. They have to be adept at sharing thoughts and feelings with the audience. Here again there is a close parallel with what happens in fictional soaps, where viewers are also given the impression that they are eavesdropping on intimate exchanges between characters, many of whom they already consider to be their bosom friends. In docu-soaps the scenes which, by the same token, acquire key significance are the ones in which one of the lead characters entrusts some hitherto unrevealed information to the sympathetic ear of the programme maker (and thus by extension to the viewer). In other words, that characteristic soap opera obsession with gossip is matched in docu-soaps by scenes where characters shift into confessional or revelatory mode and come out with those less than flattering comments on their colleagues and work mates. The particular frisson in the case of docu-soap 'confessionals' is that, when characters open up in this way, viewers can be pleasurably stirred by the thought that the person may have gone too far in giving public expression to what they themselves would have been inclined to have kept under wraps (Bethell, 1999: 15; Glynn, 2000: 217–21).

Producers of docu-soap also marshall and manoeuvre their chosen characters in the same way that storyline developers in soaps manipulate their dramatis personae. At an early stage in the production process a decision is made, for instance, as to the optimum number of characters needed for the multiple storylines that will make up the docu-soap narrative. Likewise, docu-soap producers are mindful of the need to have a mix of characters, in order to ensure that sufficient narrative interest can be generated. The strong and occasionally outrageous characters will require foils or confidants on whom they can offload. In *Pleasure Beach*, for instance, the ebullient manager Jim Rowland is paired with his comparatively taciturn lieutenant Keith Allen. A series of dramatic effects is achieved by playing off one against another. By the same token situations have to be found, or (dare one say) contrived, to encourage some form of dramatic exchange. In *Hotel*, for instance, there are several occasions when the outwardly belligerent manageress Eileen Downie confronts members of staff who have failed to carry out their appointed duties to her satisfaction. The capturing of these adversarial moments provides an important narrative component of docu-soaps and producers will always be on the look-out for characters who can be relied on to generate conflict and aggravation. As one producer commented:

> Most of the successful series have featured characters who put pressure on others … it is essential that these characters are 'larger than life': they must engage the audiences almost immediately by being 'in your face' and giving the impression that they do not care what people think of them … (Bethell, 1999: 14–15)

It should not go unremarked in this connection that participants in docu-soaps quickly latch on to what producers are looking for. Those who are given starring roles also swiftly recognize that, as the docu-soap finds a large appreciative audience, so too they acquire high commodity value by virtue of the key roles they play. This again emphasizes the kinship between star performers in soaps and docu-soaps. One might even, with some justification, claim that docu-soap stars had even more power than soap actors. A single character in a fictional soap is almost always expendable, whereas a docu-soap deprived of one or more of its leading characters (say Maureen Rees in *Driving School* or Jeremy Spake in *Airport*) is virtually unthinkable.[8]

Once the main characters have been introduced in the first couple of episodes of a docu-soap, careful thought will be given as to how their roles might be developed. Decisions are made about the amount of exposure they will be given and the narrative function that each character will be expected to fulfil within a number of separate storylines. Here story boarding can hold potentially the same importance it might have in the planning and plotting of a fictional soap narrative. The 1999 series *Builders* (BBC 1) provides a good illustration of the organization and planning that goes into a multi-part docu-soap. The programme follows the work of various teams of builders as they ply their trade in a number of different locations. The series producer, John Fothergill, when I visited him in his office at a mid-way point in the production process, explained to me how the series had been developed, in particular how the various groups of builders had been selected. He drew my attention to a large white board which chronicled, in great detail, the storylines which were already in play and those which were still at the planning stage. The graphic display indicated how characters had been attached to specific storylines and how, in some of the episodes still to be transmitted, calculations were being made about what characters combinations in which storylines could reap the best narrative reward. Material for the later episodes would be shot in accordance with the perceived needs of developing storylines and greater prominence would be given to characters whose performative ability had already been highly rated by members of the viewing public.

Such brief glimpses into the storyline planning and character manipulation that typify the docu-soap production process once again underline the genre's strong family likeness to soap opera. Both categories of programming are concerned with tracking the movements, and tuning in to the utterances of characters in contained environments. Both are ultimately pre-occupied with the entertaining tittle-tattle of uncomplicated flesh-and-blood characters.

Modes of presentation

All docu-soaps – to a greater or lesser degree – make use of structuring devices inherited from fictional serial drama. The division of the recorded material into a number of (usually) half-hour episodes is the most obvious reminder of docu-soaps' indebtedness to the soap opera format. This serialized mode of presentation is well suited to the relatively limited ambitions of the docu-soap. It also demonstrates (if further proof were needed) how this particular sub-genre has its origins as much in television as it does in documentary practice. Serial formats have always been favoured by broadcasters since they secure audience attention on a regular basis. Soap opera in this respect represents the classic example of a television genre specifically designed to encourage the greatest possible audience loyalty, with viewers integrating their consumption of soap into their domestic and family routines. The insertion of docu-soaps at regular points in the TV schedule (in some cases on two or more evenings a week) also reveals their kinship with soap opera. In both cases seriality is used to foster the illusion that events in the depicted world are moving forward at a pace not dissimilar to the one which viewers themselves inhabit (Kilborn, 1992: 92–4). It also conveys to viewers that comforting sense of being ensconced in a story world which, potentially at least, has no foreseeable ending.

The serial format also enables programme makers to present material and to manipulate characters so as to enhance narrative interest and to inculcate in viewers the desire to return to the scene of the unfolding drama, as characters reveal more of themselves or as new intrigues are unveiled. In addition to this, recurrent use is made in docu-soaps of structuring devices specifically developed by producers of broadcast serial and series drama. Pacy credits sequences are played out to the accompaniment of lively signature tunes (most notably in *The Cruise*, *Holiday Reps* and *The Matchmaker*), while end-of-episode trailers alert us to the viewing pleasures which future episodes will bring. Some of these credits sequences are presented in a highly mannered way and seem to be making rather ironic or parodic reference to those hustling credits sequences which set the tone for super-soaps such as *Dallas* and *Dynasty*. It is by such means that viewers of docu-soaps might well be encouraged to apply soap opera frames of reference when reading these texts. It is as if, when they tune in to the opening credits they are being given a signal that the events they are about to witness have been dramatically enhanced in order to maximize the show's entertainment potential.

As far as the structuring of the narrative is concerned, docu-soaps also regularly employ the standard tension building devices derived from fictional narratives. Sometimes the tension will be allowed to build within a single episode. One of the episodes of *Pleasure Beach*, for instance, centres on a self-contained bomb-alert storyline, where suspense develops around the staff's attempts to put various emergency procedures into action. The standard docu-soap convention, however, is one that allows individual storylines to build over several episodes. One such storyline is the one In *Driving School*, which centres on whether Maureen, the indefatigably incompetent learner driver, would ever succeed in passing her driving test. The other manner in which the narrative organization of docu-soaps clearly resembles that of soap is in their employment of the familiar cliffhanger and tease devices where the audience is kept on tenterhooks as to how a particular storyline will develop (Kilborn, 1992: 40–1). Unlike soap opera, however, which has tended to favour slightly more dramatic forms of leave-taking, docu-soaps, which are more character-centred than action-centred, will generally opt for less melodramatic forms of episode ending. The words of a leading character referring to coming events may often suffice, though more often than not it is left to the unseen narrator to bring the curtain down on the current proceedings and to provide brief appetite-whetting information on events covered in the next episode.

Interweaving storylines

The structuring device which arguably places the docu-soap most decidedly in the soap opera camp is that of storyline interweaving. Switching
the narrative focus between several different storylines in the course of an
episode is one of the special hallmarks of broadcast serial drama and is
responsible for some of soap opera's most characteristic effects. It assists,
for instance, in spreading narrative interest across a series of family or character groupings, thus creating the impression of a living, vibrant community. It also facilitates a switching of perspective between various settings
within the familiar location and is, as such, a device which controls the
flow of the narrative events. In particular it enables the scriptwriters to
inject pace and variety into a narrative account which, measured by other
types of dramatic fiction, is edging forward at a snail's pace. Interweaving
storylines are, in short, a way of ensuring that the audience's boredom
threshold is not taxed too severely.

Television audiences have become very familiar with the technique
of narrative segmentation and producers of docu-soap have been able to
capitalize on this familiarity. By interweaving three or more storylines within
individual episodes, producers ensure that they create the pace and variety
concomitant with this type of factual entertainment. Segmenting the
narrative in this way tends, if anything, to divert attention away from
individual storylines, since the viewer is always reckoning with the immi-
nent switch of narrative focus. This not only has the effect of introducing
the necessary variety, it also has the additional benefit of concealing the
slightness of some of these storylines. As docu-soap producers themselves concede, some storylines are so trite, insignificant and fragmented
that they would not stand up to sustained scrutiny. It is only when they
are stitched together into a larger patchwork that the narrative potential
of these stories can be realized. As producer Jeremy Mills astutely observes:

> We use the technique of parallel action and intercutting to make some-
> thing bigger than the sum of the individual parts ... It's a question of tell-
> ing narratives in a different way from traditional single strand documentaries
> when you're essentially using linear narrative ... Docu-soaps operate on
> different lines, however. When you're just about to see something happen,
> you cut away to something else, then you cut back to the original story. One
> story starts, another one starts; then eventually one gets resolved. Another
> one gets picked up, overlaps, brings in a new character and so on. There's a

strategy to the way they're constructed. You're essentially pulling people through the narrative. (Interview with the author, London, 1998)

The voice of documentary?

If docu-soaps have borrowed a considerable number of structuring techniques from soap opera, this is not to say that they have entirely forfeited their documentary claims. By virtue of the fact that they are filmed in specific locations and that the dialogue is unscripted and (largely) unrehearsed, docu-soaps are still able, for instance, to communicate a powerful sense of 'Being There'. Likewise, in spite of regular, but often rather transparent attempts to stage events and to encourage characters to perform, docu-soaps can still provide revealing glimpses of the reality behind various institutional facades.

The documentary leanings of the genre are perhaps best exemplified, however, by docu-soaps' use of voice-over narration. Unlike many other contemporary forms of documentary which have eschewed 'voice-of-God' narration, docu-soaps are heavily dependent on the device of the unseen, seemingly omniscient narrator. In traditional forms of documentary (especially in the mode generally referred to as 'expository' (Nichols, 1991: 34–8)), the commentary spoken by an on-screen or unseen narrator has been regarded as an integral part of the attempt to persuade the viewer that this is an authoritative, credible account of events. In so far as it usually seeks to communicate a single perspective on events, the commentary has an ideological significance in that it frequently presents an account which reflects a particular value system or set of beliefs. Viewers are thus guided or nudged into putting a particular interpretation on the account thus rendered (Kilborn & Izod, 1997: 58–60). In docu-soaps the voice-over commentary has a similar guiding function, but falls short of being expository in that little attempt is made to elucidate or explain. Docu-soap narration is not concerned to encourage viewers to draw wider inferences from a highlighted case, nor is it intended to stimulate a critical engagement with problems raised by a 'real world' investigation (Nichols, 1991: 126–33). It is, more often than not, simply a device for providing an explanatory context for the events occurring in the narrative (especially when audiences have to be cued for a rapid switch to a new location). Given the formal structure of docu-soaps, where viewers are being rapidly switched between different locations, some form of narrational guidance is important in order to avoid audience disorientation. In fictional narratives these locational transitions can normally be effected by resorting to some internal narrative device (often worked into a conversational exchange). In docu-soaps, by contrast, the switching between storylines has to be made that much more explicit, the act of transition usually being marked by phrases suggesting simultaneity or parallel action ('Meanwhile in the hotel foyer ...').

Recognizing the need to employ a narrator, but aware that narration can easily become ponderous or preacherly (criticism was often levelled against expository documentaries on these grounds), producers of docu-soap have made virtue of necessity by allowing the narrator to develop a distinctive persona in keeping with the generally lighthearted tone of these entertainment pieces. Though docu-soap narrators are hardly ever seen (the one exception to this is *The Matchmaker* where the lead character is also the narrator), their voices become closely identified with the programme in question. Very careful consideration is therefore given to choosing an appropriate voice for docu-soap narration. Most of those selected for the task are well known actors and actresses who have made a name for themselves in other forms of TV light entertainment, especially in sit coms and in soap opera. The use of a voice with which audiences will already be familiar draws attention to the particular functions of a docu-soap narrator. Not only are they there to play the anchoring role of providing directional links between on-screen events, they also – if not more importantly – establish the tone of the series by adopting an informal and conversational register. To this extent, narrator figures in docu-soaps acquire a significance almost equal to the lead characters. Through the familiar timbre of their voice and their generally knowing attitude, narrators become identified, in the audience's mind, with the authorial voice responsible for creating these soap-like pieces of entertainment. On these grounds alone – as well as their function as context and continuity providers – the narrator's significance in docu-soap should never be underrated.

Conclusion

After achieving such a high profile in the period 1996–99, docu-soaps became a much less visible presence in the widening body of TV factual programming. By the turn of the century new forms of the factual had arrived and some of these were proving very popular with audiences, especially the game-doc and survivor categories. Docu-soaps did continue to be produced, however, albeit in much smaller numbers than hitherto. Some docu-soaps, including the two airport-based series *Airport* (BBC) and *Airline* (ITV) have proved to be almost as long-lived as certain soaps. What has doubtless contributed to their longevity is that the airport location, with tens of thousands of travellers in transit to holiday or business destinations and thousands of workers catering for their various needs, is an ideal setting for witnessing those confrontations and exchanges which are the essential ingredients of docu-soap.

While it is the case that docu-soaps have not, as a species, become totally extinct, they have been largely displaced in the schedules by the new reality formats. The latter may contain certain vestigial docu-soap traces, but they mark a significant shift away from docu-soap scenarios and concerns. The new formats are, by and large, bolder and brasher and have a stronger voyeuristic element. They are also generally more action-centred and place much greater emphasis on developing strategies for audience involvement. Many of the new reality formats have been made with a view to capturing the attention of an international audience. This again distinguishes them from docu-soaps, for while some of the latter (e.g. *Driving School* and *Airport*) have achieved quite respectable overseas sales, they have generally not the same international penetration as their more illustrious successors. The reasons for this are not difficult to discern. Though docu-soaps can occasionally transport us to exotic locations (e.g. the Caribbean hotspots visited in *The Cruise*) and some can produce entertaining action sequences of universal appeal (e.g. the scrapes Maureen gets into in *Driving School*), they remain at heart character- and speech-focused entertainments. This makes them that much more culturally specific than the contemporary reality based game-docs which are made with half an eye to the global TV market and which lend themselves to being easily adapted to the perceived 'needs' of a culturally or nationally defined television audience.

In the final analysis, the significance of docu-soaps has to be measured in terms of the space they opened up for the creative merging of factual and fictional discourses. For all the journalistic scare-stories about them signalling the 'end of documentary as we know it', docu-soaps succeeded in reactivating interest in what could be achieved by hybridizing disparate elements from established formats. This crossfertilization of different strands has manifestly had an invigorating impact, and not just in the field of factual/documentary programming. Their influence is also discernible in various strands of light entertainment drama, especially those which focus on interpersonal relationships within a workplace environment. Like all other television formats, docu-soaps have shown themselves to be vulnerable to the vagaries of fashion. After a brief spell in the lime-light, during which time they were actively (some would say ruthlessly) exploited by commissioning editors, they have now quietly taken their place alongside the many other factual formats which compete for consumers' attention in an increasingly crowded television marketplace.

Notes

1   An additional performance requirement was that participants were expected, at regu-lar intervals, to unburden their feelings to an unmanned video camera located in the basement of the house. This confessional element was to become a staple feature of many of the later reality formats, including reality game shows.

2   On the basis of docu-soaps produced and aired in the period 1996–2000, one can make a broad distinction between a) programmes that highlight the place where the action will be staged (*Airport, Dover, Paddington Green, Pleasure Beach*) and b) programmes that, at least nominally, seem to place more emphasis on the activities of a named profession (*Estate Agents, Matchmaker, Holiday Reps, Vets in Practice*).

3   Even when serious issues are touched upon in docu-soaps, they always remain rela-tively underdeveloped and are never allowed to detract from docu-soaps' generally bright and breezy tone.

4   These cueing devices are also a way of reinforcing the 'reality claims' of the events in both a temporal and locational sense.

5   Producers themselves sometimes dispute the extent to which participants are re-quired to perform. As a member of the *Airline* production team observed: 'Contrary to popular belief, we are not looking for people who want to perform. We're looking for people who just showed a knack of being ordinary and talking about their job in a way that comes across well'. (Interview with the author, London, 1999)

6   The moment of confession has become a generic feature of many other popular factual formats, including the very successful *Big Brother* series, as discussed in Chap-ter 3. Here, as in other series belonging to the 'survivor' sub-genre, individual sub-jects are required – at regular intervals – to enter the equivalent of a confessional box.

7   It is no coincidence that Francesca Joseph, the director/producer of *The Matchmaker*, had had extensive theatrical experience before moving into TV programme produc-tion.

8   Just like soap actors, docu-soap performers also have to struggle with their new-found celebrity status. Trude Mostue, one of the stars of the highly rated series *Vets*

in Practice once admitted that her involvement in the programme had led to her whole life becoming public property. In an interview with authors of the research report *Consenting Adults?* (Hibberd et al., 2000) which examined the public's participation in various forms of TV programming, she suggested that it felt to her as if she had become 'a kind of Truman Show'.

5 Faking the real: sleight of hand in the factual domain

O, what a tangled web we weave,
When first we practise to deceive!

'Marmion', Sir Walter Scott

In the course of the 1990s, an increasing number of anxieties began to be expressed about the state of factual programming in the UK. Above all there were fears about the apparent dumbing down of programme quality. The upsurge of reality programming in all its many guises was taken to be symptomatic of this fall from grace, while the popularity of the anodyne, apolitical docu-soap was seen as providing further evidence of a lamentable qualitative decline. As if this were not enough cause for concern, a number of stories blew up in the last two or three years of the decade over the alleged faking of documentary material.[1] It was discovered that programme makers had been guilty of introducing unacknowledged reconstructions into their work or of deceptively manipulating the material in such a way as to break that all important bond of trust which exists between programme makers and members of the viewing public. As a consequence of these fakery scandals, it was feared that audiences would also lose faith in the ability of the regulatory authorities to maintain those standards of honesty and integrity among broadcasters that they were supposedly there to safeguard. A no less pressing concern – and one that was shared by broadcasters and by members of the viewing public – was that the proliferation of fakery incidents seemed to confirm the widely held belief that there had been a clear decline in ethical standards amongst programme makers and that this was due, in no small part, to their having to operate in a far more competitive broadcasting environment, without the benefit of those institutional support mechanisms on which they had once been able to rely (see Chapter 2, pp. 28–36).

To suggest, however, as some observers have done, that fakery is a widespread phenomenon which compromises the entire factual/

documentary programme making industry is a gross exaggeration. There have in fact been comparatively few incidents where audiences have been actively misled as to the status of material screened. It is for this reason the chapter heading introduces the idea of 'sleight of hand' since it draws attention away from the idea of fakery as an act of wilful deception and gives a more productive emphasis to the range of manipulative techniques deployed, more generally, in factual programme production. This is not to belittle or excuse the acts of deception that have occurred. It is simply to make the point that, in their reporting of the various fakery incidents, some observers have neither drawn sufficient attention to the particular set of conditions which proved propitious for fakery to occur, nor have they admitted that the borderline between what might be considered deceitful and what is legitimate practice is indeed remarkably thin (and that furthermore the distinctions are becoming ever more blurred).[2] As the experienced and respected documentary maker John Willis has observed:

> The line between fact and drama in documentary has grown increasingly blurred and in the struggle between journalistic truth and dramatic excitement, drama is winning. (Willis, 1998a: 6)

This chapter is therefore not so much concerned with chronicling the individual incidents of faking (though one section will be devoted to specific cases where programme makers are considered to have transgressed), but more with assessing what these incidents tell us about the state of factual/documentary TV programming, especially the forces which have driven broadcasting in the 1990s. This chapter will therefore be concerned to view what are essentially a series of localized spats in the context of sets of filming and editing practices developed by documentarists to shape their work in such a way that it does not simply reproduce the surface details of the historical world but leads to a more active and considered audience response. Throughout the chapter this emphasis will be that all forms of documentary involve, in John Grierson's much quoted phrase, a 'creative treatment of actuality' (Grierson, 1966: 13). Every documentary requires a careful selection and editing together of recorded material, most or all of it acquired with the specific intention of integrating it into a documentary account that will have its own set of formal narrative requirements. Documentary film and programme makers will always be conscious that, in a very real sense, they are framing the real. This idea of framing immediately introduces the idea of reality distortion since, depending on how a sequence is shot and how individual images are framed, a particular view of the reality thus captured is being relayed to the viewer. This is some way removed from the more active and transgressive forms of faking which will be considered shortly, but it is useful to bear in mind that the whole documentary film and programme making enterprise is concerned at one level with adjusting reality to the needs of programme makers. It is in the course of this adjustment process that certain discreet acts of cheating – or perhaps better, sleight of hand operations – will be needed to achieve the desired effect. It should therefore come as no surprise to learn that much of the debate surrounding fakery in documentary has centred on where one draws the line between the small and possibly insignificant acts of 'reality adjustment' (about which the audience would not be overly concerned) and the larger, and arguably more reprehensible acts of outright fraud, to which the audience might have more serious objection.

Remaking reality

One of the central ideas that has frequently been voiced in discussion on documentary is that one of the genre's special missions has been to encapsulate, record and reveal events occurring in the socio-historical world (Kilborn & Izod, 1997: 2–19). Documentary is, in Nichols' telling phrase, one of the 'discourses of sobriety' (Nichols, 1991: 3), helping to keep us attuned to issues and developments in the world about which we, as dutiful citizens, might wish to be kept informed. It follows from this that documentary should be sufficiently reliable with respect to the veracity of its accounts to allow them to be used as the basis for further serious reflection and debate. In so far as documentary and other forms of factual programming are supposedly primarily concerned with 'real world' events and issues, it should – so the argument goes – be possible to make a meaningful distinction between documentaries and works which are wholly fictional in their orientation. The latter will attempt, by a variety of creative means, to draw their readers or audiences into a world which has been imaginatively evoked by an authoring agent. There may be all manner of overlaps and interconnections between the world thus created and the socio-historical world, but there is an understanding that, in works of fiction, producers will have felt free to take considerable liberties with the historical events as they are known to have occurred (i.e. a degree of poetic or dramatic license will have been exercised in what is essentially a creative act). Documentary or non-fiction work, on the other hand, makes special claim on our attention by virtue of the fact that it is documenting, chronicling or otherwise engaging with the 'real world' in some shape or form, even though it may deploy a wide range of techniques, some borrowed from fiction, to achieve these goals. This is the contractual basis on which documentary operates. Any excessive deviation from this modus operandi (e.g. the inclusion of an invented scene which is not acknowledged as such) runs the risk of diminishing the work's claim to documentary status. It also – especially if such deviations are repeated in other works – can jeopardize the trusting attitude which audiences have generally displayed towards the work of documentarists.

For the analyst seeking to isolate features generally deemed to be characteristic of documentary discourse (in order to have a benchmark for establishing when works have forfeited their documentary claims), it is important to distinguish the particular narrative techniques being employed in fictional and nonfictional modes. To be more explicit: it is generally accepted that narrative has played an important role in many (some would say all) forms of documentary work. Fictional narratives produced for consumption by cinema and television audiences will frequently centre on a series of dramatic interactions between characters who speak lines or act out roles dreamed up for them by a creative scriptwriting team. Every word uttered and each gesture made by characters is carefully weighed in terms of its function in progressing the plot or the clues it provides to our understanding of personality. In narrative fiction there is, in other words, an overriding concern with the moulding and shaping of elements according to a preconceived blueprint. Likewise there will be a series of calculations concerning the supply of narrative information: when is the optimum moment for a piece of knowledge to be divulged and what information has to be withheld in order to build or intensify tension and suspense? Documentary, on the other hand, is driven by a different set of narrative priorities. In documentary, so it is claimed, the narrative may not attain the same prominence as it does in works of pure fiction. It will be employed principally as a facilitating device. It may be used to shape the account being rendered in such a way as to assist the audience's understanding of a complex argument or, alternatively, to show how certain solutions are found to resolve a particular problem (the so-called problem/solution narrative structure); or it may simply act as a powerful device for retaining audience interest, especially when other forms of dramatic excitement may beckon on alternative channels (Kilborn & Izod, 1997: 115–25). What distinguishes narrative in documentary from narrative in fictional work, therefore, is that the former should not become an end in itself. In this respect, producers of narrative fiction have a degree of freedom not possessed by documentarists. They are working to uncover a different kind of truth to the one which documentarists are seeking to access. It is as a consequence of this that creators of fiction are, as a matter of course, accorded that much vaunted poetic or dramatic license to invent, distort and manipulate their material in ways that would be considered illegitimate or beyond the pale if practised by their documentary colleagues in the interests of producing a suitably gripping story.[3]

In attempting to distinguish how narrative is employed in fictional and non-fictional work, one quickly becomes aware that, in the context of recent developments in film and TV programme making, such distinctions are increasingly difficult to sustain. So many of the operations of documentarists will involve having active recourse to strategies employed in works of fiction that it becomes a moot point as to whether it is critically productive to continue to insist on this dichotomy. Boundaries between fictional and non-fictional work become progressively blurred as producers in both 'camps' seek new ways of presenting their wares. An increasing body of TV dramatic fiction makes the claim to get close to the authentic, lived reality of contemporary life by cultivating the look and feel of documentary.[4]

One of the results of the generic blurring which has taken place over the last two or three decades is that some of the old certainties about the constituent features of particular genres have slowly evaporated. In the new order of film and television making, where hybridizing has become the norm rather than the exception, it becomes increasingly difficult to make clear generic divisions between categories which at one time may have seemed to be relatively self-contained. As Bill Nichols has perceptively observed:

> Many 'social problem' fiction films are made with as civic-minded and socially responsible a purpose as many documentaries. Thus documentary fails to identify any structure or purpose of its own entirely absent from fiction or narrative. The terms become a little like our everyday, but unrigorous, distinction between fruits and vegetables. (Nichols, 1991: 6)

Faking the real

The introductory section to this chapter raised a number of points which are important for a proper understanding of the sometimes stormy debates over fakery in contemporary documentary. This section will provide some general reflections on the practice of faking within the broader cultural and artistic sphere before examining a select number of fakery incidents.

Faking has, of course, a long and not entirely dishonourable history. It has been practised in diverse spheres of human activity, ranging from the world of business (counterfeit money), the cultural and artistic domain (forged art works) and also the sphere of interpersonal relations (the fake orgasm). As far as artefacts and objects are concerned, the practice of faking is connected with attempts to fulfil the desire of those who wish to own or have access to an original item which, in cultural or material terms, is deemed to be of high value – often on account of its unique qualities. Hence passing something off as original, when it has in fact been copied or cloned, attracts a particular kind of cultural opprobrium.

In contemporary usage the term 'fake' is almost always surrounded by an aura of negativity, but originally it was used to refer, much more neutrally, to the 'performance of an operation' (Websters New International Dictionary, second edition). It was only in the course of time that it has come to mean the practising of fraud or deception. Sometimes the fraud can be relatively trivial as in the donning of a fake moustache to attend a fancy-dress party. On other occasions the faking involves some act of dissembling in order, possibly, to gain material or emotional advantage (e.g. to fake sickness). It is in those cases where it can be shown that there has been an intention to practise deception that the perpetrators are rightly condemned (e.g. when counterfeited paintings or items of jewellery are counterfeited and sold at vastly inflated prices to an unsuspecting buyer.)

Where malicious intent can be proved, then the perpetrators' actions can become the subject of criminal proceedings. In many other instances, however, the circumstances surrounding acts of fakery and/or deception are far more obscure. Discovery of the 'fraud' may come a long time after the committing of the alleged fraudulent act and there is sometimes no unanimity as to whether a fraud has actually occurred. There has been no small number of cases, for instance, where scientists have made what have appeared to be major discoveries on the basis of convincing evidence, only for it to be later discovered that the evidence was specially concocted. One of the most spectacular instances of faking in the scientific field was the early twentieth-century Piltdown man scam, where the claim was made that a skull discovered in a chalk pit in Sussex provided irrefutable proof of the 'missing link' which would fill the evolutionary gap between ape and man. The Piltdown Man story and all the many other cases where evidence has been manufactured or falsely adduced to 'prove' a scientific theory may help us to understand the motivation of all those who, for a variety of reasons, including vainglory, commercial pressures or simply the expectation that they will be able to deliver the goods, find themselves having to fabricate evidence or massage the facts in the mistaken belief that this will enhance their professional standing or simply enable them to bring their project to a more timely conclusion.

While the production of fake evidence in order to prove a scientific thesis suggests some interesting parallels with fakery in documentary practice, examples of alleged fakery crop up with some frequency in many other fields of cultural, artistic and literary activity. Authors producing autobiographical accounts of their life experience or events they have witnessed are especially vulnerable to the charge that they have created a largely fictionalized version of events in order to project a more favourable image of themselves. They claim, in other words, to be producing an account that has documentary status, but evidence gathered from other sources suggests that many more liberties have been taken with the fashioning of material than may have been admitted. This can, in turn, lead to bitter controversy. There have been, for instance, many instances where a particular account has become the subject of often bitter controversy. The Guatemalan author Rigoberta Menchu's autobiographical book *I Rigoberta Menchu* for which she won the 1992 Nobel Peace prize, was later attacked on the grounds that it was a composite of experiences rather than an accurate 'documentary' version of events (see Ellison, 1998: 2). Likewise Binjamin Wilkominski's book *Fragments*, an alleged autobiographical account of childhood experiences in Nazi concentration camps and which later became the subject of a thought-provoking documentary *Child of the Death Camps: Truth and Lies* (BBC 1, 1999) was later revealed to be a fictionalized reworking of events, though none the less harrowing for being so (see Lawson, 1998: 17).

Documentary and the remaking of reality

All documentarists – and not just those who are producing dramatized reconstructions of past events – are vulnerable to the charge of 'reality distortion' in so far as they are, by definition, deploying a series of manipulative strategies in their attempts to represent the real. Audiences are also, for their part, well aware that when they engage with any documentary/factual account, they are putting considerable trust in the integrity of the programme maker and the institution which has commissioned the work. The readiness to maintain trust might thus be severely tested if it later emerges that all was not what it was being made out to be.

Following the recent spate of fakery incidents in the UK and elsewhere in Europe, it might at first sight appear that this bond of trust has been somewhat compromised. In June 1999, for instance, the ITV breakfast television company GMTVwas forced to suspend a producer when it was discovered that someone who had appeared on a programme about cosmetic surgery and who seemed to be just an ordinary member of the public was in fact an employee of the medical clinic administering the treatment. Earlier the same year there had been a similar furore at the BBC when it came to light that guests who had appeared on the daytime talk show *Vanessa* (which was in fact cancelled soon after the incident) had also been simulating designated roles. There have also been isolated cases of allegedly more thoroughgoing acts of fakery where whole programmes claiming documentary status had been shown, on closer investigation, to be mere simulations of the real (see pp. 108–9).

At one point in the late 1990s the proliferation of faking incidents and their extensive reporting in both the tabloid and the broadsheet press led to something approaching a moral panic.[5] The impression was given that the broadcasting industry was in a state of crisis, that the discovery of isolated incidents of fakery represented merely the tip of a very large iceberg and that there were many more scandals waiting to be revealed. The suggestion was made that, if broadcasters working in the *factual* domain were capable of pulling the wool over viewers' eyes in this way, could they ever again hope to be regarded as reliable, trustworthy reporters, let alone as 'honest seekers after truth'?

Expressions of moral outrage at the number of fakery incidents came primarily from print journalists. (There was, of course, no little irony in the fact that they should be seen to be sitting in judgement on their TV colleagues in this way when normally the boot was on the other foot!) That print journalists were themselves capable of stooping to forms of deception is illustrated by the following salutary tale. In June 1999 the *Sun* got one of its reporters to pose as a barmaid and to confess her purported addiction to sex to the producers of a documentary report to be included in the highly respected BBC 1 series *Everyman*. When the true identity of the barmaid came to light, the programme was withdrawn from the schedule, suggesting that the Corporation accepted some responsibility for not being stringent enough in checking the credentials of a key witness. It later transpired, however, that the reporter had signed an 'honesty clause' in the appearance contract she had concluded with the programme makers. The signing of the honesty clause, introduced to prevent programme makers from being hoodwinked by false guests or undercover journalists, enabled the BBC in this instance to take legal action against the *Sun* on the grounds that their reporter had embarked on a 'calculated and lengthy deception [which went] beyond reasonable limits' (cited in Gibson, 1999: 1).

With the benefit of hindsight, it is possible to view these individual fakery incidents and the stir they caused in a slightly broader perspective than many observers at the time were prepared to. The inclination on the part of many was to explain the deluge of fakery in terms of a vaguely defined 'drop in standards' or attribute it to the journalistic laziness of programme makers. More thoughtful observers, however, drew attention to what they saw as the root causes of the malaise. Three principal reasons, all of them related to working conditions in the current broadcasting environment, were put forward:

1   There has been mounting pressure on programme makers to deliver work against ever tighter deadlines and to operate with smaller budgets. Sometimes, in order to gain a commission, programme makers have found themselves making promises about completion dates or about the inclusion of 'authentic material' which have proved impossible to realize without the taking of a few liberties (Winston, 1999: 8).

2   The changes in the broadcasting environment over the last few years, especially the growing fragmentation within the television industry, have meant that there are now far fewer checks and balances built into the programme making process. As one industry observer has

commented: 'One of the difficulties is that television is now a very fragmented business. Researchers move from company to company in search of work. Career development is random, training erratic and budget pressures means that usually researchers have left a production before the crucial editing stage begins' (Willis, 1998a: 6).

3   The move, in the majority of European countries, to introduce lighter-touch regimes to regulate broadcasting has meant that programme makers may not feel under the same pressure as they once did to adhere strictly to the codes of practice governing their operations. This is in spite of the fact that the penalties for the more flagrant acts of deception can actually be quite severe in that the failure to comply with the broadcasting codes of practice can have serious consequences for the offenders.[6]

A 'cause célèbre'

Whatever the root causes of the purported faking malaise in the late 1990s, the fact remains that makers of factual/documentary programming became subject to ever closer scrutiny (some felt they were victims of a witch-hunt) as journalists sought to discover more examples of illegitimate practices relating to the faking of programme material. The proliferation of fakery incidents had already given rise to the belief that 'where's there's smoke there's fire' and for a time there was a distinct air of nervousness amongst broadcasters lest some new scandal should be unearthed. What no one could have anticipated, however, was a scandal of the proportions surrounding *The Connection*. This programme was an hour-long, award-winning documentary produced by Carlton Television and originally shown in 1996 in ITV's *Network First* series (at that time the one ITV slot reserved for serious documentary work). *The Connection* made the claim to be a serious investigation into the smuggling of heroin from Colombia into the UK, but subsequent investigations revealed it to have been largely faked.

The programme bore all the outward marks of a well researched documentary. The programme makers seemed to have been able to gain 'unprecedented access' to key members of the Colombian drugs cartel masterminding the operation and also to have obtained dramatic footage chronicling the various stages in the drugs' journey from Colombia to London. *The Connection* had been watched by 3.7 million viewers when it was first broadcast in 1996, many of them attracted by the pre-transmission trails which promised startling revelations about illicit drug-running activities. The programme subsequently went on to garner no fewer than eight international awards, which must have been especially gratifying for the makers Carlton who earlier had been lambasted by the Independent Television Commission for the allegedly low and superficial character of its factual programming. No one at the time of the programme's initial transmission raised any serious doubts about the authenticity of the material, but some two years later a team of journalists from the *Guardian* published a deeply disturbing report which showed that not all that had been shown in the programme had been been as it seemed. This was not the type of 'reality adjustment' which involved a little tinkering at the edges, it was more in the nature of a wholesale forgery.

The Connection was shown to have offended against the legally-binding ITC programme code on a number of counts including the following:

- an individual introduced as a high-ranking member of a notorious Colombian drugs cartel was in reality someone with low-level connections to the underworld who had agreed to play the role of the number three figure in the cartel
- the so-called 'mule', the courier filmed bringing the drugs into the UK, did not, as claimed, have drugs secreted in his stomach, but had been filmed swallowing some innocuous mints
- contrary to the claim of the programme that the courier got through Customs at Heathrow, he was in fact stopped by immigration officials and sent back to Colombia
- the journey from Colombia to the UK, which the programme presented as a single journey was in fact filmed in two legs, some six months apart
- the journey itself was not part of a drugs mission masterminded by the cartel; it had been set up by the programme makers; and even the plane ticket had been paid for by a member of the production team.

On the strength of these proven allegations the makers of *The Connection* were fined £2 million by the regulator. The revelations about the faking of *The Connection* did set alarm bells ringing in the industry, especially as the incident had received such high profile coverage in the press. The price paid by the individuals most directly involved was also a high one, not just in financial terms but also in terms of their loss of prestige. This incident and others relating to documentary 'fakery' also led to the broadcasters and the regulatory authorities tightening the guidelines and codes of practice relating to factual/documentary production. In particular it encouraged the debate as to how the judicious but more extensive use of on-screen labelling might be the necessary prophylactic to guard against further charges of fakery.[7] In the case of *The Connection*, for instance, the allegations of fakery were in large part based on the total lack of acknowledgement by the programme makers that many of the 'documentary sequences' were dramatized enactments or simulations. It is one of the ironies surrounding *The Connection* saga that, with relatively few emendations, the programme could have easily passed muster. If the producers had been up-front in declaring their account to be a 'factually-based drama-documentary' or if the label 'dramatic reconstruction' had been systematically attached to the simulated scenes, then the programme would not have been subject to charges of extensive misrepresentation and would not have become the cause célèbre it eventually became. In making this point, however, one has to remember that members of *The Connection* production team would have been as aware as anyone that authentic scenes, shot apparently at great personal risk and forming part of a drama-filled package, have a much higher commodity value than scenes more dutifully and honestly identified as dramatized reconstructions.

In the year following the scandal concerning *The Connection* there was a spate of press revelations about diverse acts of faking and deception in factual/documentary programming. From a cursory reading of these articles, one could easily form the impression that fakery was so rife at this time that audiences would have been well advised to be deeply sceptical about the veracity of any account to which the factual label was attached. In reaching this judgement about factual programme makers' alleged propensity to play fast and loose with reality, little distinction was made between different types of factual/documentary programme, nor did those sitting in judgement pay much attention to the audience's capacity to reach their own conclusions about the 'reality status' of what they were being shown.

Another controversy which flared at this time and which throws some more light on what is at issue in the debates over fakery centred on the

Channel 4 documentary *Rogue Males* (1998) about rogue builders. The programme's declared objective was to show, using a traditional documentary format, the workings of the black economy. A subsequent investigation by journalists, however, revealed that the cowboy builders who appeared in the programme had been impersonated by friends of the director. The scene which created the most stir was the one in which two men are caught in flagrante stealing pallets from a builder's yard. Perhaps not surprisingly this scene proved, on further investigation, to have been reconstructed. The director, Dominic Savage, when challenged on the Channel 4 programme *Right to Reply* (March, 1998) as to why had not chosen to label it as such, provided the rather lame excuse that he had beforehand 'made it right with the owner of the yard'. Seeking to explain himself further, he added that such incidents of petty theft occur so regularly that, in simulating one for the camera, no great liberties were being taken with the truth. This issue of the legitimacy of reconstructing regularly occurring incidents will be returned to later in the chapter. With regard to the controversy surrounding *Rogue Males*, the point can simply be made here that, as with *The Connection*, the director has chosen to *encourage* the assumption that this was an actual break-in and also to foster the belief that he had shown considerable journalistic resourcefulness in getting his camera where the action was.

With *Rogue Males* the charge against the programme maker was based on the contestable proposition that the public had been hoodwinked by a wilful act of deception (the inclusion of faked or invented scenes). Likewise with another Channel 4 documentary *Chickens: Too Much, Too Young* (1997) concerning the activities of young rent boys in Glasgow, key scenes in what was assumed to be a straight documentary account were later shown to have been set up by members of the production team. One of the rent boy's clients was, it later transpired, a member of the production team. In the case of both *Rogue Males* and *Chickens* … action was taken against those thought responsible for perpetrating the deception. With the former, Channel 4 felt moved to issue a formal apology to viewers, while with the latter the ITC chose to impose a hefty £150,000 fine on the broadcaster. While clearly designed to have some deterrent effect and to reassure the public that those charged with maintaining broadcasting standards were taking all necessary steps to put their house in order, the imposition of fines did little in itself to address some of the underlying issues exposed by the fakery controversies: those relating to the *audience's* understanding of what was being communicated and to the highly pressurized conditions under which an increasing amount of factual programming was produced. Producers were still having to operate in an environment not entirely conducive to the maintenance of the highest standards. Likewise there was a feeling in some quarters that the imposition of heavy fines on wayward programme makers might actually prejudice freedom of expression (Winston, 1999). The argument was that, if the penalties for transgression were severe, producers would regrettably but understandably seek refuge in bland, non-challenging reports which would not cause offence.[8]

Hoaxing

As probably could have been predicted, few of the fakery scandals of the late 1990s led to widespread manifestations of public outrage that broadcasters were failing in their basic duty to be honest and transparent in their dealings with the viewing public. The public had already learned to adopt a due measure of scepticism with regard to the credibility of much media output. Broadcasters did recognize, however, that they had made it that much more difficult to defend themselves against the charges of fakery by the very fervour with which they had hyped the programmes in the first place. Promoting documentaries such as *The Connection* on the strength of the 'dramatic footage' they contained or of the 'remarkable access' that the programme maker had been able to gain, proved to be a major hostage to fortune when it was later discovered that the scenes in question had been dramatically enacted. By the same token, of course, the heavy promotion of these action-centred documentaries by ratings-hungry broadcasters provides further evidence of the kind of pressures on programme makers which may lead to the taking of certain liberties.

There is, therefore, more than a little irony in the fact that it was as a direct consequence of the heavy trailing of a new documentary series that – with the controversy surrounding *The Connection* still raging – another piece of deception involving factual programme production should come to light. This time, however, the deception was practised, not by the programme makers but by the subjects chosen to appear in the documentary. *Daddy's Girl* (Channel 4, 1998) was the first in a new series of documentaries exploring father–daughter relationships. Channel 4 had aired several promotional trails for this programme and one of these had been seen by the real father of the daughter who appeared in one of the trails. He promptly rang the broadcaster to inform them that the 'father' in the programme was none other than his daughter's older boyfriend. Stuart and Victoria, the couple in question, had a highly developed sense of the kind of material which today's producers regard as 'good television' and succeeded in pulling the wool over the eyes of the programme makers as to the true nature of their relationship. Later, when called upon to explain themselves, the couple were at pains to point out that they viewed their actions – which had, of course, involved letting quite a large circle of friends in on the deception – as merely a pleasurable prank.

In a later programme entitled *Who's Been Framed?* (Channel 4, 1999) which provided a post mortem examination of how the producers of *Daddy's Girl* had been deceived, Stuart and Victoria describe in some detail how they had, with relative ease, been able to dupe the show's producers into believing their story. Just as talk-show guests are expected to be adept at producing tailor-made performances, so in *Daddy's Girl* Stuart and Victoria had been able to turn the tables on the programme makers by providing the production team with a story which contained all the required ingredients. What the case of *Daddy's Girl* therefore reveals is the high degree of complicity (see also Chapter 4, pp. 107–9) between programme makers and their subjects when all parties have something to gain from certain types of factual programme making. Subjects key into the performance expectations of producers, while producers may be willing to turn a deaf ear if certain details of a life-story almost beggar belief. In the *Who's Been Framed?* programme Stuart makes the revealing comment: 'It was only acting. It was as if we were directing our own film' and goes on to remark that, in acting as they did, he and Victoria 'got strong indications of what the programme makers were after ... They seemed to be after the unusually close relationship between father and daughter'. In other words, the programme makers were not going to let doubts about the possibly questionable authenticity of the couple's account get in the way of a good story.

For some the *Daddy's Girl* hoaxing episode may well have seemed like a defining moment in the post-modern world of television, but for others it provided yet further proof that standards were indeed slipping in the factual programme making industry. In the case of *Daddy's Girl* what appears to have happened was that members of the production team were indeed willing to turn a blind eye to what must have struck them as inconsistencies or dubious aspects of the couple's story because it appeared to contain such taboo-breaking dramatic potential. That this could happen gave more than a little cause for concern. While this incident, and the other fakery scandals previously alluded to, did not in themselves prove that fraud and deception were rife in contemporary programme making, they did seem to point to a worrying tendency.

What all the incidents revealed was not a picture of widespread fraudulent activity amongst programme makers but one of an industry having to adapt perhaps all too rapidly to the demands of the new broadcasting age. Fakery may not have been endemic within the industry, but as the competitive pressures became more intense, so the likelihood became greater of corners being cut. This is not to excuse the more blatant acts of deception that have occasionally been practised; it is simply to provide an explanation for the various instances of liberty taking that did occur.

As emphasized throughout this book, there was no aspect of broadcasting or programme making activity in the 1980s and 1990s that was *not* subject to radical transformation. The fakery incidents might be regarded as the inevitable collateral damage which has resulted from this transformative process. Until the late 1980s documentary programme making could still be regarded, in many respects, as continuing in the Griersonian and Reithian public service tradition, with acknowledged centres of excellence within the established broadcasting institutions. This situation changed quite radically in the course of the 1990s as new modes and systems of programme production were introduced and as the broadcasting industry became increasingly fragmented. Programme makers' primary allegiance today is likely to be towards one of the small independent production units to which they are temporarily contracted. No longer do they identify, to the extent they once did, with that broader documentary tradition, so preoccupied are they with the accomplishment of short-term goals. Though producer inexperience may have played its part in some of the fakery scandals, the malaise – if this it is – is clearly more systemic, rooted as it is in the prevailing conditions under which most factual programming is nowadays produced. As Paul Hamann, head of documentaries at the BBC for much of the 1990s, observed as the decade drew to a close:

> With the explosion in factual programming over the last eight years schedulers from all companies want more documentary production because it's cheaper and more bankable than light entertainment. This, however, means younger people with less experience are taking the reins. Some of the things [relating to faking] I have heard are clearly down to inexperience. (Carter, 1999: 20)

Fall-out after fakery

The spate of faking and hoaxing incidents in the late 1990s led, understandably enough, to much soul-searching as to the origins of and remedies for this malaise. The particular concern of broadcasters was whether all these press revelations about fakery would diminish the audience's readiness to believe the veracity of any documentary account. By the same token, programme makers were fearful that the somewhat tarnished reputation that documentary/factual programme making was acquiring might lead to a reluctance on the part of potential contributors to become involved in future documentary projects.[9] As the then controller of editorial policy at the BBC, Phil Harding, warned in the course of a debate at the 1999 Edinburgh International Television Festival:

> The audience has to be able to know what they're seeing is true … if the audience don't believe what they're seeing on one chat show, they won't believe what they're seeing on another chat show and they won't start to believe any of the documentaries or any of the investigations. Once you let one thing go, that then becomes a cancer that can spread throughout all television. (Walker, 1999: 3)

Faced with a growing tide of criticism about falling standards and shoddy working practices, broadcasters and regulatory bodies set about revising the various codes of practice under which programme makers in the UK are required to operate. Regulatory bodies such as the Independent Television Commission (ITC) and the Broadcasting Standards Commission (BSC) also investigated complaints about fakery and alleged malpractice by programme makers.[10] The ITC, for its part, paid particular attention to revising that part of its Programme Code relating to factual programming, while the BBC in its *Producers' Guidelines* went to considerable lengths to spell out to programme makers how vigilant they would have to be as they faced up to the challenges of the digital age. As the Director-General Greg Dyke states in the preface to the 2001 *Producers' Guidelines*:

These Guidelines are a working document for programme teams to enable them to think their way through some of the more difficult dilemmas they may face. Risk-taking is and must remain an essential part of the creative process at the BBC. What the Guidelines can do is to help us to make sensible calculations about those risks by leaning on the experience of others who have been in similar situations. (BBC, 2001; 2)

The revision of programme making guidelines and codes of practice sent out clear signals that broadcasters were intent on putting their house in order. The problem for programme makers working in the factual domain, however, is that a requirement to adhere strictly to regulatory guidelines may not in itself be sufficient to prevent confusion or misunderstandings arising. The simple act of labelling a sequence as a 're-construction' or as 'library pictures' is in itself no guarantee that other types of deception are not being practised. The public's understanding of some of the quite complex issues underlying alleged fakery has not been helped by the way in which some observers (mostly newspaper journalists) have simply subsumed diverse instances of alleged deception under one generalized heading of 'fakery', without differentiating sufficiently between individual categories of programming. Thus, certain acts of minor reconstruction whereby, say, a character in a relatively lighthearted docusoap is asked to repeat a routine action for the benefit of the camera have, on occasions, attracted almost the same degree of opprobrium as more thoroughgoing cases of deception such as occurred in *The Connection*. As Shaun Williams, chief executive of the UK producers' alliance PACT, opined at the the height of the controversies over fakery:

One of the problems (about the fakery scandals) has been a blurring of a number of quite separate issues. There's a big difference between hoaxers unknowingly used, reconstructions and blatant deception and fakery. (Carter, 1999: 20)

Reconstructing reality

Many of the misunderstandings and complaints about alleged faking in factual/documentary programming in recent years have related to the practice of dramatic reconstruction. Reconstruction has, of course, featured prominently in the whole history of documentary, so it might be salutary to remind ourselves what issues are at stake when reconstructional techniques are being employed. In the light of some of the recent scandals, broadcasters have also been forced into a careful reappraisal of what constitutes legitimate practice in the field of dramatic reconstruction. This current section will therefore draw quite heavily on what broadcasters have had to say, as it frequently reveals a degree of insight which some critics have chosen to overlook in their rush to suggest that most, if not all programme makers are involved in some kind of deception.

In the early history of documentary, debates over about the employment of reconstruction were not conducted with the same vehemence as they are today. The need to employ quite extensive reconstruction was quite literally imposed on documentarists by the severe limitations of recording equipment available at the time. Scenes of postal employees sorting letters in the mail train in the well known documentary *Night Mail* (1936) all had to be shot in the studio. Likewise some of the sequences involving close-up shots of herring in John Grierson's *Drifters* (1929) were also produced in a studio setting. Nowadays – when the camera can literally go anywhere: into the deepest recesses of the human body or far into outer space and where images of events happening in these places can be transmitted direct to our television screens – one might imagine that documentarists would no longer have quite the same need to resort to reconstruction. Having the technological ability is not, however, the same as being able to actually deliver the goods. Actuality and dramatic live footage has achieved such a high commodity value that programme makers find themselves as actively involved as ever in the process of reconstructing reality. As programme maker Bernard Clark has commented:

> Twenty years ago, the documentary maker would only be able to show 'the sort of things that happen' … Today, technology enables the presentation of things actually happening. And the pressure is on to deliver more and more of this sort of material. But unless a programme-maker is on-hand shooting 24 hours a day, reconstruction – even at at the most superficial level – is inevitable. A key concern is the degree to which reconstruction is used, and when it would be presented as such rather than purporting to be 'reality'. *It is a highly subjective area.* (Carter, 1999: 20, my emphasis)

Mindful of the pressures under which today's generation of programme makers operate, regulators and broadcasters have, as suggested, sought to supplement the guidance they give on where to draw the line between permissible and illegitimate acts of reconstruction. In the codes and guidelines produced by the ITC and the BBC, it is accepted that the use of dramatized reconstruction in factual programmes is a legitimate technique to illustrate or recapture events which were, for whatever reason, not recorded as and when they occurred. Both sets of guidelines lay considerable emphasis on the need to be up-front with the audience, in terms of being clear as to what status the reconstructed or invented sequence has in the overall context of the work. Adequate labelling is thus seen as the best way of avoiding any confusion or misunderstanding (broadcaster-speak for 'pre-empting complaints about faking'). As the BBC *Producers' Guidelines* put it:

> The reconstruction or re-staging of events in factual programmes can be a great help in explaining an issue. It must always be done truthfully with an awareness of what is reliably known. Nothing significant which is not known should be invented without acknowledgment. Reconstructions should not over-dramatise events in a misleading or sensationalistic way. Reconstructions would be identified clearly so that no-one is misled. Repeated labelling may be necessary to achieve this. (BBC, 2001: 45–6)

Though eminently well intentioned, such injunctions only go part of the way towards clarifying some of the knottier issues surrounding reconstruction, including the difficulty of being able to make an effective distinction between what is a reconstructed event and what is an event that has been specially staged for the camera. And if one were to pursue the question of labelling to its logical conclusion, one could also easily make the case for all factual/documentary programming being prefaced by a label advising viewers that what they are about to see is a representational re-enactment (in the sense that all documentary work involves the framing, editing and reconstituting of material). There is nowadays, however, much greater acknowledgement than once there was that some form of intervention lies at the heart of all documentary work. The key point is that the audience should have some knowledge and understanding of the processes by which the material has been gathered and put together. In the words of the BBC guidelines:

> There are few factual films which do not involve some intervention from the director, even those which are commonly described as 'fly on the wall' or observational documentaries … However, production methods, especially in television with single camera location shooting, sometimes mean that it is impossible to record all events exactly as they happen. *Many of the techniques that are used to overcome this have long been part of the accepted grammar of programme making. The conventional skills employed to edit sound*

and picture together are widely understood and accepted by the audience. (BBC, 2001: 46, my emphasis)

The important point to note here is that it is accepted that the final court of appeal in these matters should be the viewer. Being able to share with an audience some of the problems programme makers may have faced in reaching editorial decisions as to what or what not to include is seen as one of the defining characteristics of 'legitimate practice'. The key criterion is whether or not you, as a producer, can satisfactorily explain the decisions you have taken to representatives of the people's court.

This idea that the production team should either implicitly or explicitly be sharing with the audience the perspective from which the programme is being made is an important one. It has not always featured prominently enough in the fakery debates, possibly because those who have rushed to judgement on allegedly errant programme makers have more often than not spoken *for* the audience rather than going to the trouble of canvassing the audience's own views on the matter. Audiences, or more specifically focus groups representing the views of audiences, have by and large signalled that they have maintained confidence in the integrity of programme makers in spite of the recent fakery incidents (Hibberd et al., 2000). Producers have also, for their part, under the pressure of heightened scrutiny of their activities, been more prepared than once they were to consider how they communicate their intentions to the audience. As Peter Dale, head of documentaries at Channel 4 has observed:

> The most positive thing to come out of these recent controversies is an increased sense of vigilance and impetus for debate ... In between breaking a code and playing safe is a grey area that is highly subjective. Negotiating this comes down to sharing clarity of purpose – everyone understanding what a particular programme is doing, and why. (Carter, 1999: 21)

Being clear about a particular factual programme's intention from the producer's perspective is one thing. Successfully conveying this to an audience is quite another matter. Let me illustrate this by referring to a recent example where the 'signalling of intent' clearly did not, at least in the eyes of some, have the desired effect. In July 2001 Channel 4 broadcast a spoof documentary in the *Brass Eye* series which addressed the highly sensitive issue of paedophilia. Following many hundreds of complaints from viewers, both the ITC and the BSC ruled that Channel 4 had been guilty of 'unacceptable practice'. Though the regulators defended the channel's right to air disturbing and provocative material, they judged that on this occasion the labelling of the programme had been insufficient and viewers had not been well enough prepared for a documentary-style spoof investigation. In the words of the ITC ruling: 'The programme had caused unnecessary offence to many people' (*Independent*, 7 September 2001: 1). The regulators' requirement that Channel 4 issue an on-air apology for the 'offence' once again draws attention to that 'grey area' identified by Peter Dale. When a programme is deliberately designed to provoke its audience, too much labelling is inevitably going to reduce its potential impact. The difficulty for the broadcaster, therefore, is judging how best to communicate the underlying intentions of the piece without diminishing the programme's satirical bite.

The *Brass Eye* programme had, it must be remembered, been found wanting not because it was considered to have misled or deceived the audience through the inclusion of faked material, but because it had offended against two of the ITC codes relating to taste and decency (hence the demand for an apology rather that the imposition of a fine). The regulators felt moved to take action because the programme had, in the words of the ITC ruling, 'caused gratuitous offence'. The controversy surrounding the programme and the action taken by the regulators once again demonstrates, however, the difficulties of legislating in this field. While the regulators could, on this occasion, point to the fact that a number of individual viewers had chosen to express their outrage or discomfiture, there was still a feeling in some quarters that the steps taken represented an unwarranted curtailment of free expression.

More generally, there is evidence to suggest that members of the television audience take an altogether more even-handed, more clear-sighted and on the whole sensible attitude to these issues (including those of fakery) than many commentators choose to acknowledge. Or expressed in slightly different terms: audiences have a greater scepticism about the 'reality status' of much of what they see than many working in the broadcasting industry might imagine. There is an awareness on the part of the viewers that what they are consuming is highly processed material and their responses are determined accordingly. Annette Hill, for instance, in her audience research work has shown that many in the British TV audience (in one sample more than 70 per cent) actively distrust the 'reality' of stories in factual entertainment programming (Hill, 2001: 36–50). Moreover, this scepticism seems to be growing. In a poll commissioned for the 1998 series *On Air* (BBC 2) which considered among other matters the issue of fakery, 46 per cent of respondents thought that factual programmes took more liberties with the truth than they did five years previously (even though viewers were still disposed to believe more in what they saw on TV than what they read in their newspapers). When the same group of respondents was asked to comment on the 'builders' yard' incident in *Rogue Males* (see pp. 134–5) the majority declared themselves not to be unduly exercised by the 'slight deception' that had been practised. Likewise, when asked about their views on the use of unacknowledged reconstructions in docu-soaps, there was a broad consensus that this was all part of an acceptable trade-off. Viewers were happy to accept that there would need to be the occasional piece of dramatic restaging in the putting together of these lightweight entertainment packages. Because they were lightweight in character, no great offence was taken that some sleight of hand had been practised to achieve the desired ends.

Fakery in wildlife programming

The issue of 'reality staging' will be returned to in Chapter 6, but in concluding this we will consider a category of programming which has of late been exposed to close critical scrutiny, (possibly because the issues relating to fakery have been so hotly debated). The sphere of programming that has, perhaps unexpectedly, found itself in the dock is wildlife documentary. The charges levelled against it are that, if audiences knew what trickery was being practised in the way that accounts of wildlife and natural history were put together, they might take a very different view of the material they were watching. This is not, the argument goes, fakery on the grand scale as practised in *The Connection*, but nevertheless some of the issues involved are sufficiently close to those which cause concern in other types of factual output as to warrant closer investigation. Once again the key questions relate to the potential misleading of an audience: can wildlife film makers be accused of similar acts of deception as other factual programme makers who manipulate human subjects to their own ends? Are what purport to be accounts of life in the wild far more reliant than ever we would imagine on shots of animals in zoos, with these shots being regularly intercut with footage obtained in 'genuine' wildlife locations? And, perhaps most important of all, do audiences feel in some way misled if such mixing and matching practices are not signalled to them either through the commentary or through some form of labelling?

Just as with the general categories of factual/documentary programming, the whole debate about fakery in TV wildlife programming has to be set in the larger context of contemporary television and the requirement for particular types of programming. Over the years wildlife and natural history programming has been one of the staple ingredients of broadcast output. Indeed, in today's highly competitive television environment, wildlife and natural history have, if anything, achieved even higher profile. There are now a number of dedicated wildlife/natural history satellite channels (Animal Planet, The Discovery Channel, National Geographic). Likewise some of the company mergers in the 1990s have been inspired by the desire of major players (such as the Discovery Channel and the BBC) to achieve economies of scale in the production of wildlife material in the knowledge that these categories of programming were not subject to the same vicissitudes of fashion as other TV genres. As John Willis has observed:

> Every channel scheduler needs a supply of natural history. Wildlife programmes are timeless enough to be repeated almost endlessly ... In the longer term, natural history is top dollar because the genre has shelf-life. Wildlife libraries are hugely valuable assets. Dialogue-free and with no stars to ask for large salaries, they are the perfect international television product. (Willis,1998b: 4)

Like every other form of factual programming, however, wildlife has, of late, been required to deliver its due measure of dramatic or gripping entertainment. Programmes featuring the more savage, aggressive or predatory aspects of animal behaviour are especially highly prized for their 'chill appeal', while footage which captures hitherto unrevealed moments of animal life is also much sought after. In presenting us with this material for our edification and visual delight, wildlife producers will frequently draw attention to selected aspects of the film making process. The patience, resilience and stamina of those doing the filming are lauded, while the devising of innovative techniques to capture a particular aspect of animal behaviour sometimes becomes the subject of an introductory documentary promoting the new series. On the other hand, a discreet silence is usually maintained about other parts of the production process, especially regarding how certain shots may have been obtained and what criteria were employed in the assembling of particular sequences. Silence in itself does not, of course, suggest that anything reprehensible has occurred. Audiences will, after all, have become familiar over the years with many of the conventions employed by wildlife film makers. They will, for instance, have become accustomed to the frequent use of anthropomorphic modes of narrative presentation in wildlife programming. Viewers recognize that this belongs to the 'established grammar of film making' and make due allowance for this in the interpretation they put on the representations of wildlife behaviour depicted in the programme or film. There is, however, a fine line between what might be regarded as legitimate practice, where most viewers will accept that film makers have resorted to certain types of artifice in the attempt to produce a revealing account of animal behaviour, and more questionable practice where untenable short-cuts have been taken in order, say, to heighten dramatic tension or to fit things in with the dramaturgical requirements of a developing story.

The codes and guidelines under which UK programme makers operate make a series of suggestions as to what constitutes acceptable practice in relation to wildlife filming (see BBC, 2001: 186–90). There are, however, as one might have anticipated, diverging views as to how these guidelines should be interpreted. Some in the wildlife film making community take the pragmatic view that natural history programme making will inevitably mean filming animals in captivity, if for no other reason than the rapaciousness of exploitative human beings has driven many forms of wildlife from their natural habitats. It is also the case that filming an animal in the wild might, on occasions, expose the film makers to risk and danger or, alternatively, bring such a degree of disturbance to the wildlife environment as to drive animals away from this habitat (another instance of the consequences of documentary intervention!) There are thus some sound reasons why film makers consider that the inclusion of 'captive sequences' in wildlife programming is justifiable, provided that the main motivation is to portray what would naturally happen in the wild and provided that no extravagant claims are made that the recording has been made in the wild. Already here one sees a grey area opening up. Programme makers may not exactly be actively encouraging the belief that everything seen in the final edited version has occurred in the wild, but the absence of any explicit commentary to this effect might actually foster this illusion. This may explain why a substantial minority of film makers still cling to the belief that the unacknowledged filming of wildlife in zoos, which may create the illusion that the animals are enjoying the freedom of the wild, should be resisted since it is deceiving the audience as to the true state of affairs.

There is no question that fuel has been added to the fire in this particular debate by the recent furore over fakery in other categories of factual programming. And just as with the wider issue of reconstruction in documentary, so too in wildlife filming the debate about the staging or mixing of scenes is by no means a recent phenomenon. One of the most celebrated instances which shows how far film makers are prepared to go in adjusting reality to the dramatic needs of a story is provided by the film *White Wilderness* (Disney, 1959). In one remarkable scene hundreds of apparently suicidal lemmings are seen leaping off a cliff to what one presumes to be their certain death. It was only after several scientific experts had wryly observed that this flew in the face of all the known patterns of lemming behaviour, that members of the production team admitted that the whole sequence had been set up. The lemmings had not plunged to their death of their own volition but had been pushed.

Provided there is a reasonable degree of honesty and transparency on the part of programme makers in the way in which these techniques are deployed then wildlife producers can hardly be accused of 'wilfully deceiving' their audience. Indeed sharing with the audience details of how certain footage has been obtained can, as already suggested, enhance viewers' appreciation of the wildlife events being depicted. When all is said and done, wildlife programming is governed by a similar set of imperatives to those which hold sway in other types of factual programming. The basic requirement is for a type of factual entertainment that will hold the attention of viewers in an ever more crowded marketplace. In this respect the filmed activities of animals, which are still the main source of attraction in most wildlife documentaries, might be regarded in the same light as the activities of those human performers in some of the contemporary game-docs. After all, encouraging an audience to gawp voyeuristically at the antics and cavortings of a group of housemates in a contained TV environment is not so dissimilar to the situation in wildlife docs where groups of animals are filmed competing for territorial advantage and are seen indulging in various bonding, feeding and mating rituals. In both these instances the viewer is being invited to experience the excitement of an unfolding drama and film makers are concerned to present events in such a way as to maximize the dramatic potential.

In the case of wildlife documentaries then, the concern among some observers is not so much that viewers are being actively misled about the true nature of animal behaviour, but that they are being deprived of the opportunity to become conversant with some of the more pressing issues affecting conservation and the survival of certain species. As one commentator has observed:

> While the spectacular programmes of individual animals and species have flourished, programmes dealing with conservation have slipped in the schedules, and environmental issues have been pushed to the margins. (Coward, 1997: 45)

The more pressing questions which have to be asked about wildlife programming on TV relate not so much to charges of fakery (in the form of the occasional mixing of 'captive sequences' with those shot in the wild) as to the changing balance of natural history provision. With the continuing popularity of wildlife TV programming (it is still the most popular form of non-fiction material after news and sport) and with so much money being invested in blockbuster series such as those produced and/or narrated by David Attenborough, the hunt for dramatic wildlife footage in contemporary TV programming continues unabated.[11] The concern is that the commercial imperative is now so strong that, like many other categories of factual programming, wildlife is becoming just another form of factual entertainment. And since it is well known that entertainment relies on a number of standard components, it is perhaps not surprising that these factual categories are beginning more and more to resemble each other. We have already noted, for instance, the increasing number of wildlife programmes which lure viewers with the promise of action-packed scenes featuring spine-tingling acts of predation (e.g. Fox TV's *When Animals Attack*) and other types of violent encounter. There are distinct parallels here with the chase-and-arrest sequences in some of the A & E reality formats. Likewise those drama-rich sequences in wildlife docs which focus on a creature's desperate struggle to stave off the incursion of a competitor, have a clear affinity with scenes in popular people-centred documentaries such as *Neighbours from Hell* whose subject is the often violent territorial feuds which can be played out in the human jungle.

Conclusion

Debates on fakery have often been clouded by the knee-jerk tendency on the part of some journalists to treat all 'offences' as if they were third-degree crimes. There has been a disinclination to seize the opportunity provided by the coming-to-light of particular instances of fakery to consider some of the wider issues relating to documentary production and reception. What is needed is a more open debate about the challenges that programme makers confront in attempting to represent reality on the screen. This would include a greater acknowledgement of the pressures under which producers are now required to operate. It would also recognize that the range of work covered by that slippery term 'documentary' is now extremely broad and that different audience expectations arise according to whether the programme in question is more serious in its orientation or primarily conceived as lightweight entertainment.

There is some evidence to suggest that today's audiences are much more adept at reaching their own judgements concerning the 'reality status' of programming than some broadcasters and critics might imagine. It is also the case that audiences, on the whole, generally have a more sceptical attitude to media output than once they did. One might even go so far as to suggest that – especially with the new reality formats – viewers are actively encouraged to engage with these texts in the full knowledge that the scenarios they introduce have all, to a greater or lesser extent, been specially contrived for television. Thus, for the viewer, one of the pleasures offered by the new generation of reality formats is the knowledge that what is being offered for consumption is manifestly 'staged reality'. The fact that nowadays so much is so unambiguously staged has meant that the focus of concern has now shifted away from anxieties about the 'reality status' of factual programming material.

After a period in the late 1990s in which there was an apparently unrelenting preoccupation with faking in documentary, there are now a fresh set of concerns surrounding the new reality formats. As well as misgivings (some of them media-fuelled) about the potential psychological damage which participants in these shows may suffer as a result of such high-profile media exposure, there are also anxieties about what this degree of audience involvement in what is so palpably staged reality signifies in cultural terms (see Greer, 2001). Given the unprecedented popularity of a show like *Big Brother*, a lot of attention has been focussed on a particular type of reality staging, one in which contestants produce self-performances in highly contrived, made-for-TV situations. One must not underestimate, however, the significance of another factual category in which self-performance skills are, arguably, harnessed to somewhat more serious ends, in the category of programming epitomized by the *Country House* sub-genre which requires volunteer participants to act out roles in contrived made-for-TV scenarios. Unlike the *Big Brother* and *Survivor* shows the programmes belonging to this new sub-genre do not include an elimination element in their format design. Their primary aim remains that of delivering easily digestible factual entertainment, but such shows can still claim to have what might be regarded as a slightly more serious purpose. They are, namely, aspiring to illuminate some aspect of the contemporary or historical world while still offering audiences the pleasurable, game-doc inspired spectacle of watching a group of real-life individuals producing performances in response to a challenge that television has thrown down. An increasing number of such programmes have emerged in recent years and it is this particular brand of reality staging that will be examined in Chapter 6.

Notes

1 For a period in 1998, following the scandal surrounding *The Connection*, (a documentary about the smuggling of heroin from Colombia to the UK which proved to be largely faked), stories about fakery in documentaries or about fake guests in talk-shows regularly featured in the broadsheet and the tabloid press.

2 In making this point, I am not seeking to let programme makers off the hook or to find excuses for shoddy working practices. I am merely underlining the importance of putting the individual incidents into some sort of context and of bearing in mind that television programme makers (especially those working in the areas of news and current affairs) have always been subject to much tighter regulation than print journalists.

3 For more on the nature of fiction and its relevance to documentary discourse see Branigan (1992): 192–4.

4 The TV drama series *The Cops* (BBC, 2000) for instance, an award winning drama about rank-and-file police officers, deliberately set out to affiliate itself to documentary by the style of its camera work and by the warts-and-all approach to its subject matter.

5 There, was, of course, a certain irony in the way that documentary programme making was being hauled into the glare of publicity in this way. Just a decade previously fears were being expressed about documentary being an endangered species. In the course of 1999, seldom a week passed without there being some new scandal about unscrupulous documentarists playing fast and loose with reality.

6   Another well-publicized faking incident involved the German news journalist Michael
    Born. In 1996 he was given a four-year prison sentence (later commuted to two years)
    for setting up what was in effect a cottage industry in faked documentary reports
    (Mapplebeck, 1997a: 10–12).

7   It was still felt in some quarters, however, that the brouhaha surrounding *The Con-
    nection* and other cases of alleged or proven fakery, and in particular the imposition
    of heavy fines, was disproportionate to any 'damage' that the audience might have
    suffered as a result of being allegedly hoodwinked in this way (see Winston, 1999: 8).

8   Brian Winston has suggested that the prominence given to individual acts of fakery
    has the ideological advantage of making it appear that factual programmes that have
    not been thus exposed can 'safely' be regarded as wholly truthful, non-biased ac-
    counts in which programme makers have adhered to high journalistic standards
    (Winston, 1999: 9).

9   Molly Dineen, one of Britain's best known contemporary documentary makers, also
    blamed the high-profile docu-soaps for the growing disinclination of some people
    to appear in more serious types of documentary work: 'Docu-soaps are incredibly
    slack. To look at it selfishly, they're queering my pitch, they make some people stars
    and they're not particularly offensive, but there's a feeling of mockery and piss-tak-
    ing that has made people very wary' (cited in Dugdale, 1999 : 6).

10 Particularly careful consideration was given to the reframing of the codes relating to
    the dramatic reconstruction of events, so as to avoid any confusion arising as to the
    'reality status' of the presentation. (See in particular ITC Programme Code: Autumn
    1998: Section 3.7).

11 And just as other factual categories are seeking to engage the attention of the viewer
    through the use of innovative presentational techniques, so too a new breed of wild-
    life programmes has developed since the late 1990s which foreground gung-ho wildlife
    presenters such as Steve Irwin and (more recently) Mark O'Shea and their confron-
    tations with a range of dangerous animals and reptiles.

6 Staging the real: new modes of reality formatting

What might be regarded as one of the more positive outcomes of the fakery controversies of the late 1990s was the impetus it gave to the debate on some of the key issues surrounding documentary discourse. Programme makers felt constrained to stand back and indulge in some critical reflection about their production practices; regulators felt duty-bound to revise the codes and guidelines relating to factual programme making; and audiences – if they needed any reminding – were also made more aware of the role they were being allotted as targeted consumers and also of the power they held as television became more and more consumer-oriented.

What has particularly informed this debate is the recognition that all documentary, to a greater or lesser degree, involves some form of staging. Successive generations of documentarists and programme makers may have sought to persuade us that their work has a special claim on our attention by virtue of the fact that it brings revelations about the real world. They have not always been as eager to concede that these revelations are the result of active intervention on the part of a film or programme making team. Fly-on-the-wall documentarists may attempt to convince us that they are quasi-invisible observers of events which would have happened that way whether or not the camera team had been present. In reality, however, all documentary is based on some form of purposive intervention where the reality to be captured is inevitably going to be shaped by a number of factors: by the preconceived notions of the incoming chroniclers, by the insistence of the chronicled that they give their version of events (which may or may not accord with the chroniclers' view) and by the type of narrative format which the film makers choose to employ (Kilborn & Izod, 1997: 199).

Staging is, in this sense, an inherent part of the documentary process and has become part of the accepted grammar of film and programme making. Roger Graef, a documentary film maker who has been very closely identified with the fly-on-the-wall tradition is, for instance, more than happy to concede that 'the vast majority of documentary film making is going to involve some kind of staging' (*On Air*, BBC 2, November 1998). According to these criteria then, the environment or location where the filming occurs takes on certain stage-like characteristics. Likewise the performative contributions of documentary witnesses are subject to enough directorial management and control to warrant the use of the term 'staging' to describe what is being undertaken. In short, since documentary is committed to finding appropriate means to represent reality, even in those cases where events are not being openly and explicitly restaged, documentarists can be seen to be shaping their material according to certain dramaturgical requirements. With respect to the aforementioned 'contributions of documentary witnesses', for instance, the impression is often given that they are spontaneous utterances. On closer examination, however, they prove not to have been as unrehearsed as one might have been led to believe. A certain amount of stage-managing will be seen to have been necessary to generate apparently spontaneous remarks. By the same token, it will not always be acknowledged that the selection of witnesses may itself be subject to rigorous selection criteria which take into account their performance ability.[1]

If some of the operations in the production of traditional documentary involve, at least implicitly, a form of staging, a more explicit form occurs in the widespread use of reconstruction practices. Documentary's constant endeavour to produce for its audiences compelling, arresting and sometimes thought-provoking accounts of the real has resulted, throughout the genre's history, in documentarists resorting to reconstruction techniques. Various forms of historical evidence, including eyewitness testimony, official records and other contemporary accounts, provide the basis for an imaginative, but factually-based reconstruction of events. In the vast majority of cases, the aim has been to produce an account which is grounded in historical reality. In some cases the basis for the dramatic staging, or the evidential starting point, is not provided by a known historical event, but by some factually informed conjecture. Dramatic, hypothetical scenarios are created along the lines of: in what way would a known reality be transformed if, let us say, a sudden and unpredictable event were to occur? Such imaginative enactments can have strong audience appeal and also have an additional provocative function in that they prompt viewers to use the conjectural account of the film maker as a starting point for drawing their own conclusions.[2]

Staging and restaging events has played a significant role in the history of documentary (Paget, 1998; Rosenthal, 1999) and has provided documentary with opportunities for extending the range of its appeal and for addressing its audience in ways that can be both emotionally poignant and intellectually challenging. Consider, for example, Peter Watkins' debut film *Culloden* (BBC, 1964), in which he explores the circumstances in which thousands of Scottish clansmen perished at the hands of the English army. In this drama-documentary account Watkins has one scene in which actors representing soldiers from opposing armies speak direct to camera in the manner that one might expect if contemporary television reporters were covering such an event. This, for its time, innovative restaging of the battle against the original backcloth of Culloden Moor, arguably prompts viewers to indulge in a more critical form of engagement with the issues raised than would a more traditional mode of documentary chronicling. Another instance from documentary history where staging is used to produce a response that could be obtained in no other way is in Claude Lanzmann's 1985 film *Shoah* (an oral history of the holocaust). In the scene in question Lanzmann films a holocaust survivor, Abraham Bomba, cutting people's hair in a barber's shop in today's Tel Aviv. Bomba, we have been told, was once employed as a barber in the Treblinka death camp where he had the grim task of cutting off the hair of women and children prior to their being murdered in the gas chambers. At Lanzmann's prompting, Bomba is asked to recall some of the detail of those terrifying events. The pain involved in this act of remembering is clearly almost unbearable; and at one point Bomba breaks down and pleads with Lanzmann to stop. For the audience, however, this simple but profoundly affecting piece of imaginative restaging brings home both the enormity of what has happened and the intense emotional and psychological burden of having to live with the memories. It is through what is in effect a contrivance that Lanzmann creates a wonderfully evocative, though intensely painful bridge between the everyday barber-shop of the present and the nightmare horrors of the past.

In both *Culloden* and *Shoah* staging is employed as a quite legitimate device to assist in the discovery of a deeper truth and to convey emotion that, arguably, could not have been evoked by any other means. The power and appeal of such stagings lies in their ability to create the aura of facticity, while at the same time making a strong imaginative appeal. In both cases it is a staging device which provides the bridge back to the historical events the documentarist is seeking to reinvoke. With *Shoah* it is the person of Bomba himself and the haircutting activity which provides the link. With *Culloden* it is the geographical location which acts as the triggering device. In both cases, however, the respective staging devices are – in an almost Brechtian manner – made transparent to viewer (Kleber & Visser, 1990: 19–37). This very transparency might in itself be regarded as part of a more general attempt to activate within the audience an informed and critical response.

Created-for-TV formats

While film makers throughout the history of documentary have had recourse to a whole range of staging and reconstruction techniques, the 1990s saw an exponential growth in the number of programmes which were wholly based on the idea of the set-up. All documentary work is, as already argued, to a greater or lesser extent the result of some act of intervention. It is the case, however, that in some instances the processes by which the film or programme makers have intervened are made more explicit than in others. This can be done by including references to the documentary production process, by sowing the seeds of doubts within the viewer's mind about the nature and reliability of evidence offered in the body of the text (the classic example of this is Errol Morris's *The Thin Blue Line* (1987)) or by encouraging the audience to reflect on their role in putting a particular interpretation on the text in the light of their own experience or knowledge. Those documentaries which display some or all of the above features are are usually referred to as belonging to the reflexive mode (Kilborn & Izod, 1997: 75–80). Generally speaking, the documentaries which display these reflexive traits tend to be found outside the mainstream of factual/ documentary programming, since texts which problematize the viewing experience or which deliberately seek to provoke critical engagement on the part of the TV viewer are not normally the kind of material which will find favour with commissioning editors.

However, whole swathes of documentary/factual programming have come on stream in the 1990s that display certain features of the reflexive mode while manifestly displaying a marked entertainment orientation. The programmes in question openly acknowledge their dependence on the creative intervention of a programme making team, indeed part of their selling proposition to TV audiences is their celebration of the fact that reality has in some way been heightened or 'brightened up' as a result of television intervening. The term which TV producers themselves use for this type of operation is 'reality formatting'. It aptly describes how scenarios are set up and situations contrived for television's specific needs. It also confirms the extent to which what is subsequently presented is, to all intents and purposes, a wholly televisual phenomenon. Reality game-shows are the most obvious example of 'reality formatting', in that they have been so clearly fabricated for the purposes of TV entertainment. There are, however, a range of other programmes which could be included in this category. Indeed it is significant that critics increasingly use the term 'created-for-TV' as a generic label for this style of programming. What these created-for-TV formats all have in common is that, implicitly or explicitly, they emphasize the highly mediated quality of the screened events.

Of all the 'created-for-TV' formats which have been introduced into the domain of factual programming since the late 1990s, it is the make-over shows which have come to dominate the early evening schedule of mainstream networks in recent years and perhaps best exemplify reality formatting.[3] Whether the subject of the intended transformation is the home, the garden or the person, the structuring principles of the make-over sub-genre remain the same. A team of telegenic professionals moves in on the domain of 'ordinary' people. With or without the knowledge of the latter, they effect the make-over and then, in the final climactic or pay-off scene, the audience registers the shock, anger or delight of all the made-over individuals. Make-over programmes thus adhere to the tried-and-tested storytelling device where an initial 'problem' is satisfactorily and harmoniously resolved in a classic problem/solution narrative trajectory. These programmes generally adopt a lighthearted approach to their subject and most make-over operations are conducted in the spirit of postmodern playfulness. There is, for instance, a shared expectation that a mood of goodhumoured bonhomie will prevail between the teams of gardening or DIY experts sent out on the make-over mission and the ordinary members of the public who become part of the make-over performance. The other important ingredient in these created-for-TV make-over formats, which in no small measure may account for their ratings success, is their strong wish-fantasy appeal. They positively invite the imaginative involvement of the viewer. What would it be like if *my* home or *my* garden were to be subject to this kind of transformation? How would I feel if *I* were to become embroiled in such a television spectacle? What pleasures would I derive from sharing the television stage with celebrity TV performers?

If part of the appeal of make-over programmes lies in their ability to engage viewers in this type of conjecturing, they have certain features in common with the 'hypothetical' programming category referred to above. At the same time they also share a number of traits with that much larger genre of 'television-meets-the-people' programming which relies on TV programme makers' ability to dream up ever more ingenious ways of entrapping ordinary members of the public in embarrassing situations, so providing a rich vein of popular TV entertainment.[4]

The classic example of the TV 'sting' genre is *Candid Camera*, but this long-running programme from the 1950s has been followed by a whole series of shows, usually fronted by a well-known TV celebrity, which are based on a similar formula. Programmes such as *Beadle's About*, *Noel's House Party* or *You've Been Framed* will usually involve the playing of a practical joke on targeted victims and enabling the audience, through strategic camera placement and explanatory commentary, to be witness to the victims' growing embarrassment and discomfiture, but also to their profound relief when, in the climactic scene, everything is revealed to have been a television prank. Following the rather crude set-ups of the early years, some of the more recent examples of the 'sting' genre have, in relative terms, become more sophisticated and necessitate quite elaborate planning operations. The series *Make My Day* (Channel 4, 2002) for instance, was again dependent on the targeting of unsuspecting victims and arranging for them to be involved in a sequence of ever more bizarre events occurring in the course of what they assumed to be just another ordinary day at their office or workplace. Setting up this exercise was, in itself, a major logistical exercise not only requiring the active collaboration of all the victim's workmates, but the discreet placement of more than fifty concealed cameras to film the target's reactions to these contrived events.

The staging of 'real-life': the example of *The Truman Show*

The point being emphasized here is that contemporary modes of the factual have become increasingly dependent on various types of set-up. This brings us back, perhaps inevitably, to Peter Weir's *The Truman Show* (1998), since this film, more than any other single text in recent times, contains a telling reflection of the lengths to which contemporary television is prepared to go to produce compelling real-life entertainment. Since the film highlights so many of the practices which today's generation of factual programme makers have adopted, particularly with regard to 'reality staging', we will explore parts of the film in a little more detail.

The film centres on the character of Truman Burbank (played by Jim Carrey) who becomes the unwitting star of a non-stop, twenty-four hours a day documentary soap opera. Everything that occurs in his life is fashioned and shaped for the requirements of real-life TV entertainment and some 5,000 surveillance cameras are on hand to record every moment of his waking and sleeping life. It soon becomes evident to the viewer, however, that all those with whom he comes into contact are merely actors playing the designated roles of friends, relatives and fellow residents of Seahaven, the purpose-built town where the action is set. The concept on which *The Truman Show* is based is that the global television audience, having become satiated with the glossy, plastic world of TV creation, has developed a craving for something that is apparently less mediated and has much greater claim to reality status. As Christof, the fictional originator of the show, suggests at one point in the film:

> We've become tired of watching actors give us phony emotions, bored with pyrotechnics and special effects. While the world he [Truman] inhabits is counterfeit, there's nothing fake about Truman himself. No scripts, no cue cards. It's not always Shakespeare but it's genuine. That's how he can support an entire channel. (Niccol, 1998: 75)

The central or guiding idea of the film is based upon the essentially monstrous proposition that television has been able to wholly appropriate a person's life for the purposes of TV entertainment. The narrative project of *The Truman Show* is thus to chart the various stages in Truman's slow recognition that he is a prisoner in this created-for-TV paradise. Truman himself, once the 'reality' of the situation has dawned, becomes ever more reluctant to play this role. A series of skilfully interpolated sequences where the cracks in this most elaborate of reality simulations begin to show through, reveal his dawning recognition that the world which he inhabits is entirely phoney and that he is the victim of a highly elaborate frame-up. Finally, in the film's dramatic climax, Truman succeeds in detaching himself from the totally controlled environment in which he has been contained for almost thirty years and escapes into the world of reality. The heavily ironic ending suggests that human beings still have it within them to resist the media's blandishments – or as Truman tersely puts it in the course of his final showdown with Christof: 'You never had a camera in my head' (Niccol, 1998: 106).

In many ways *The Truman Show* is a satirical swipe at the whole 'real-life' entertainment industry and reveals the lengths to which TV producers are prepared to go in their quest for new audience-friendly reality formats. In the film it is the character of Christof who has come up with the original concept for what would later become 'The Truman Show', a concept based upon the not entirely unfounded proposition that TV audiences will be willing to follow, breath by breath, the course of an individual's life from the cradle to the grave. Once the show had been launched, it quickly acquired a momentum of its own and Christof becomes increasingly aware of the need to create storylines which will 'keep the drama alive' (*ibid*.: xiv). This requirement to lend a helping hand in the development of compelling storylines is paralleled in the practices of certain contemporary producers, as they strive to maintain audience interest in situations which would otherwise be boring in the extreme. In the case of 'The Truman Show', prodigious efforts are needed to set up that contained environment into which the unwitting Truman is to be inserted:

> What Christof proposed to Moses (CEO of Omnicam) was unprecedented and staggering in its scope. He showed Moses plans for a new studio on a large parcel of land in Burbank, California … This Bubble or Dome was to cover an entire town. Christof had the plans adapted for what he called Seahaven. Here we would watch Truman grow to manhood, facing all the trials and tribulations we all face, but in a controlled environment. Thousands of concealed mini cameras would be built into the 'set' to cover every angle of the town, both exterior and interior … This would be nothing less than a record of a human life from birth to death, every single moment live-to-air, and would create television history. (*Ibid*.: xv)

The energy and resources required to maintain this elaborate 'real-life' fiction become the subject of much humour throughout the film; likewise the ever more desperate attempts by the show's producers to retain the services of their star performer in whom they have so much invested, especially in the latter part of the film when Truman is plotting his escape. Here again *The Truman Show* provides some ironic commentary on the employment of real-life performers in contemporary factual formats. The film not only satirizes TV's flagrant manipulation of volunteer participants, but also raises a series of ethical questions concerning invasion of privacy and the consequences for individuals of having celebrity forced upon them. While it is true that, unlike Truman, the majority of real-life performers in today's TV reality shows have given their informed consent to participate, there is plentiful evidence to suggest that many have seriously underestimated the costs of allowing the media to exploit them in this way (Hibberd et. al., 2000: 73–4). Some of them may be able to capitalize on the short-lived fame that television exposure brings them. For others, however, the experience may bring with it the more uncomfortable recognition that their lives are, in one sense, no longer their own.[5]

Though *The Truman Show* is in certain respects quite a dark film, carrying as it does Orwellian echoes of Big Brother surveillance, it is primarily lighthearted and humorous in its tone. It gently mocks the frantic efforts by the show's production team to maintain the ludicrously elaborate fiction, while at the same time concealing from Truman the 'true' state of affairs. Hints are regularly dropped in the narrative about the faked character of Truman's surroundings, beginning with the theatrical light fixture that crashes down into the street near his home and culminating with the scene in the Control Room, reminiscent of NASA's Mission Control, which reveals the huge logistical effort required to bring images of Truman to the worldwide audience. Much of the humour of the film derives, therefore, from this ridiculing of some of the more exploitative aspects of real-life television: the way in which situations are contrived and the growing requirement that subjects play out some designated role. One of the pleasures that *The Truman Show* offers *its* audience, for instance, is its carefully calibrated exposure of lapses on the part of the production team and actors hired to play the various supporting roles. Here again the film is suggestive of one of the pleasures that real-life audiences of reality programmes allegedly derive from watching these shows: the opportunities that they provide for viewers to discern where a gap opens up between simulated and authentic reality. These are the moments which some critics have described as 'flickers of authenticity', when the ability of an actor to sustain a performance falters and when elements of that individual's true persona begin to shine through (Roscoe, 2001: 13–14).

The Truman Show does not just point the finger of blame – if one can call it that – at the all-powerful media machine. It also seeks to illuminate the presumed nature of an audience's involvement in the type of reality programme on which the fictional 'Truman Show' is so clearly modelled. What the film amply demonstrates is that the power of reality television is only as strong as the readiness of the audience to become voyeuristically absorbed in the most trivial and intimate details of Truman's life. The world which he inhabits may be revealed to us (the real audience) as nothing more than an elaborate set-up, but the recurrent shots of the gawping TV audience (in bars, in workplaces and in homes) as they hang on Truman's every word, speak volumes about the nature of the collective audience response to reality television. As one commentator has observed:

> *The Truman Show* explores the relationship between the media and its audience, asking questions about the way the viewer and the viewed are simultaneously exploited and – here's the rub – are happy with such a state of affairs ... [The audience] revel in Truman's adventures, enjoying the spectacle, while expressing sympathy for his plight. It is apparent that these voyeurs perceive no ethical problem in holding both views as Truman is merely a consumer product who exists for their entertainment ... Such ironies abound in the film. Truman is world famous, but doesn't know it. People love Truman, but this love is conditional on his remaining ignorant of the truth. What keeps people watching is the possibility he might just discover what they know. (Greenslade, 1998: 5–6)

In the fictional scenario of *The Truman Show* the whole elaborate world of Seahaven has been set up with the intention of securing the attention of a worldwide audience. This is in order to enable advertisers to sell a range of goods and services which appear to be endorsed by the good Truman. The irony is, of course, that Truman himself is merely a commodified product developed to act as a consumer lure. Vast fortunes are made by the companies who, through a sophisticated system of product placement, are able to get their advertising messages across to the global consumer. When all is said and done, then, the fictional world created by 'The Truman Show' and all the 'reality staging' conducted therein, is but a pretext for the real business of shifting consumer goods.

Reality set-ups

Opinion is divided as to whether *The Truman Show* should be best regarded as 'Kafka-inspired allegory of real life' (Whitehouse, 1998: 9) or as a sustained critique of some of the practices of contemporary reality programming. Wherever one places the emphasis, the film certainly provides some telling commentary on how adept today's generation of TV programme makers have proved themselves to be at developing a variety of reality formats which can be generically grouped under the portmanteau label of 'real-life' factual entertainment. Doubtless, the film's success is also in part attributable to the audience's recognition of how accurately it satirically targets the key ingredients of today's reality formats: the contriving of situations, the contributions of real-life performers and the frequent recourse to secret filming techniques.

It is one of the particular achievements of *The Truman Show* that it so accurately describes the relationship between the audience and the television entertainment they so hungrily consume. Part of the 'message' of the film is that, as a member of the television audience tuning in to this type of reality show, you are aware of the extent to which you are being drawn in to a highly contrived, if not exploitative form of entertainment, but still retain sufficient detachment to be able to delight in the performance ability of the participating players (see Greenslade, 1998: 5–6). This ability to be simultaneously absorbed and yet to be acutely aware of the strategies being employed to secure one's involvement may, in part, explain the phenomenal success of shows like *Big Brother*, where audiences are constantly being encouraged to conjecture what new ploys might be adopted by the show's producers to add more spice to the proceedings.[6] In offering these various performance-oriented entertainments to viewers, television makes no attempt to conceal the fact that everything is an elaborate televisual contrivance. The controlling hand of television is a visible presence throughout each show; indeed one of the identifying features of the genre is the manner in which attention is sometimes drawn to some detail relating to the set-up. In *Big Brother*, for instance, the hand of control is symbolically represented by the 'Big Brother' voice of authority, an unseen agent who instructs housemates on what tasks they are to perform and to whom they are required to address their 'private' thoughts and grouses. The disembodied voice of 'Big Brother' is one of the many contrivances to reinforce the idea that we have entered a sphere where everything is aspiring to the conditions of a television performance.

A distinction must be made here, however, between the different types of set-up – or, more accurately, between the purposes which different types of reality set-up are required to serve. In the case of the game-doc reality format, the aim of the set-up is to produce a series of exchanges between – and performances from – participants which can form the basis of an extended piece of TV entertainment with pronounced voyeuristic appeal. In producing these performances, participants are under no illusion that the principal expectation of their puppet-master controllers is to let their personalities shine through and to indulge in various forms of witty, spontaneous interaction – with the aim of encouraging particularly strong forms of audience identification. While these made-for-TV shows are clearly not making any serious claims to enlarge the store of human knowledge, there are other types of reality programming which have come on stream in recent years where the set-up is linked to somewhat less trivial ends. These formats still depend on the performance ability of participants, but at the same time they reveal some overlap with more traditional forms of documentary. The programmes are, in other words, still governed by the entertainment imperative, but the subjects with which they engage have at least some relevance to the wider world of public affairs. And even though they do not treat these subjects in any great depth, the programmes in question are sufficiently issue-oriented as to provoke at least some critical reflections on the part of their audience.

Like the game-doc formats with which they share certain common features, these programmes depend for their success on a producer's ability to come up with contrived scenarios in which a group of volunteer participants act out certain roles. Just as with the game-doc, no attempt is made to hide the fact that everything the audience gets to view has been specially devised for television, though the forms of creative intervention will differ according to individual programme requirements. It is possible, however, to make a crude distinction between the type of programme in which 'real-life' individuals retain their own identities but are manoeuvred into alien environments (with a film crew in attendance to report on how they fare) and the increasingly popular category of programmes where a group of non-professionals (people like you and me) will agree to act out delegated roles, all in the interests of producing a piece of historically-inspired entertainment (see pp. 166–7). Both types of programming rely on a large measure of television assistance in setting up situations and both are sometimes promoted on the grounds that they are conducted in the manner of a sociological experiment.

Programmes in the first category of 'formatted reality' are exemplified by the series *Back to the Floor* (BBC 2, 1997–) and *Living with the Enemy* (BBC 2, 1998–). Both employ classic 'what-if?' scenarios. *Back to the Floor*, for instance, is based on the premise: What would be the outcome if someone who had 'made it' in his or her profession were to temporarily relinquish their customary role and to become an ordinary shop-floor worker for a week? Each programme in the series therefore combines the promise of dramatic entertainment (Will the boss involved in the role reversal be up to the job and will she or he experience some form of comeuppance?) with that of making a number of documentary-like revelations about life on the shop-floor and about the problems of running the organization. In the case of *Back to the Floor*, the fact that shop-floor workers are made aware of the boss's identity before filming begins means that there is not the same dramatic pay-off as if the incomer were not to be thus identified. Nevertheless the basic set-up of the series provides an opportunity for giving a dramatic spin to what would otherwise be a more sober account of working practices. That it should be the bosses themselves who are seen gaining sometimes painful insight into deficiencies or failings of their organization also gives a particular frisson to these *Back to the Floor* narratives.

The series *Living with the Enemy* is based on a similar kind of television contrivance, but this time depends on TV producers being able to persuade people with opposing views or values to spend time in each other's company. But just as *Back to the Floor* created situations in which people were required to meet challenges they would not normally confront, so *Living with the Enemy* sets its sights on extracting dramatic mileage from placing ideologically opposed people under the same roof for a trial week. *Living with the Enemy* clearly has certain features in common with those game-doc reality formats in that in both cases the protagonists/contestants are put together in a controlled environment and then set the task of achieving some modus vivendi with those with whom they are thus closeted. Though the declared aim of the *Living with the Enemy* series may resemble a sociological experiment in which people with very different views seek common ground, the principal aim of the series, of course, is to generate the requisite amount of dramatic entertainment. Thus, while some of the programmes in the series may have given insight into the values and belief systems of particular social groups, they have also provided a platform for those with a penchant for indulging in amateur dramatics.

Given the series' dramatic imperative, success is often down to the producers' skill at casting characters and setting up situations which generate lively and entertaining confrontations. In a programme transmitted in 1999, for instance, a mild-mannered Young Conservative, James Hellyer, agrees, at the instigation of the programme makers, to enter the lions' den represented in this instance by the colourful, drug-using collective Exodus. Just four days into the week-long experiment in living together, James lodged a complaint with the local police about the drug-taking activities of the group, thereby raising the dramatic tension of the programme by several degrees. In a later programme an animal rights protester goes to stay with a hunt-loving farmer, while in yet another a gay couple living in Soho agree to play host to a couple of macho rugby players from the north of England.

Each programme in the *Living with the Enemy* depends on there being an ideological gulf separating the opposing parties. It is the enormity of this gulf that provides the trigger for the dramatic exchanges which programme producers hope will ensue. There is also a recognition on the part of subjects that they are expected to tailor their performances according to the programme's needs. As one reviewer wrote revealingly at the time:

> Paul and Mark [the gay Soho couple] *slipped into the role* of sensitive, caring liberals feeling all hurt by the bullying crassness of their northern guests, whilst the latter *knew it was their job* to pile on the outrage. (Sweeting, 1998: 19, my emphasis)

The series producer of *Living with the Enemy* confirms this point about how participants adapt to the contrived situation when he writes:

> What is always surprising is that on paper there is no way they [the opposing parties] are going to get on, but in a real life situation, they have to. When they are living in someone's home, they don't react in that really dogmatic way. They sound people out, trying to work out what the areas they disagree on are going to be, and as the week progresses they attack in those directions. They don't just turn up and start arguing. (Morris, 1999: 17)

Programmes like *Living with the Enemy* therefore rely on participants' ability to enter into the generally playful and lighthearted spirit which governs these made-for-TV encounters. And for members of the audience, just as with the game-doc formats, one of the pleasures of watching these programmes is monitoring how the participants cope with the challenges that performing in such a contrived situation brings. In what ways do they seek various forms of accommodation with the enemy? Do they sometimes let their guard drop and reveal those 'flickers of authenticity' as the pressure of maintaining their 'ideological' role becomes too much for them? How successful are the programme makers at contriving situations that will generate drama? The very fact that such questions can be posed reinforces the point being made here that such exercises in 'reality formatting' all tend to be be measured by the degree of entertainment they produce rather than the insights they provide into what might have contributed to the formation of protagonists' strongly held views and what forms of social action might be needed to bridge these ideological divides.

Another programme type which has enjoyed considerable popularity since the late 1990s involves taking certain elements of the performance-oriented reality formats, but giving these a slightly more serious spin. The programming in question has sometimes been categorized as historical re-enactment, though these particular attempts to bring history to life rely on a different set of techniques to those employed in conventional drama-tized reconstructions. Thus, while series such as *The 1900 House* (Channel 4, 1999), and the two follow-up series *The 1940s House* (Channel 4, 2001) and *The Edwardian Country House* (Channel 4, 2002) all resemble drama-documentaries in that they present dramatized reconstructions of the un-recorded past, they also include a number of ingredients borrowed from contemporary reality formats. Each of the afore-mentioned programmes (and others which have been spawned by the sub-genre's popularity with viewers) operate with a similar concept. This involves gathering together a group of lay volunteers and conveying them, via the television equivalent of a time machine, to an historical location, for example to a townhouse which has been specially prepared for this particular TV exercise to repli-cate the living conditions of 1900. Such programmes are clearly seeking to capitalize on the popularity of game-doc entertainments but also base their appeal on the more serious proposition that they are trying to reproduce historically accurate scenarios which might promote better understanding of what it might have been like to live through those times. The popularity of such programmes is partly attributable to a more general nostalgia for the past, but it is their affinity with the game-doc reality formats which – possibly more than any other factor – accounts for their ratings success. Series such as *The 1900 House* and the clones which have followed it, all focus on events which, we are invited to imagine, might have taken place within a domestic, i.e. contained environment of long ago. Programmes on the other hand which have attempted to repeat this formula, but which have shifted the location away from the broadly defined domestic sphere have generally not been as well received. An example of the latter is *The Trench* (BBC 2, 2002), a four-part series which attempts to recreate the daily life of soldiers serving in the First World War. Using various types of documentary evidence, the producers of the programme simulate the type of conditions to which soldiers in the trenches would have been exposed at that time. A team of twenty-four lay volunteers, who, incidentally, had had just eleven days of army training by way of preparation, were then invited to relive the nightmare experiences which soldiers might have gone through. The problem for the series was that this type of simulation is not always sufficiently appropriate to what the series is attempting to convey. For instance, in order to reinforce the sense of authenticity, the series makes regular use of historical, eyewitness testimony. The often harrowing verbal accounts of what soldiers went through, when juxtaposed with the sequences where the lay volunteers attempt to re-enact day-to-day life in the trenches, almost inevitably draws attention to the degree to which events have been sanitized. As one of the volunteer combatants noted: 'All right, so we've stood up to the freezing cold and experienced the terrifying tedium of sentry duty. But in terms of experiencing the permanent presence of death, we've barely scratched the surface' (Middleton, 2002: 40).

Drama at any cost?

As demonstrated in the previous section, not all the programmes in the 'formatted reality' category escape the criticism that they are tilted too heavily in the direction of factual entertainment. On the other hand, most of them still retain vestiges of documentary seriousness and public service credibility in the way they encourage at least some form of critical engagement with contemporary or historical issues. The same cannot be said for another category of programmes which are also masquerading as quasi-documentary but which are clearly intent on selling themselves on account of their sensationalist appeal: the sub-genre of programmes which have mostly been commissioned by the ITV network and which contain the term ' … *from Hell*' in their titles. The suggestion to audiences is that the incidents to be featured will often include examples of deviant or extreme behaviour where individuals set out to wreak revenge on their neighbours or where, alternatively, they are seen to be the unfortunate victims of crime or acts of malice. Programmes in this 'People behaving badly' category, whether they be *Neighbours from Hell* (ITV, 1997), *Weddings from Hell* (ITV, 1998) or *Divorces from Hell* (ITV, 1998) are all intent on generating as much dramatic excitement as possible from the subjects they cover. One of their more unsavoury characteristics is that, like the more sensational talk-shows, they tend to focus on victim humiliation. Thus, while feuds between neighbours can be a serious and disturbing business for those at the centre of the disputes, the series *Neighbours from Hell* seems only concerned to pick up on the dramatic conflicts that arise from the disputes and to reduce everything to the level of a freak show. That these programmes have much in common with the freakshow is clearly signalled in producers' preoccupation with the dramatic, nicely captured in the following piece of programme listings blurb:

> All across Britain neighbours are fighting, suing and spying on each other in increasing numbers. This documentary highlights a series of both tragic and farcical feuds and draws on home video footage to illustrate the level of hostility that sometimes exists. (*Radio Times*, 14 July 1997)

When a programme claims that its very *raison d'être* is that of 'highlighting … tragic and farcical' feuds, it is clear that producers will be primarily concerned to maximize the amount of drama and voyeuristic titillation delivered by the programme. While it would be going too far to assert that everything in these shows is staged, there is evidence to suggest helpful advice is sometimes given to contributing participants as to how they can spice up their performance in accordance with the dramaturgical requirements of pacy drama. Those who agree to participate are well aware what type of performance is being sought from them, even though their appearance in such programmes frequently shows them in a dubious light, if not exposes them to public ridicule.[7]

When events are restaged for the camera in programmes of this type, considerably more liberties can be taken in the setting-up of dramatically entertaining situations. Consider, for example, the following case of a person who, together with a colleague, had agreed to make a contribution to a *Holidays from Hell* programme. The subject in question had entered the media highlight several months previously, after she and a friend had been caught up in a life-threatening avalanche incident. The event was widely reported in the press and broadcast media, and the victim had already been the subject of numerous newspaper and TV reports.[8] Approached by the producers of the *Holidays from Hell* programme, our subject was quite taken aback to discover what kind of contribution was expected of her. I quote her comments in some detail, as they show the lengths to which producers are prepared to go in restaging events:

> They [the programme makers] spent a whole day with us … They were here for a total of 8 hours. We had to dress up in ski gear and stand outside our front door and pretend to be going on holiday. We were also provoked into saying what they wanted. They engineered the programme to what they wanted. They wanted us to be quite dramatic … wanted us to cry and say what a terrible experience it was and how you felt in the avalanche: impending death and everything. They wanted us to be quite graphic about our emotions … The problem was that it had all happened two months previously, so it was very hard to get emotional about it … I was quite taken aback. I felt a bit of an idiot, 'cos I felt as though it was just churning over old ground really. They wanted you to relive the nightmare. (Interview with programme participant, October 1999, Hibberd et al., 2000)

An episode such this clearly illustrates how far some factual programme makers are prepared to go in bending reality to their own ends. Small wonder, then, that observers continue to express concern about a type of programming which often encourages and generally panders to lowest common denominator tastes (Mapplebeck, 1997a: 10–12). There is also the fear that this preoccupation with nightmare neighbours and with other manifestations of antisocial or deviant behaviour provides yet further evidence of the dumbing down that is supposedly endemic in contemporary TV.

Staging the imagined past

It should by now have become abundantly clear that the staging of events, using a variety of techniques, has played a key role in many of the recently developed factual formats. Many of these formats have depended on the audience's fascination with the performances of ordinary, but celebrity-seeking individuals. Others have involved the painstaking recreation of historical locations and encouraging audiences to share in lay performers' sometimes stumbling attempts to re-enact for an audience of today the spectral what-might-have-been sequences of an imagined past. Interconnections exist between all these different formats, as producers have sought to incorporate ingredients of already successful genres into new forms and styles of programming. That drive to produce imaginative revisitations of the past, for instance, which resulted in series such as *The 1900 House* and *The Trench*, is also discernible in another brand of factual programming which developed in the late 1990s. The programmes in question, *Walking with Dinosaurs* (BBC 1, 1999) and *Walking with Prehistoric Beasts* (BBC 1, 2001) are usually regarded as an offshoot of natural history programming, but on closer inspection can be seen to have features in common with other forms of factual entertainment.[9]

Both series (and ones which will doubtless supersede them) are of interest for our present concerns as they employ some of the most extensive and elaborate forms of staging that we have encountered in any type of factual programming hitherto. This time the creative intervention involves a major technical tour de force on the part of the production team in that they have attempted – largely by the use of cutting-edge computer animation – to recreate the sights, sounds and above all creatures of the Jurassic Age. The success of both series is thus dependent on the public's continuing fascination with these great lumbering beasts which once roamed the earth, but equally on producers' skill in dressing up these natural history lessons in the kind of garb which has made them compulsive viewing for large TV audiences. Using other terms of reference, the *Walking with ...* series combine the enlightening aspirations of natural history documentaries with the more visceral attractions (simulated encounters with prehistoric beasts) of action-packed drama. The *Walking with ...* programmes thus base their appeal on two potentially very powerful audience-engaging devices: first, the promise of gaining insight into the dinosaur world (on the basis of painstaking examination of fossil remains, DNA testing etc.) and second, the lure of being conveyed into the living presence of creatures which have for so long have had such a powerful hold on the collective imagination. The re-enactment sequences make extensive use of computer-generated images but are also dependent on the more recently developed techniques of animatronics which ensure that dinosaurs are brought to life in such a way that the illusion of a real-life encounter is created.

Like other styles and types of factual programming examined in this book, the *Walking with …* series can also be viewed as part of broadcasters' attempt to popularize factual/documentary output in order to maximize its appeal. *Walking with Dinosaurs* (which cost £6 million and took three years to make) was built up to be a ground-breaking media event and the series was very heavily promoted. An hour-long 'how-we-did-it' documentary *The Making of Walking with Dinosaurs* was also aired immediately before the screening of the first episode, detailing how some of the special effects had been achieved. Beside exhibiting some of the self-congratulatory traits usually found in this type of appetite-whetting 'behind-the-scenes' programme, this particular 'making of' account illustrates some of the difficulties that producers encounter when they attempt to reconcile the instructional aspirations of serious documentary with the need to produce an action-packed piece of dramatically enthralling entertainment. As one critic has observed:

> The behind-the-scenes information and visuals from the 'making of' program, with its narrative of technology mixed with art and science, situated 'construction' as a spectacle in its own right, giving visual evidence of construction to viewers eager to understand how such realistic constructions were possible. (Richards, 2001: 74)

For all the promotional hype about the ground-breaking qualities of the series *Walking with Dinosaurs* and despite the fact that it succeeded in delivering very high ratings (thirteen million viewers), *Walking with Dinosaurs* is remarkable not so much for what distinguishes it from other contemporary formats, as for what it shares with them. First and foremost there is the strong performance orientation of the series. No pains are spared in creating the illusion that viewers are being magically transplanted into the living presence of prehistoric beasts, where the drama is played out as if it were occurring in the here and now. Imagined events from the lost, unrecorded world of the dinosaurs, especially ones involving spectacular confrontations or acts of predation, are (re)enacted in such a way as to enhance their dramatic appeal. The idea of staging is thus central to the whole concept of the *Walking with …* series. This is also evident in the way that viewers are actively positioned as if they were living witnesses of an ongoing drama. The flow of the narrative is not characterized by that traditional documentary to-ing and fro-ing between the present of the truth-seeking documentarist and the past of the historical subject under investigation (here dinosaurs). It takes the form, rather, of a sustained dramatic simulation of *imagined* dinosaur activity and behaviour. This emphasis on the dramatic puts *Walking with Dinosaurs* and its successor(s) in the same league as Spielberg's film *Jurassic Park* (1993). Both offer, through the medium of advanced computer technology, the illusion of direct access to the dinosaur world. And just as the diegesis of *Jurassic Park* conveys a powerful sense of presence in an alien world, so too *Walking with Dinosaurs* creates the illusion that we are on some kind of prehistoric safari. This illusion is reinforced by the voice-over commentary, spoken by Kenneth Branagh, which provides a running commentary on events. The mating, feeding and hunting activities of dinosaurs are reported on as if they were happening in the here and now, rather than being more pointedly contextualised within their historical framework.

The need to create a strong sense of immediacy is already signalled in the title of the series and is a clear sign of the entertainment imperative which is virtually omnipresent in all forms of contemporary factual programming. This immediacy is, however, only bought at a certain cost. For while the producers of *Walking with Dinosaurs* have undeniably succeeded in creating some visually dramatic sequences, doubts remain as to whether these presentational and storytelling techniques are wholly appropriate to what is being depicted. Several critics, for instance, have taken exception to the accompanying commentary which at times seems so at variance with the spectacular visual drama being enacted as to create an unintentional humorous effect. Other observers have been more concerned that the producers, in choosing a format intended to create the maximum visceral impact, had 'missed an opportunity to produce a world-class science programme and had gone for the softer option of making a dinosaur soap opera instead' (Barrett, 1999: 8). These remarks, coming as they do from a scientist who had worked as an adviser on the *Walking with Dinosaurs* series, are worthy of closer examination, especially as they alert us to some of the problems that programme makers encounter when they attempt to restage events on the basis of relatively slim evidence, especially when there are pressures to maximize the entertainment appeal of a series which claims to be scientifically rigorous. The truth is, of course, that these dual aims are not wholly compatible. The desire to produce an educationally enlightening series can sometimes be undermined by an overly dramatic narrative. Thus, while Dr Barrett is suitably impressed by the 'way in which the disparate pieces of information gathered by paleontologists have been worked together to attempt an impression of the dynamics of a living ecosystem', he is positively hostile to those elements of the series which push it inexorably in the direction of dramatic entertainment. He laments the requirement for a 'continual narrative – an unbroken story that leaves little room for discussion or qualification' and concludes that "it is impossible for the viewer to decide whether they are witnessing something that is considered to be likely, possible, merely hypothetical or just plain wrong (*ibid.*, 1999: 8).

Some of the points raised in these remarks take us back to the debate about fakery and related issues raised in Chapter 5. The suggestion here is not that producers of the *Walking with ...* series are guilty of hoodwinking the public, but that the attempt to produce these entertainment-oriented accounts may prove counterproductive in that at least some viewers may feel that their intelligence is being underestimated, or even insulted, if they sense they are being cajoled into believing that the account given is claiming the status of scientific fact when it is actually far more speculative in character. In other words, viewers may well prefer to apply their own frames of reference in drawing conclusions about dinosaur behaviour on the strength of evidence supplied. At least some in the audience may have favoured an approach which made the evidence available and then allowed viewers themselves to undertake the necessary imaginative work. As Dr Barrett concedes, however, mainstream television has always had a problem in dealing with that which is the subject of speculation or conjecture. As we have repeatedly seen, the economics of contemporary broadcasting place such a high premium on accessibility that producers will always be under heavy pressure to come up with scenarios that are visually and dramatically enthralling. Blockbuster series have, by definition, to be big and bold, but this boldness always comes at a certain cost.[10] The entertainment potential of the *Walking with ...* programmes is unquestioned, as the ratings prove, but it is far more difficult to make the case for their documentary aspirations. As Dr Barrett himself, rather plaintively, concludes:

> The BBC spent a huge amount of time and money on *Walking with Dinosaurs* and consulted a large number of paleontologists to obtain the most up-to-date information. Given this huge body of expertise, wouldn't it have made more sense to take these diverse opinions, drop the pseudo wildlife

programme approach, and produce a factual series more akin to the excellent BBC productions *Earth Story* and *The Planets*? (*ibid.*)

Construction and deconstruction

For all the doubts cast upon certain aspects of the series *Walking with Dinosaurs* and *Walking with Prehistoric Beasts*, it has been generally acknowledged that they bear eloquent testimony to the technical and creative ingenuity of highly-skilled programme makers. It is these same skills which are amply lauded in much of the publicity which preceded the launch of the series. Getting a programme talked about and generating pre-launch excitement is the aim of any good publicist, but in the case of *Walking with Dinosaurs*, there was a risk that revealing how everything had been contrived was potentially a double-edged sword. While giving the audience some information about how, say, the animatronic techniques developed to bring dinosaurs to life, might be appetite-whetting, showing too much about the staging and filming techniques might have been counterproductive. Just as magicians usually refuse to show how tricks are done, so too programme makers will normally be wary about revealing too much about how certain effects had been achieved. With *Walking with Dinosaurs*, there was a clearly a worry that too much information about the workings of the dinosaur models and of the whole staging operation could detract form the visceral impact of the 'dinofest' experience (Lawson, 1999: 17).

Giving the audience insight into how a text is made can, on the other hand, be viewed as a strategic move on the part of the programme maker to enable viewers to read the text with a greater measure of detachment and, potentially, reach a deeper level of understanding of what the text is seeking to convey. Questions relating to how much of what goes into the making of a documentary should be shared with the audience are part of a much wider debate, which in some ways goes to the heart of the documentary enterprise. In Chapter 5 we have commented on the misunderstandings and problems which can arise when that which is contrived or fabricated is not adequately labelled as such, or where the 'reality status' of a particular sequence is not signalled clearly enough. The 1990s, however, have seen an increasing number of examples in which programme makers have delighted in talking about the 'constructedness' of their products or about how they have resorted to a whole series of artful techniques in putting together these accounts of the real. Some critics have taken this preoccupation with the constructedness of texts and this desire to establish a more knowing relationship with the viewer as symptomatic of a postmodernist stance, while others have been more concerned to emphasize that it is part of a deliberate attempt to refresh the language of documentary by exposing the conventionalized character of traditional forms of documentary address.

Drawing attention to how documentarists put reality together, especially to the way in which events are staged for the camera, is a favoured strategy of those who wish to challenge or stimulate viewers into more critical and reflective engagement with the text. A good illustration of this is provided by the work of Nick Barker who in heavily stylized series such as *Signs of the Times* (1992) and *Unmade Beds* (1997) deliberately sets out to unsettle his audience and provoke them into adopting a more questioning attitude to more 'mainstream' modes of documentary expression (Bruzzi, 2000: 155–63). As viewers contemplate the staring faces and statuesque poses of subjects in *Signs of the Times*, for instance, Barker is clearly hoping that they will recognize that this is a revelatory upstaging of the traditional mode of documentary address: presenting subjects articulating thoughts on camera (the talking head) or allowing thoughts to be be communicated to us via a voice-over device while the subject is seen engaging in some activity not necessarily connected with the topic being discussed. While some would argue that Barker's work has brought a much needed breath of fresh air to documentary discourse, one has to say that – in the current highly commercialized broadcasting environment – opportunities for this type of innovative, thought-provoking and heavily stylized work remain severely limited. In the eyes of television executives, attempting to provoke the audience into new ways of seeing by such provocative means is regarded as a highly risky strategy.

The mockumentary impulse

Within today's ever more ratings-conscious television environment one of the most common ways of encouraging a reflective and critical response on the part of the audience has been through the various types of spoof, parody and pastiche. These have become a noticeable feature of the factual landscape in recent years and have become the subject of extensive critical examination (Roscoe & Hight, 2001). The parodying of specific documentary programme-making techniques has now advanced, however, to the point at which a distinct volume of work has emerged which constitutes a separate sub-category, to which the label 'mockumentary' is sometimes attached. Just as with other parodic or satirical practices in art or literature, mockumentaries poke fun at the strategies customarily employed by documentary makers to attract and hold the attention of viewers. It goes without saying that, for their parodic offerings to have the desired effect, mockumentarists rely on a reasonable level of audience familiarity with the sets of conventions employed in documentary. In a media-saturated age, with individuals constantly exposed to the burden of information overload, it might be claimed that some form of parodic activity is a healthy and wholly justified response (if for no other reason than it draws attention to the huge efforts invested in buying audience attention).

It could also be argued that the outpouring of mockumentary or spoof-like material is attributable in no small measure to the wildfire proliferation of factual/reality formats in recent years, which has in turn led to audiences becoming overly familiar, or ultimately just plain bored with, what they are being offered. From the programme maker's or documentary institution's point of view, the scheduling of the occasional spoof or mockumentary has an important additional function. Not only does it acknowledge that audiences gain pleasure from the act of parodying in itself (the humorous recognition that particular formal means are being used to elicit a particular effect); it is also tantamount to an acknowledgement that broadcasters may well have taxed the viewers' patience by overexposing them to particular TV formats. Viewed from this perspective, the inclusion of the occasional mockumentary in a broadcaster's schedule might almost be seen as an attempt to re-establish good faith with the audience. Viewers are credited with having sufficient insight, knowledge and awareness to share and delight in the various types of debunking being attempted. Thus, in addition to doing duty as an entertainment vehicle, mockumentaries can help restore to viewers a sense of their own viewing competence, in that one of the promised pleasures is being able to recognize the conventions that are being satirically targeted.

All films and programmes belonging to the broad mockumentary category have that much in common in that they alert us to at least some of the ways in which reality has been staged. In this respect they are clearly related to that larger body of documentary work to which the label 'reflexive' is sometimes attached (Kilborn & Izod, 1997: 75–80; Nichols, 1991: 56–75; Renov, 1993: 135–50). Reflexive documentary has as one of its goals the desire to expose some of the techniques by which documentary achieves some of its characteristic effects and to question some of the claims that have traditionally been made for the genre, especially the idea that observational documentaries could attain a high level of transparency. Reflexive documentaries therefore subject their own formal qualities to scrutiny and reflect upon the processes by which material has been gathered and shaped according to conventionalized programme-making practices. Above all they challenge or provoke an audience into reconsidering sets of relations which they hitherto may have taken for granted. As Nichols has noted:

> In its most paradigmatic form the reflexive documentary prompts the viewer to a heightened consciousness of his or her relations to the text and of the text's problematic relationship to that which it represents. (Nichols, 1991: 60)

One of the key features of reflexive documentary in general and of mockumentary work in particular is the frequency with which producers resort to various types of irony and parody in their attempt to expose how the targeted category of programming works on its respective audience. It might in this respect be argued that, in the case of documentary, there were stronger grounds for attempting this kind of exposure given documentary's claim to be revealing allegedly important truths, while often concealing the degree of manipulation being practised.

In examining the role played by mockumentary work in contemporary factual programming, an important distinction needs to be made between work which is destined for consumption by a television audience and documentarists who are primarily targeting a cinema audience. In other words: While there will, in practice, be considerable overlap in the parodic techniques employed by TV programme makers and independent film producers, those who receive commissions primarily from television will not have the same expressive freedom in terms of the subjects they treat and the techniques they employ. This is not to suggest that producers of factual/documentary programming for television are less capable of satirical or critical reflections on their working practices. It is simply that the work they produce has to compete for a place in the schedule with many other types of programming material. For this reason, limits are set as to the extent to which they can be seen to be problematizing the relationship between text and audience.

In a more media literate age, audiences have developed a generally more sceptical attitude to what they see and hear on their television screens. Programme makers have, accordingly, been keen to develop new ways of speaking to their audience which acknowledge this greater degree of viewer knowledge and awareness. This may not always take the form of a 'full-blown' reflexive or satirical work which may prove to be inimical to television's primary task of keeping an audience on board (see Corner, 1996: 24–6). There are, however, a number of other ways in which audiences can be reminded that broadcasting is, among other things, about the delicate management of a relationship between producers of texts and those who feel that tuning in to these same texts may bring them certain rewards. Television's primary commitment may be that of continuing to churn out entertainment-oriented material for consumption by a mass audience, but there still has to be some recognition that television – in maintaining the all-important relationship with its viewers – can afford to be occasionally self-deprecating and even at times ironically detached.

The gently mocking finger

Over the years television, especially in the UK, has developed a number of different ways of gently poking fun at itself. This may be done out of the recognition that it was sometimes wont to take itself too seriously. It may also reflect a collective acknowledgement on the part of producers that the medium itself, especially during the period when it was dominated by public service ideals, was on occasions guilty of being patronizing or condescending to its audience. The introduction of material which gently chided the medium (or more accurately the programme makers) for these shortcomings was not only calculated to reveal a degree of self-critical awareness, it was also a way of maintaining good faith with the audience.

Given the great diversity of programming which has emerged in television's short history and the zeal with which broadcasters have sought to court the public's attention, there has been no shortage of targets at which satirical barbs can be aimed. In the annals of British broadcasting, the late-night satire show *That Was the Week That Was* (BBC, 1962–63) provides an early example of a programme that succeeded in pricking the pomposity of public figures, but also was delightfully irreverent about the medium itself, especially that tendency to take itself far too seriously. In those early days of television, spoofs that mocked the sobriety of current affairs and documentary presentations were also not unknown. A 1960s edition of BBC *Panorama*, for instance, featured an item in which Richard Dimbleby, *the* authoritative voice of current affairs broadcasting at the time, was seen, against a suitably rural backdrop, discoursing seriously and soberly on the prospects for the Italian spaghetti harvest that year. Only slowly did it dawn on viewers that the date of transmission (1 April) might throw some doubt on the veracity of the account. Since this time British television has continued to be mildly irreverent about its own activities and to poke fun at some of the excesses in which it is wont to indulge. It is, in this respect, not without significance that some of the programmes which satirize the medium have become more firmly lodged in the collective memory than the objects of their ridicule. The series *Not the Nine O'Clock News* (BBC, 1978–82), for instance, acquired the status of a cultural icon by gently parodying styles and techniques of current affairs and documentary discourse (Strinati & Wagg, 1992: 275–6).

The 1980s and 1990s have, however, seen a quantum leap in this mildly subversive activity. In the field of television drama, for instance, the American series *Moonlighting* and *thirtysomething*, with their visual playfulness and their strategies for narrative subversion, both point to a far more knowing relationship with the audience than had been the case with TV drama up to that point. Some of the same tendencies are discernible in certain categories of factual/documentary programming produced in the 1990s, so this section will examine how and to what ends, these forms of subversion are practised. As illustrated throughout this chapter, there has been a general leaning towards 'reality staging' in many of the recently developed factual formats. Attention is drawn to the setting-up of situations, to the rules which govern participants' involvement and, quite frequently, to the unseriousness of the whole exercise. There is, in other words, no attempt to conceal the fact that this is principally a televisual reality that is being projected. Viewers are, for their part, encouraged to be dubious about certain aspects of the account(s) being rendered and not necessarily to take everything at face value. The BBC docu-soap *The Matchmaker* (BBC 1, 1999) provides a good example of this. The series takes as its subject an exclusive dating agency in the south of England and this organization's efforts to secure suitable partners for its clients. In certain respects the series falls in line with standard docu-soap expectations. Characters are encouraged to indulge in deliberately over-the-top performances. Storylines are neatly interwoven to create the necessary pace and variety. Nevertheless there are some significant deviations from standard docu-soap practice. There is a gentle all-pervading irony in the series and viewers get a strong sense that many of the featured meetings and events have been specially contrived. In addition, rather than rely on the standard docu-soap device of the unseen, all-knowing narrator, *The Matchmaker* allows Alun Jenkins, the eponymous head of the dating agency, to provide his own often heavily ironic narration. This deliberate subversion of a particular generic convention brings a double benefit: firstly it provides an amusing tongue-in-cheek commentary on the 'showman' function of the narrator in other docu-soap productions and secondly, it allows the producers of the series to develop the matchmaker character as a lynchpin star of the show. In particular, it enables the programme makers to generate a good deal of humour by pointing up the lamentable gulf between his personal and professional aspirations and his actual achievements in the dating field.

Though *The Matchmaker* exaggerates, if not parodies various aspects of the docu-soap, it still retains a sufficient number of generic features to allow it to be recognized as belonging to the docu-soap genre and to be promoted as a docu-soap production. There is, on the other hand, a growing body of TV programming which more openly parodies the factual formats which have leapt to prominence in recent years. Whether one classifies this material as 'spoof' or 'mockumentary' is possibly of secondary importance. The key questions are: What light do programmes of this type throw on the operations of television in an image-dominated culture and also what do they tell us about programme makers' perception of the likely responses of the intended audience?

Various attempts have been made to explain the proliferation of spoofs, parodies and mockumentaries in recent years. The most frequently cited explanations are, first, it reflects the distinctively postmodernist aspiration to reveal the extent to which conventional discourses shape and control what is communicated; second, it represents an acknowledgement by broadcasters that audiences are likely to experience 'viewer fatigue' after heavy exposure to particular factual forms (especially the heavily promoted reality formats which have shot to prominence in recent years); and finally, it contains a recognition that the very earnestness, which has become an endemic feature of certain forms of documentary/factual programming, positively invites a satirical or parodic response.

Television has, as already suggested, devised various ways of reflecting critically on its own operations. Comedy shows will frequently feature sketches where television celebrities and personalities are the target of satirical jibes or where features of well-known TV genres are exposed to gentle ridicule. In the context of UK television in recent years, certain figures have become virtually synonymous with this kind of deflating or subversive activity. Chris Morris, for instance, has established a reputation for himself as a humorist par excellence, specializing in sometimes highly original satirical attacks on journalistic and broadcasting practices. His radio series *On the Hour* (BBC, 1991–92) and its television successor *The Day Today* (BBC 1, 1994) parodied and caricatured the activities of news and current affairs broadcasters by playing up the gulf between the earnestness of their address and the frequently banal content of the actual message. Morris's Channel 4 series *Brass Eye* (1999–2000) continued in this vein and was likewise concerned with lampooning broadcasting conventions and with humiliating the politicians and showbusiness folk who rely on the oxygen of publicity that the medium provides.[11]

While Morris has been wideranging in his satirical attack on broadcasting and its representatives, others have been more concerned to home in on the factual/reality formats which have, of late, become such a prominent feature of the television landscape. The six-part series *That Peter Kay Thing* (Channel 4, 2000) for instance, was a programme which, among other things, gently mocked the ubiquitous docu-soap, in particular the latter's obsessive concern with transforming participants into larger-than-life characters expected to deliver a suitably tailored performance. Actor/comedian Peter Kay turns this particular generic requirement to his own advantage by delivering a virtuoso acting performance in which he takes on fifteen different roles, with each character as quirky as the next. The parodic intentions are further reinforced by the producers' decision to employ Andrew Sachs as the programme's narrator. Sachs's voice was already familiar to viewers as narrator of such classic docu-soaps as *Hotel* and as the actor who played the Spanish waiter Manuel in *Fawlty Towers*. In *That Peter Kay Thing* the gulf between the serious docu-soap-like commentary provided by Sachs and the often hilarious or bizarre events being enacted on screen is an additional pointer to the humorous, spoofing intentions of the series.

Another instance of spoofing being used to good effect is provided by *We Are History* (BBC 2, 2001) a series of ten-minute spoof history documentaries slotted into the schedule immediately following *Battlefields* (BBC 2, 2001) a serious documentary investigation of battles in the Second World War. Each programme in the *We Are History* series parodies some aspect of TV historians' attempts to bring history to life for the viewer. A particular butt for the programme's satirical sniping is TV's fondness for reconstructions of historical events. The *We Are History* series also raises important questions about the nature of historical evidence, especially in those sequences where the presenter comes up with readings of key moments in history which are delightfully at variance with traditional interpretations. While series such as *We Are History* are primarily satirizing the studied intensity and passionate conviction with which TV historians address their audience, other programmes set out to provide what might be seen as a more thoroughgoing exposure of the documentary form. The series *People Like Us* (BBC 2, 1999, 2000) for instance, could be regarded as a sustained critique of the character-centred reality formats which have proliferated since the early 1990s.

Each programme in the *People Like Us* series focuses on the attempts of a less than competent documentary investigator (wonderfully played by Chris Langham) to provide a probing, behind-the-scenes account of a particular occupation or profession. It soon becomes apparent, however, that everything is a front for an extended parodic demolition of the styles and practices traditionally associated with observational documentary. The figure of the documentary investigator, usually so articulate and self-assured, is here transformed into a bumbling incompetent (echoes here of Michael Moore's *Roger and Me*). Rather than slipping into the role of unobtrusive, mediating agent, Mallard, the investigator, invariably becomes involved in the events, sometimes with amusingly disastrous consequences. Likewise, rather than winning the confidence of his interview partners and putting them at their ease, Mallard will frequently antagonize them.[12]

By the same token, *People Like Us* deliberately subverts the visual style and filming techniques employed by those working in the observational mode. Camera wobble to convey 'authentic reality' and the exaggerated use of the zoom to signal 'a deeply emotional moment' are just some of the techniques which are mildly pilloried in this series. Perhaps the favourite target for parodic critique in *People Like Us*, however, relates to styles of narration practised in contemporary factual/documentary formats. The voice-over, for instance, is a long-established narrational device for providing contextual information and guidance as to where events are taking place (especially in docu-soaps where the viewer is constantly being switched backwards and forwards between different storylines). In *People Like Us* all these narrational conventions are wickedly subverted. Mallard's persona as a hopelessly incompetent investigator – established via his embarrassingly naive questions and his wholly inappropriate responses and interruptions – is reinforced by the pedantic, circumlocutory commentary which accompanies the on-screen events. While this narrational excess is in itself a source of considerable humour in its own right, it also acts as an effective reminder of the role played by commentary in many other forms of documentary, where it plays a vital role in securing and maintaining viewer interest and involvement.

Just as with any other form of parody, *People Like Us* presupposes a reasonable level of viewer familiarity with the conventions of the targeted genre. One might even claim that the pleasures of watching such series are commensurate with the viewers' knowledge of the working methods of documentarists and of the language of documentary. As observed in Chapter 3, one of the required skills of today's generation of programme makers is the ability to coax a compelling performance out of those who are persuaded to participate. One of the achievements of a programme like *People Like Us* – and of others which employ similar parodying techniques – is that they effectively deconstruct these popular formats. It is thus a *knowing* laughter which is generated. Audiences are still entertained, but are at the same time being invited to consider some of the more serious implications of television's ever growing intrusiveness, together with the media's compulsive need to make performers out of people. The point to make here is that the TV programmes which display parodic intentions are not just subverting the styles and techniques employed in documentary/factual discourse. They are also, in some measure, imitating these same constructional and narrational techniques in order to realize their own entertainment potential.[13]

Conclusion

The desire to maximize entertainment potential is the point to which one inevitably returns in any discussion of the changing factual landscape. Some opportunities remain for the development of innovative and even mould-breaking work and certain programme makers have succeeded in coming up with formats which have breathed new life into the genre. The major investment, however, both in terms of creative energies and material resources, has been in attempts to devise reality formats with wide popular appeal. In the public mind, therefore, 'reality' becomes more and more equated with a phenomenon closely associated with the idea of performance. 'Reality' becomes increasingly something that is staged by groups of semi-professionalized lay-performers for the entertainment requirements of consumers. Just as in their consumption of soap opera, those who hungrily devour this commodified, staged reality may retain an awareness of how things are contrived and set up for their benefit. But also, just as with the debatable claim that soap opera can engage with important real-life issues, so with many of the factual formats we have been examining, their ability to be revealing about the world and its affairs seems increasingly compromised by the entertainment needs they are required to fulfil.

Notes

1 Documentary makers also often speak of the need to 'cast' a documentary.
2 One of the best known examples of the hypothetical documentary is Peter Watkins' powerful and harrowing film *The War Game* (1965) which considers what – on the strength of all the known evidence – would the likely effects be of a nuclear attack on a British city. (See also remarks in Conclusion, pp. 196–7 on two other 'hypothetical' drama-docs *Smallpox 2002* (2002) and *Gas Attack* (2001).)
3 Some of the better known UK examples of this popular sub-genre are *Changing Rooms* (BBC 1), where homes are transformed, *Ground Force* (BBC 1), where gardens are tamed and refashioned and *Location, Location, Location* (Channel 4) where the focus is on property upgrading.
4 Entrapment of this kind has now become so routine that it can be probably described as a sub-genre in its own right.
5 A particularly significant detail in *The Truman Show* is that Christof, the arch manipulator and exploiter, is someone who jealously guards his own privacy.
6 In many ways television operates hand in hand with the tabloid press in promoting these programmes. Broadcasters use the press as a valuable publicity tool and are happy to feed journalists with inside stories about participants. The press, for its part, is happy to feed off the public's continuing fascination with these shows.
7 Likewise they are aware of the kind of amateur video footage that producers are looking for to provide documentary evidence of the various crimes and misdemeanours being committed by those with whom they are in conflict.
8 The 'circulation' of subjects round different types of TV programme is an increasingly

common phenomenon. Recent research (Hibberd et al., 2000: 8) has discovered that almost 50 per cent of participants in factual/documentary programmes have already appeared in one or more television programme.

9   Some observers regarded the series *Walking with Dinosaurs* (BBC 1, 1999) as part of the BBC's attempt to win back the public service high ground by bolstering its natural history output, after the Corporation had suffered adverse criticism in the previous three years or so for the alleged dumbing down of its programming.

10   There is a distinct irony in the fact that a blockbuster series such as *Walking with Dinosaurs*, which tells the story of the rise of a species soon to be rendered extinct, draws attention to the sad dearth of documentary accounts addressing important contemporary natural history issues such as environmental protection and animal conservation.

11   One of the more controversial aspects of the 1999 series was the way in which Morris inveigled politicians and showbusiness personalities into participating in this show, in the mistaken belief that they were contributing to a programme concerned with exploring serious issues.

12   Part of the programme's tease is that we hardly ever encounter Mallard as a fully-framed figure. His bumbling presence is, however, occasionally signalled through brief fragmented shots of an arm or a leg intruding into the frame as he fights the losing battle to assert his authority.

13   The extent to which ironic and parodic playfulness have come to pervade the new broadcasting ecology is further evidenced by the popularity of work produced by and/or featuring such talented performers as Steve Coogan (*Knowing Me, Knowing You with Alan Partridge* (BBC, Radio 4, 1993)) and Ricky Gervais (*The Office* (BBC2, 2000)).

Conclusion

When surveying the broad range of TV programme output since the late 1980s, few would disagree that one of the more striking features has been the growth in the number of popular reality formats. Some have taken this as indicative of a general qualitative decline, as broadcasters became more and more subject to the pull of commercializing forces. Others have viewed developments in a more optimistic light, refusing to join in what appears to be a ritual lament about declining standards and focusing more on the new energies that have been released as broadcasters have had to vigorously compete for viewer attention in a period of rapid change. Peter Bazalgette, creative director of Endemol UK (the company responsible for *Big Brother*), has in recent times emerged as the spokesperson of those who take the latter view. In his 2001 Hugh Wheldon Memorial Lecture (organized by the Royal Television Society) he sought to quash the myth that there had ever been a Golden Age of television and drew listeners' attention to the diversity and inventiveness of much contemporary TV programming. Summarizing the points raised in his lecture, Bazalgette concludes:

> Television is still relatively young and until the 90s it was stuck with a number of constraining genres such as light entertainment, documentary and game shows. In the past decade these have been thrown up in the air by European producers. So much so, in fact, that American TV – long the world leader – now looks to us for new ideas...We should not be complacent about British television. But I do believe we should blast the trumpet against the Golden Ageists. In terms of choice, quality, inventiveness and investment viewers are better served now than ever. (Bazalgette, 2001: 11)

While it is easy to spot in these words the attempt by an industry insider to defend television against charges of dumbing down, Bazalgette's remarks do at least alert us to what has to be taken into account when producing a balanced assessment of recent developments in factual programming. The hybridizing impulse ('Throwing constraining genres up in the air' in

Bazalgette's phrase) can certainly be seen to have had an energizing impact. Likewise, for all critics' dark mutterings about constant cloning and recycling, viewers do nowadays have access to a much wider range of factual/documentary material than at any other time in broadcasting history – much of it made available by specialist channels who, besides generating new programme material, have become adept at raiding the broadcasting archives to discover 'forgotten' documentary treasures (Richardson & Meinhof, 199: 10–12).

What Bazalgette, in his upbeat assessment of what he calls the 'new Golden Age of television', neglects to emphasize, however, is that almost all these developments – including those in factual TV programming – have been broadcaster-led. Programme *makers* have, for the most part found themselves, to an increasing degree, in the position of *product providers*, producing work to the specifications of the major broadcasters. This is not to deny that some new life has been breathed into the factual domain as a result of the demands for more 'audience-friendly' types of material (Roscoe, 2001: 18). This new, commercialized broadcasting environment has meant, however, that the number of programmes which could be defined as 'documentary' (using Griersonian criteria) are diminishing and are being superseded by styles and categories of programming which exhibit far more 'portmanteau' qualities. The new formats have, in no small number of cases, been developed in direct response to the demand of broadcasters for particular types of material which could be accommodated in designated parts of the schedule.

The development of the new factual formats has resulted, at least in part, from the desire to seek new ways of connecting with the viewer. Sometimes, as with *Big Brother* and *Pop Idols*, a key element in the concept has been the attempt to involve the audience, via various interactive means, in a series of 'media-steered' events. Programmes such as these also raise important questions about the nature of 'mediated interaction' (Corner, 1999: 13; Thompson, 1995: 81–118) and the role played by the contemporary media (especially television) in reflecting, and contributing to our changing notions of what is 'public' and what is 'private'. What conclusions, for instance, are we to draw from the fact that millions of viewers are able to become so enthralled by the televised game-playing activities of a group of celebrity-hungry individuals? Why does so much kudos seem to be attached to being selected to appear in such high-profile events, where one is effectively sacrificing one's privacy in exchange for what is often a very brief, though intense period of media exposure? And what is it that viewers get out of participating vicariously in such events?

Attempting to answer these questions raises, in turn, a number of important issues relating to popular culture and the role of the media as a potentially socially progressive, democratizing force or as a tool which serves largely consumerist ends. The popularizing imperative which we have seen in operation in the majority of the new reality formats: the high premium placed on entertainment and the preoccupation with 'real-life ordinariness' ('*The Simpsons*, but for real' (Selway, 1993: 67)) has certainly proved to be a winning formula as far as gaining the attention of viewers is concerned. It has also encouraged and fostered in audiences forms of sensitive engagement where viewers will be very alert to the manner in which they are being addressed and be highly critical (even be prepared to switch to another channel) if they sense that programmes are becoming overly formulaic or are simply cloned versions of a show which has achieved high ratings on another channel. This idea of 'viewer competence' (the suggestion that audiences develop a level of generic awareness about programming material offered for their consumption) provides a useful critical tool for gaining insight into how texts are both produced and received by the audiences at which they are aimed.

Conversationalism

The increasing slippage (or should it be overlap?) between the private, more intimate spheres of human experience and the more public world of television is a phenomenon that has almost become an identifying feature of contemporary media discourse. Entertainment is also merging increasingly with information, and where issues of more public import are addressed, high priority is given to what one might call the 'accessibility factor'. Norman Fairclough, in his highly instructive analysis of media discourse and today's broadcasting practices remarks on the 'tendency of public affairs media (news, documentary, magazine programmes, dealing with politics, social affairs, science, and so forth) to become increasingly *conversationalised*' (Fairclough, 1995: 10). Conversationalisation – the tones, colourings and intonational patterns of ordinary conversational exchange – thus becomes not just a structuring component of all the entertainment-oriented reality formats; it has begun to colonize other areas of programming (including 'serious' documentary) which now also have to measure up to the new accessibility criteria. In one respect, of course, it is highly laudable to employ a discursive register which promotes understanding of sometimes difficult issues. On the other hand there is clearly a connection between conversationalism and the adoption of a more consumerist approach towards the audience. As Fairclough observes:

> [The] increasing construction of audiences as consumers and the increasing pressure on producers to entertain can be seen as part of a normalization and naturalization of consumer behaviour and the representation of people across the whole range of programmes (quiz shows, soap operas, sport, drama, news, and so forth) ... Also, because marketization undermines the media as a public sphere, there is a diversion of attention and energy from political and social issues which helps to insulate existing relations of power and domination from serious challenge – people are constructed as spectators of events rather than participating citizens. (*Ibid.*: 12–13)

This line of argument suggests considerable pessimism with regard to what others see as the democratizing potential of the new media order. So deeply have the broadcast media become embedded in existing power structures that even when it might *appear* that ordinary people are being given a voice, closer inspection reveals that their participation is severely constrained. Any talk about democratizing potential has, therefore, to be accompanied by the recognition that the broadcaster is still effectively calling all the shots.

The confessional impulse

Much the same can be said with respect to the confessional discourse which has become such a characteristic feature of contemporary media output (whether in the form of talk-show revelations, of intimate exchanges between game-doc performers or the sometimes startling disclosures made by docu-soap participants). Clearly, the readiness of individuals to air publicly what moves, disturbs or elates them might be taken to reflect a significant, and largely healthy shift in attitude within the wider society concerning what areas of human experience can be openly talked about. Above all, it signals the overcoming of old taboos. On the other hand, as some of the more extreme examples of TV talk-shows have taught us, this openness, this readiness of ordinary people to give vent to their private feelings and concerns has resulted in some of the most exploitative forms of TV programming yet encountered. And while the generally more heavily regulated environment of European television has mostly shielded us from the more extreme forms of 'toxic talk' and histrionic display to be found on American TV, where ritual humiliation of subjects has virtually become par for the course, the explosion of talk-centred reality formats in Europe since the early 1990s gives more than a little cause for concern that marketization is beginning to take its toll. To be more specific: the participation of 'ordinary people' in the various types of reality programming we have been looking at is almost always a more heavily constrained involvement than they – or for that matter large numbers of the viewing audience – might imagine. The contractual basis which enables them to appear requires their agreement to deliver a kind of 'self-performance' in situations or scenarios dreamed up by a TV production team. In the majority of reality game-docs, for instance, participants can be under no illusions that what is expected of them is the delivery of an audience-pleasing performance. Likewise, in the 'softer' forms of contemporary documentary individuals are sometimes manouevred into positions and required to act out roles (see Chapter 6) where they are made to appear little more than caricatures. One programme maker, disturbed by what she clearly regards as a dubious trait in today's entertainment-led, character-centred documentary coins the term 'victim voyeurism' to describe this caricaturing tendency:

> TV subjects are increasingly drawn from the social caricature of the Mad, the Bad and the Sad ... These victimised subjects have become nineties TV icons, a new documentary A-list: the Mad, a motley crew of stalkers, new age therapists and the man who bit his dog; the Bad, *Crimewatch* baddies in balaclavas, photofits and dodgy reconstructions; and the Sad, disabled children, troubled transvestites and starving donkeys. (Mapplebeck, 1997b: 5)

What gives Mapplebeck and critics of like persuasion particular cause for concern is not only the exploitation of the subjects by the media machine, but what audiences themselves will take out of these voyeuristic exercises.[1] Such forms of programming revel in the depiction of belligerent interactions and various other forms of attention-seeking behaviour. There is also a worrying concentration on scatty, disorientated or otherwise dysfunctional individuals. Hardly ever is an attempt made to explain the behaviour we are witnessing. And even though producers, when challenged, will always contend that the full informed consent of participating individuals has been gained, many observers remain concerned that these shows carry uncomfortable echoes of the freak show (Dovey, 2000).

The challenge for any critic exploring recent developments in factual/documentary programming is not so much to assess what these developments tell us about the current state of television as to describe the particular forms of pleasure that audiences derive from the new reality formats. Work undertaken by Annette Hill and others into audience response suggests, for instance, that viewers – while demonstrating a capacity to become intensely involved in media events such as *Big Brother* and *Pop Idols* – are also able to take a decidedly more detached and sceptical view, not least because they recognize (and possibly even delight in) the ways in which these formats are targeting them as consumers (Hill, 2001). It is for these reasons that – although raising concerns about the attrition of serious documentary from the schedules of mainstream broadcasters – this study does not join in the general chorus of lament. The development of the docu-soap, the game-doc and the other reality formats discussed here should not be viewed as symptomatic of an overall qualitative decline, but rather as an an attempt to re-animate factual TV genres.

For all the marketization pressures under which today's generation of programme makers are required to operate, it is a tribute to their ingenuity and creative inventiveness that they have found ways of regenerating and extending the factual genres. Such initiatives and experiments are more than mere glimmers of hope amidst the all-encircling gloom; they indicate that at least some broadcasters are more prepared than they are sometimes given credit for to challenge their audiences into new ways of thinking and seeing. The hybridizing impulse, already singled out here as a dominant shaping influence in contemporary forms of the factual, does not necessarily have to serve distinctly populist ends. It can also be part of an attempt to move the genre on in other, more formally experimental ways. Take, for example, the collaborative work between the British documentary film maker Brian Hill and the poet Simon Armitage. Both have, over the last few years, been involved in a number of experimental projects which have sought to develop a new form of poetic documentary. *Saturday Night* (BBC 2, 1996), *Drinking for England* (BBC 2, 1998) and *Killing Time* (Channel 4, 2000) are all examples of work which explores the expressive potential of combining documentary and specially written verse. In each of these works, ordinary men and women are filmed in a variety of working and domestic situations and these sequences are then poetically illuminated by the verse that Armitage has written. This is far from being 'art for art's sake'. The underlying intention is not so much to explore the poetry in everyday life as to stimulate the viewer into a new form of engagement with pressing contemporary issues. *Drinking for England*, for instance, examines people's relationship and attitudes to alcohol. The starting point for this series was a series of interviews in which Hill asked a number of individuals to reflect on their attitudes to drink. Working from this taped material Armitage then produced a number of poems, which the original interviewees were then invited to recite or sing in the fitting surrounds of pub or club. The documentary, in its final edited form, thus combined some of the performance-oriented traits of the new reality formats with echoes of the poetic documentary, a form or tradition which stretches back to such well-known classics as *Song of Ceylon* (1935) and *Night Mail* (1936), the latter with its inclusion of the catchy specially composed W. H. Auden poem 'This is the Night Mail Crossing the Border'. While Hill's and Armitage's collaborative work may furnish further proof that there is nothing wholly new in the world of documentary, the very fact that a place can still be found in the schedules for this kind of formally innovative work suggests that not everything in the factual/documentary domain is being reduced to dumbed-down blandness.

There still remains, however, that darker vision of a broadcasting world in which more serious forms of documentary work are steadily eroded, to be superseded by the more entertainment-oriented formats. In the colourful phrase of one media observer: 'Once the proud lion of the television jungle, documentary is increasingly being tamed into the role of performing dog concerned not with insight but ratings' (Midgley, 1998: 45). Debates continue as to how the alleged slide into mediocrity might be halted when television is required more and more to adhere to market-led principles. Some UK observers felt that their worst fears were being confirmed when the BBC decided to subject its flagship current affairs series *Panorama* to a major refurbishment exercise and to shift it to a far less favourable slot in the schedule (Kampfer, 2001: 9). While some view this move as symptomatic of a regrettable ghettoizing of serious programming on television, others view these developments in far less apocalyptic terms.

They see the new digital order as providing a fresh outlet for work that both seriously engages with the contemporary world and extends the stylistic range of existing factual genres. The launch of new digital channels such as BBC 4 ('Radio 4 with style', in the words of a BBC press release) has rekindled hopes that television of the twenty-first century will be able to free itself of what, to some, appears to be the stranglehold of ratings-driven, entertainment-led forms of programming.

Events occurring outside the confines of the television world (if such are nowadays conceivable!) may also, on rare occasions, have an impact on the production and transmission of certain types of TV programming, including factual/documentary work. In the wake of the terrorist attacks on New York and Washington on 11 September 2001 there was a feeling in some quarters, for instance, that there would have to be a significant reappraisal of news and current affairs broadcasting. More specifically, there was a conviction that, from now on, the public would have much less of an appetite for those frothy, lightweight and sometimes cynical forms of programming which had come to dominate the mainstream schedules (Hughes, 2001: 16). There was even an expectation that the attack and the ensuing war in Afghanistan would act as a wake-up call to broadcasters, who for far too long were considered to have neglected international subjects in favour of those of more parochial concern. The recognition that values and priorities need to change is not the same, however, as being able to effect a significant shift in broadcasting policy. Indeed, at the point of writing, some eighteen months after the attack on the Twin Towers, there are very few signs of any significant change of attitude on the part of those who have a determining influence on the commissioning and scheduling of TV programming. In the UK there may have been a marginal increase in the number of programmes which provide an international perspective on contemporary events, but this falls far short of qualifying as a sea change. Commercial considerations remain the major determinants in deciding what gets commissioned and aired. In a broadcasting environment which continues to be dominated by marketplace thinking and where there is now an almost endemic resistance to risk taking, the best that possibly can be hoped for is the preservation of some balance within overall factual programming provision between work which treats factuality as diversion and programmes which attempt to engage their audience in more demanding ways.

The situation in which factual/documentary programme making currently finds itself is neatly encapsulated in an exchange which took place at the 2001 Sheffield International Documentary Film Festival. In a special session devoted to 'The Future of Documentary', Channel 4 Director of Programmes Tim Gardam provided a relatively upbeat assessment of the genre's future, claiming that more people than ever before were finding time to watch culturally demanding programmes. Warming to his theme, he went on to suggest that programme makers were beginning to respond to the challenge of producing work which reflected what he referred to as the 'cultural revolution', that period in recent history spanning the period from the collapse of the Soviet Union up to the attacks of 11 September. Responding to these stirring words, Christopher Hird, the Chair of the Festival Committee and himself a practising film-maker, felt moved to point out that this was all very well, but that if not enough *broadcasters*, especially the all-powerful commissioning editors, were prepared to take risks with their audience, then viewers would still be deprived of the consciousness-raising fare for which Gardam was pleading. Documentary would, in Hird's estimation, continue to be subject to the same forces of erosion as the institutions of public service broadcasting (see Hughes, 2001: 16–17).

This brings us back finally to the question raised earlier in the book as to whether, at least as far as television is concerned, we are indeed, as some would have us believe, moving into a post-documentary age. It is John Corner's contention that documentary, already 'notoriously imprecise since its coinage … will undoubtedly weaken further as a defining category at a time when electronic mediations of real life have never been so extensively enjoyed' (Corner, 2000: 687–8). On the basis of what we have seen of developments in the factual TV domain in the course of the 1990s, it is difficult to reach any other conclusion about documentary's prospects, though it is salutary to remember John Willis's remarks on documentarists' proven ability to survive against all the odds, even when they are having to operate in decidedly unfavourable conditions (Willis, 2000: 102). Of one thing, however, one can be reasonably certain and that is that the forms and structures once associated with 'classic documentary' will become increasingly absorbed into the many hybridized formats which since the early 1980s have become such a feature of the factual landscape. Likewise it is fairly safe to predict that the public's engagement with actuality based material is likely to take on increasingly interactive forms, as all of us become accustomed to living in a totally wired world.

While it goes without saying that developments in the domain of factual/documentary programming will be shaped by the dictates of the new audio-visual age (in which the global potential of programme material and multi-media forms of distribution will become even more important), there are certain dangers in trying to claim too radical a break with past traditions and practices. The point being emphasized here is that 'classic documentary', even in those allegedly golden-age days, has always been subject to diverse determining forces from within the institution of television. The medium has, in other words, always been a more heavily constraining one than some observers would have us believe. 'Pure' documentary has always, therefore, been something of a misnomer, since the categories of programming to which the documentary label has been applied are hardly ever, in practice, defined or understood in these terms. Those involved in programme production have always been aware of the 'cross-over' possibilities between individual TV genres, in particular between news, current affairs and documentary.[2] In addition, those tuning in to the ever widening range of programmes broadly categorized as 'factual' will, as we know, be actively matching and comparing what they see and hear in the one programme with the bewildering array of other TV images and programme material contained within their memory store. As far as individual viewers are concerned, then, there has always been a greater blurring of boundaries than has been allowed for in some critical assessments (see Corner, 1999: 60–9).

This blurring of boundaries – both between factual formats themselves and between fictional and non-fictional genres – has become far more marked in the 1980s and 1990s. Nevertheless, this hybridizing tendency, the creation of new formats by amalgamating different generic elements to appeal to new audience tastes, must still be regarded as a continuation of a phenomenon discernible from television's earliest days. Just as with other forms of hybridizing or interbreeding activity, however, certain of the emergent new growths will lack the vigorous qualities associated with the older varieties, while in other cases the process will result in the release of new energies. Far from being a dissipating force, hybridizing can sustain and re-animate genres – and in the case of factually based broadcast material will enable audiences to connect or engage with contemporary issues which may bring new insights and understandings.

There are two recently aired programmes, both of them dramas but with a strong documentary element, which show what television is still capable of achieving even in these heavily marketised times. *Gas Attack* (Channel 4, 2001) and *Smallpox 2002* (BBC 1, 2002) are both factually based dramas combining a range of documentary and dramatic techniques in addressing a topic of great public concern: the threat of bio-terrorist attack, especially in the light of the anthrax scare(s) in the United States and elsewhere following the events of 11 September 2001. *Gas Attack* works from the 'What if …?' premise, namely: What would be the likely outcome if an anthrax bomb were to be released by a neo-Nazi terrorist group amidst a group of asylum seekers housed on a Glasgow estate. *Smallpox 2002* operates along similar lines, but here the audience are asked to project themselves imaginatively into a possible future scenario. From the time perspective of 2005, the film chronicles 'The Great Smallpox Pandemic of 2002' following the release on the streets of New York, of the deadly smallpox virus by a lone suicide terrorist.

In watching the fictional dramas *Gas Attack* and *Smallpox 2002*, then, audiences will inevitably be re-invoking some of the TV-delivered images of actual terrorist attacks and the subsequent anthrax alarm. This is what gave them such poignancy and relevance, because the dramatic scenarios of both have a strong predictive quality and also key into that general sense of nervousness and heightened tension.[3] As the director of *Smallpox 2002* has observed:

> For all of us making *Smallpox 2002*, the prolonged sensation of déja vu that followed the terrorist attacks in America has been a haunting experience. Scenes and words from our fiction have been played back to us live. A year ago my biggest concern was that the scenario we predicted might seem too implausible to swallow. Watching recent events has proved just how close to reality this fiction has become. (Dan Percival, 2002 <http://www.bbc.co.uk/ drama/smallpox 2002/making_dan4.shtml>)

In singling out these two factually based dramas for special consideration in these closing remarks, I am mindful of the old adage that 'two swallows do not make a summer'. The domain of factual/documentary programming in UK television is still dominated by those 'softer' reality formats which are constantly tilting in the direction of popular entertainment. The fact that programmes such as *Gas Attack* and *Smallpox 2002*, both of which do not shy away from tackling unpalatable truths, can still get screened on

UK television channels does give some reason for hope. Television may be becoming more and more of a marketplace but one of the basic principles of marketplace operations is that a wide variety of different tastes have to be catered for.

Notes

1   Broadcasters and programme makers always claim they take every reasonable precaution in advising individuals of the possible negative consequences of media exposure. A number of well-documented cases show, however, that the prospects of producing some memorably dramatic TV moments sometimes override the proper concern for participants' psychological and emotional well-being. The most frequently cited case is that involving a young man Jonathan Schmitz who was driven to murder following the humiliation he felt he was subjected to on a 1995 programme in the series *The Jenny Jones Show* in the United States.

2   Some of the drama-documentaries emanating from Granada Television's Drama-Documentary Unit had their origins, for instance, in the work of television journalists working for Granada's *World in Action* team (Kilborn, 1994a: 59–76).

3   Both these works, though they were initially commissioned long before the attacks of 11 September 2001, undoubtedly acquired additional credibility and resonance by the uncanny resemblance the fictional dramas bore to the 'real-life' events.

Bibliography

Andersen, R. (1995), *Consumer, Culture and TV Programming*, Boulder, Colorado, Westview Press

BBC (2001), *BBC Producers' Guidelines: The BBC's values and standards*, London, British Broadcasting Corporation

Barrett, P. (1999), 'A bone to pick', *Guardian* (Part 2), 11 October: 8–9

Baudrillard, J. (1993), *Baudrillard Live: Selected Interviews* (ed. M. Gane), London, Routledge

Bazalgette, P. (2001), 'Golden Age? This is it', *Guardian* (Part 2), 19 November: 10–11

Beard, S. (1993), 'The artful fly on the wall', *New Statesman & Society*, 15 October: 34–5

Beckett, A. (2000), 'Growing pains', *Guardian* (Part 2), 23 March: 2–3

Bellos, A. (1997), 'Punch ups, freaks, the dying …', *Guardian* (Part 2), 4 May: 20–1

Bethell, A. (1998), 'Pleasure plus principle' *Guardian* (Part 2), 2 February: 4–5

Bethell, A. (1999), A job, some stars and a big row', *Sight and Sound: Mediawatch '99*, 9 (3): 14–15

Birt, J. (1999), 'The BBC is a civilising force and it must be protected', *Guardian*, 7 July: 18

Branigan, E. (1992), *Narrative Comprehension and Film*, London, Routledge

Bremner, R. (1998), 'We all star in our karaoke culture', *New Statesman*, 25 September: 24–6

Brooker, C. (2001), 'Screen burn', *Guardian (The Guide)*, 24 November: 52

Brown, M. (1999a), 'Squaring the circle', *Guardian* (Part 2), 29 March: 10

Brown, M. (1999b), 'Culture shock', *Guardian*, (Part 2), 3 May: 8–9

Brown, M. (2000), 'One big happy family?', *Guardian*, (Part 2), 17 April: 2–3

Brown, M. (2001), 'Is there a documentary in the house?', *Guardian* (Part 2), 27 August: 8–9

Bruzzi, S. (2000), *New Documentary: A critical introduction*, London and New York, Routledge

Buscombe, E. (ed.) (2000), *British Television: A Reader*, Oxford, Oxford University Press

Caird, R. (1993), 'Television's Lost Tribe', *Daily Telegraph* (TV and Radio), 22 May: 18–19

Caldwell, J. (1995), *Televisuality: Style, Crisis, and Authority in American Television*,

New Brunswick, NJ, Rutgers University Press

Campaign for Quality Television (1998), *Serious Documentaries on ITV*, Report

Campaign for Quality Television (1999), *Serious documentaries on ITV: An Endangered Species*, Report

Campbell, D. (1999), 'The end of a beautiful friendship …', *Guardian*, 7 June: 8–9

Carter, M. (1999), 'When first we practise to deceive', *Broadcast*, 9 April: 20–2

Cathode, R. (1998), 'Voyeurs from hell', *Sight and Sound*, 8 (2): 35

Ciprian, E. (1998), ' The walls have eyes', *Guardian* (Part 2), 2 July: 2–3

Clark, M. (2000), 'Documentary in crisis', *New Statesman*, 23 October: 41–3

Corner, J. (1996), *The Art of Record: A Critical Introduction to Documentary*, Manchester and New York, Manchester University Press

Corner, J. (1999), *Critical Ideas in Television Studies*, Oxford, Clarendon Press

Corner, J. (2000), 'What can we say about 'documentary?', *Media, Culture & Society*, 22: 681–8

Cosgrove, S. (1999), 'The core values of Channel 4', unpublished lecture given in the Media Research Seminars series, University of Stirling, 15 November 1999

Coward, R. (1997), 'Wild shots' *Guardian* (Weekend), 6 December: 34–45

Dale, D. (1993), The Neighbours from Hell', *Daily Telegraph*, 21 April: 17

Dovey, J. (2000), *Freakshow: First Person Media and Factual Television*, London, Pluto Press

Dugdale, J. (1999), 'Slipping on docu-soaps', *Guardian* (Part 2), 18 October: 6

Dugdale, J. (2000), 'The same, but different', *Guardian* (Part 2): 4–5

Dunkley, C. (2000), 'It's all downhill from here', *Financial Times* (The Arts), 20 September: 20

Ellison, M. (1998), Writer of wrongs', *Guardian* (Part 2), 16 December: 2–3

Fairclough, N. (1995), *Media Discourse*, London and New York, Arnold

Fishman, J. (1999), 'The populace and the police: Models of social control in reality-based crime television', *Critical Studies in Mass Communication*, 16 (3): 268–88

Fox, C. & M. Ryan (1999), 'Culture Wars: Dumbing Down, Wising Up' (Booklet to accompany conference organized by LM Magazine in London, March 1999): 3

Gentleman, A. (2001), 'TV to die for', *Guardian* (Part 2), 20 March: 6

Geraghty, C. (1991), *Women and Soap Opera: A Study of Prime Time Soaps*, Cambridge, Polity Press

Gibson, J. (1999), '*Sun* sued over "fake TV" with BBC', *Guardian* (Part 2), 30 June: 1

Glancy, J. (1998), 'Never mind the quality', *Guardian* (Weekend), 21 November: 50–62

Glynn, K. (2000), *Tabloid Culture: Trash Taste, Popular Power, and the Transformation of Television*, Durham and London, Duke University Press

Goffman, E. (1969), *The Presentation of Self in Everyday Life*, Harmondsworth,

Penguin Books

Greenslade, R. (1998), 'Trapped in television', *Guardian* (Part 2), 5 November: 5–6

Greer, G. (2001), 'Watch with Brother', *Observer* (Arts Review), 24 June: 1–2

Grierson, J. (1966), *Grierson on Documentary*, London, Faber (first published 1946)

Harvey, S. (2000), 'Channel Four Television: From Annan to Grade' in Buscombe (ed.): 92–117

Hibberd, M., R. Kilborn, B. McNair, S. Marriot, & P. Schlesinger (2000), *Consenting Adults?*, London, Broadcasting Standards Commission

Hill, A. (2001), '*Big Brother* 2000,: the real audience' in *Ethics and Mass Communication in Europe* (ed. V. Porter), London, Centre for Communication and Information Studies, University of Westminster: 36–50

Holland, P. (1997), *The Television Handbook*, London and New York, Routledge

Horsman, M. (1999), 'Tomorrow's world', *The Guardian* (Part 2), 29 November: 2–3

Household, N. (1998), 'Alder Hey – it's been a privilege', *Radio Times*, 30 May–5 June: 27–8

Hughes, P. (2001), 'Factual's reality check', *Broadcast*, 19 October: 16–17

Independent Television Commission (1998), *ITC Programme Code*, London, Independent Television Commission

Izod, J. & R. Kilborn (eds) (2000), *From Grierson to the Docu-soap: Breaking the Boundaries*, Luton, University of Luton Press

Jwarg, A. (1991), 'Points of fact', *Time Out*, 18–25 September: 146

Kampfer, J. (2001), 'The callow youths on our screens have had their day in the sun', *Guardian* (Part 2), 5 November: 9

Kilborn, R. (1992), *Television Soaps*, London, Batsford

Kilborn, R. (1994a), 'Drama over Lockerbie: a new look at television drama-documentaries', *Historical Journal of Film, Radio and Television*, 14 (1): 59–76

Kilborn, R. (1994b), '"How Real Can You Get?": Recent Developments in 'Reality' Television', *European Journal of Communication*, 9, : 421–39

Kilborn, R. (1996), 'New contexts for documentary production in Britain', *Media, Culture & Society*, 18: 141–50

Kilborn, R. (1998), ' Shaping the Real: Democratization and Commodification in UK-Factual Broadcasting', *European Journal of Communication*, 13 (2): 201–18

Kilborn, R. & J. Izod (1997), *An Introduction to Television Documentary: Confronting Reality*, Manchester and New York, Manchester University Press

Kilborn, R., M. Hibberd, & R. Boyle (2001), 'The rise of the docusoap: the case of *Vets in Practice*', *Screen*, 42 (4): 382–95

Kleber, P. & C.Visser (eds) (1990), *Re-interpreting Brecht: His Influence on Contemporary Drama and Film*, Cambridge, Cambridge University Press

Lawson, M. (1998), 'Secrets and Lies', *Guardian* (Part 2), 1 November: 17

Lawson, M. (1999), 'In Spielberg's footsteps', *Guardian* (Part 2), 4 October: 17

Lister, D. (2001), 'Sex is a Channel 4-letter word', *Independent*, 9 January: 8

Livingstone, S. & P. Lunt (1994), *Talk on Television: Audience Participation and Public Debate*, London and New York, Routledge

McFadyean, M. (1993), 'Family entertainment?', *Guardian* (Part 2), 19 April: 13

Mapplebeck, V. (1997a), 'The Tabloid Formula', *DOX* (*International Documentary Magazine*), (13): 10–12

Mapplebeck, V. (1997b), Voyeurs and victim TV', *Guardian* (Part 2), 1 December: 4–5

Meech, P. (2000), 'Trailing documentaries', in Izod et al. (eds):103–10

Middleton, C. (2002), 'Back to the Western Front', *Radio Times*, 9–15 March: 38–43

Midgley, C. (1998), 'On the road to the docu-ode', *The Times*, 1 November: 45

Morris, M. (1999), 'Enemy mine', *Guardian* (Part 2), 15 September: 17

Morrison, J. (2000), 'ITV criticised for 'derivative' entertainment shows', *Press Association News*, 25 May: 1–2

Morrow, F. (1998), 'The slippery slope', *Time Out*, 17–24 June: 172

Mosley, I. (ed.) (2000), *Dumbing Down: Culture, Politics and the Mass Media*, Exeter, Imprint Academic

Mulholland, J. (1998) 'What's up docs?' *Guardian* (Part 2), 26 January: 6–7

Niccol, A. (1998), *The Truman Show* (Screenplay, Foreword, and Notes), London, Nick Hern Books

Nichols, B. (1991), *Representing Reality: Issues and Concepts in Documentary*, Bloomington, IN, Indiana University Press

Nichols. B. (1994), *Blurred Boundaries: Questions of Meaning in Contemporary Culture*, Bloomington, IN, Indiana University Press

O'Sullivan, T. (1994), 'The Harsh Reality', *Broadcast*, 15 April: 21

Paget, D. (1998), *No Other Way to Tell it: Dramadoc/Docudrama on Television*, Manchester and New York, Manchester University Press

Postman, N. (1985), *Amusing Ourselves to Death: Public Discourse in the Age of Show Business*, London and New York, Penguin Books

Powell, R. & H. Solomon (1992), 'Real to Reel', *Broadcast*, 9 April: 32

Prebble, S. (1993), 'Compete to Survive', *Daily Telegraph* (TV and Radio), 22 May: 6

Puttnam, D. (1998), 'Saving its soul', *Guardian* (Part 2), 26 October: 6–7

Renov, M. (ed.) (1993), *Theorizing Documentary*, London, Routledge

Richards, M. (2001), 'Digitising dinosaurs', *Media International Australia*, 100: 65–80

Richardson, K. & U. Meinhof (1999), *Worlds in Common? Television Discourse in a Changing Europe*, London and New York, Routledge

Rofekamp, J. (2000), 'What's in store … The future of auteur documentary', *DOX* (*International Documentary Magazine*), 32: 8–11

Roscoe, J. (2001), 'Real entertainment: Real factual hybrid television', *Media Inter-*

national Australia, 100: 9–20

Roscoe, J. & C. Hight (2001), *Faking it: Mock-documentary and the Subversion of Factuality*, Manchester and New York, Manchester University Press

Rosen, J. (1990), 'The Revenge of the Real' *Listener*, 29 November: 37–8

Rosenthal, A. (ed.) (1999), *Why Docudrama? Fact-Fiction on Film and TV*, Carbondale and Edwardsville, IL, Southern Illinois University Press

Rothman, W. (1997), *Documentary Film Classics*, Cambridge, Cambridge University Press

Schlesinger, P. & H. Tumber (1993), 'Fighting the the War against Crime: Television, Police, and Audience', *British Journal of Criminology*, (33)1: 19–32

Selway, J. (1993), 'Clichés come alive in Oz', *Observer*, 18 April: 67

Strinati, D. & S. Wagg (eds) (1992), *Come On Down? Popular Media Culture in Post-war Britain*, London and New York, Routledge

Sweeting, A. (1998), 'Stand by to repel viewers', *Guardian* (Part 2), 8 October: 19

Thompson, J. (1995), *The Media and Modernity: A Social Theory of the Media*, Cambridge, Polity Press

Walker, A. (1999), 'Anger over fake panellist stunt at TV festival debate', ·*Scotsman*, 31 August: 3

Watson, P. (2000), 'I am like a poacher' (Paul Watson interviewed by F. Verster), *DOX* (*Documentary Film Magazine*), 31: 10–12

Webster, R. (2000), 'Planes and boats in train', *Observer* , 27 August: 5

Wells, M. (2001), 'There's no such thing as reality TV', *Guardian* (Part 2), 5 November: 2–3

Whitehouse, C. (1998), 'Bubble Boy', *Sight and Sound*, 8 (8, New Series): 9–10

Willis, J. (1998a), 'The faking of real TV', *Guardian* (Part 2), 11 May: 6

Willis, J. (1998b), 'Fall of the wild', *Guardian* (Part 2), 12 October: 4

Willis, J. (2000), 'Breaking the Boundaries', in Izod & Kilborn (eds), *From Grierson to the Docu-soap*, 97–102

Winston, B. (1995), *Claiming the Real: the Documentary Film Revisited*, London, British Film Institute

Winston, B. (1999), 'Witchhunt', *DOX* (*Documentary Film Magazine*), 23: 8–9

Winston, B. (2000), *Lies, Damn Lies and Documentaries*, London, British Film Institute

Wyver, J. (1989), *The Moving Image: An International History of Film, Television and Video*, Oxford and New York, Basil Blackwell and BFI Publishing

Index